The BOB DYLAN *Companion*

The

BOB DYLAN

Companion

Four Decades of Commentary

Edited by

CARL BENSON

Schirmer Books
New York

Schirmer Books
1633 Broadway
New York, New York 10019

Library of Congress Catalog Number: 98-35862
Printed in the United States of America
Printing number
10 9   8   7   6   5   4   3   2   1

Library of Congress Cataloging-in-Publication Data

The Bob Dylan companion : four decades of commentary / edited by Carl Benson.
       p.   cm.
    Discography: p.
    Includes bibliographical references (p.   ) and index.
    1. Dylan, Bob, 1941–   —Criticism and interpretation.
2. Singers—United States—Bibliography.
I. Benson, Carl.
ML420.D98B57   1998
782.42162'0092—dc21
[B]
                                                                98-35862
                                                                    CIP
                                                                    MN

Contents

PART FOUR   Rolling Thunder

1975–1985

PART FIVE   Knocked Out Loaded

1986–1990

Introduction
Watching the River Flow

Bob Dylan has made a career out of self-transformation. To the cynical, his shedding of skins has been a combination power trip and lust for fame; to the devoted, it has been an honest, public airing of an ongoing identity search. Either way, Dylan remains maddeningly relevant—no matter how uninterested he appears in his own career, how slap-dash his performances and recordings; seemingly out of left field and with the resourcefulness of a sorcerer, again and again he comes up with the goods, and we cannot ignore him.

Lately, Dylan is back in fashion big time. He's won a Grammy, a Kennedy Center Honor, fancy metals and ribbons from European governments; there are over seventy-five amateur Web sites dedicated to his every move; and he's returned to his roots as a would-be Delta bluesman with *Time Out of Mind*, a collection that melds the twangy '50s, the folksy '60s, the self-absorbed '70s, and the self-righteous '80s to create a neo-rockabilly, wizened, angry, and grumpy music. Sure, the echoy production is annoying, and some of the lyrics lazily constructed, but, hey, give the old guy a break.

Peaks and valleys are part of any career. And some of these ruts have been created by critics with their own agendas. Nobody liked Dylan's born-again phase because, let's face it, most Dylan fans and 99.9 percent of the music press is not sympathetic to born-again blather. And Dylan's self-righteousness certainly was exaggerated when he thought he had a direct line to the Truth; nonetheless he was still Dylan, and not everything he created when he was bathed in Godliness was trash by any means. In many ways, Dylan's new neo-folky-ism is just as annoying, but his critics and audience are more sympathetic to a raging bluesman than to a proselytizing prophet.

How many artists could create so many different (and convincing) career phases? Most of his contemporaries are happy if they master one style. Dylan was the greatest of all the social-protest songwriters but knew when it was time to give the style up; he achieved pop stardom (scoring a couple of top-ten hits in the '60s at a time when anger still had a place on the charts) without giving up his individuality; he pioneered country-rock; brought the '70s wave of self-confession to new heights in songs about love gone wrong; wrote and performed some of the most idiosyncratic Christian rock every attempted; and now is celebrating roots rock.

Before Dylan, professional songwriters wrote material that sweet-voiced singers took up the charts. Dylan took the folk tradition of performing and writing his own material and gave it an extra twist. He proved that the best possible interpreter of his material was (ironically) one of the least talented singers and guitarists around: himself. Even when he tried to hide his voice (remember *Nashville Skyline?*), he was still the world's most limited singer; and he continues to display great limitations as an instrumentalist. If anything, age has only brought new limitations to Dylan's vocal skills, yet he continues to be a compelling vocalist. Dylan showed everyone how these limitations could be strengths, and he ushered in the era when anyone could be a performer. The door was wedged open, and in flew everyone from hoarse-voiced guitar strummers to ear-shattering punk rockers.

This book traces Dylan's career through contemporary writings, reviews, and interviews. Part One documents his arrival in New York City as a would-be folksinger. Included are diaries from Izzy Young, the folk-store manager and promoter who helped Dylan get established; Robert Shelton's famous early review from the *New York Times* that did so much to launch his career; the love-hate relationship that quickly developed between Dylan and his folkie cohorts, many of whom never achieved his popular success, as documented in numerous articles from folk magazines *Sing Out!* and the *Little Sandy Review*; and a later radio interview in which Dylan reflects on his beginnings in more honest terms than he could muster when living through the events.

Part Two traces his first folk-rock years. It includes many of the so-called interviews and press conferences that Dylan gave at this time, pulling the legs of his friends and enemies. It also documents the initial hostility to Dylan's "going electric" during his famous European and Australia tours of 1965–66.

Part Three covers the post-motorcycle-crash Dylan and his first "resurrection," as a country crooner on *John Wesley Harding* and *Nashville Skyline*. The self-mocking *Self Portrait* is retrieved from critical oblivion.

And a new rebirth—as confessional singer/songwriter—is documented in a discussion of the sessions that created the classic album *Blood on the Tracks*.

Part Four documents Dylan's further transformation, from God-like figurehead of the Rolling Thunder Revue years to follower of God as a born-again songster. The famous Nat Hentoff piece on the first Rolling Thunder Revue travesties Dylan's Zeus-like need for power and control over his cohorts. The critical reaction to Dylan's conversion is documented in an interview by long-time friend Robert Hilburn and an interesting concert review from the period that appeared in the *Boston Globe*. In addition, there is the fascinating description of Dylan's relation with religions—Jewish, Christian, and other—in the essay "Tangled Up in Jews."

Part Five documents Dylan's search for a new identity as arena rocker in the mid-'80s. Mikal Gilmore gives two frank appraisals of Dylan's working style during this period, while Lynn Van Matre uses the occasion of the issue of the *Biograph* box set to review Dylan's career to this point.

Part Six gives various perspectives on the latest "new" Dylan. Eric Weisbard's "The Folk Slingers" compares Dylan's performance work to that of folklorists Alan Lomax and Harry Smith in a fascinating discussion of what constitutes folk music in the modern media age. The flood of honors given the composer—culminating in the Kennedy Center Honors—is discussed by both conservative and more friendly critics. And Dylan's most recent album and performances are dissected and given their due place in his career.

Carl Benson

Acknowledgments

Thanks to Jessica Myers Carlin for her assistance and support in compiling this volume. Thanks to the many contributors for their willingness to contribute—and suggest other contributions—to make this a well-rounded look at Dylan's life and career.

Shortly after his arrival in New York at a Carnegie Hall hootenanny, 1962. *Photo copyright © David Gahr.*

Part One

NEW YORK TOWN
1961–1965

THE MISSING SINGER (1968)

Other Scenes, December 1968

Izzy Young is the legendary founder of New York's Folklore Center, a small, second-floor combination music store, concert venue, and overall hangout spot located on Greenwich Village's famed MacDougal Street. A left-leaning old-school radical, Young befriended Dylan when the young singer/songwriter came to town and presented his first major New York concert, on Saturday, November 4, 1961, at the 200-seat Carnegie Recital Hall. In 1968, Young published his diaries recording some of his early conversations with Dylan, revealing that the singer/songwriter was already weaving his many myths. Among the many whoppers are Dylan's claims to have personally known and played with traditional performers such as the bluesman Mance Lipscomb and to have supplied songs for rockabilly legend Carl Perkins.—CB

October 20, 1961

Bob Dylan came to Greenwich Village early in 1961 and quickly established himself as the most important singer musician songwriter to come out of the then burgeoning folk music scene. The Folklore Center on MacDougal Street was one of his regular haunts where he'd daily arrive, park himself in back of the Center, and sing his new songs to a usually delighted audience. [Today] he came in to talk about his feelings about folk music. I didn't use a tape recorder then so I have to edit slightly to connect the pieces of the rambling talk.

—

Bob Dylan. Born in Duluth, Minnesota, in 1941. Moved to Gallup, New Mexico. Then until now lived in Iowa, South Dakota, Kansas—North Dakota for a little bit. Started playing in carnivals when he was 14—with guitar and piano. Has been practicing piano at Bob Shelton's house. Started playing harmonica two years ago. Always interested in singers, didn't know the term folk music until he came to New York. Been in NYC since January 1961. Got a scholarship to University of Minnesota—went there for five months—went to classes for five days and left. Arvella Gray, blind street singer from Chicago, taught him blues songs about 4–5 years ago. Used to know a guy Mance Lipscomb, from Navasota, Texas. Listened to him a lot. Met him through a grandson—a rock and roller. He heard Woody Guthrie records in South Dakota—Dust Bowl album. Term "folk music" is a name. Sings a lot of old jazz songs, sentimental cowboy songs, top forty hit parade stuff. People have to name it something so they call it "folk music." Now very few people singing that way. It's all right but call it "folk music." Stuff I do is nearer to "folk music." Now singing old blues and Texas songs. I don't want to make a lot of money, want to get along. The more people I reach—and have the chance to sing the kind of music I sing—people have to be ready and see me once already. People often say first time—this isn't folk music. My songs aren't easy to listen to. Favorite singers are Dave Van Ronk, Jack Elliott, Peter Stampfel, Jim Kweskin and Rick Von Schmidt. Joan Baez? Her voice goes through me. She's OK. Whenever I go, I go I guess. Like a matchbox—too many matches in a tiny box. Not a planned concert [on November 4]. I can offer songs that tell something of this America, no foreign songs. The songs of the land that aren't offered over TV or radio and very few records. Offering a chance to hear them. Start recording for Columbia next week. Out probably the first of the year. Groups are easy to be in. I've always learned the hard way. I will now, too. When you fail—yourself. Dressed the way he does just because I want to dress this way. Started writing his own songs 4 or 5 years ago. First song was to Brigitte Bardot, for piano. Thought if I wrote the song I'd sing it to her one day. Never met her. Has written hillbilly songs. Carl Perkins from Nashville, Tennessee, sings them. Talking Blues on topical things. "California Brown Eyed Baby" has caught on. Wrote "Bear Mountain Song" overnight because of Noel Stookey (who was working at the Gaslight then). Never sing it the same way twice—never saw the event just heard about it. No one really influencing me now—actually everything does. Can't think of anyone in particular now.

October 23, 1961

Played piano with Bobby Vee—would have been a millionaire if he stayed with him, etc. Played piano North West to Montana. Sang for one day at Cafe Wha playing harmonica to Fred Neil. Bob was bored stiff.

"Dead Man's Hand" and "Aces and Eights"—believes in them. Believes in cards. Plays a lot of cards. It's time to cash in when you get "Aces and Eights." The other things I believe in are logical—the length of his hair—less hair on the head, more hair inside the head & vice versa. Crewcut—all hair cluttering around the brain. Let my hair grow long to be wise and free to think. Has no religion. Tried a bunch of different religions. Churches are divided. Can't make up their minds, neither can I. Never saw a God, can't say till I saw one. Got a free ride to New York— came to see Woody Guthrie—came to the Folklore Center—saw girl playing with a banjo. O God, this is it, this is New York. Everyone is playing banjo faster than I've been playing guitar. Couldn't really play with them. Used to see Woody whenever he had enough money. Met him once before in California before I was really playing—think Jack Elliott was with him. I think Billy Faier was there too. I was in Carmel—doing nothing. During the summer. Woody impressed me. Always made a point to see him again. Wrote a song to Woody in February of this year. Was going to sing all Woody songs—Jack Elliott and Cisco Houston came out with them. Woody carries the paper Bob wrote the song on. Woody likes Bob's song. Haven't sung anything really funny. Woody doesn't like Joan Baez or the Kingston Trio—Baez for her voice is too pretty and Trio because they can't be understood. Sort of like New York: don't know really. I like to walk around, just walk around. Like to ride motorcycle—was a racer in North and South Dakota and Minnesota. First guitar I had, strings were two inches away from the fingerboard. I had a flatpick but I couldn't play it. Got a Martin for a present. No one ever taught me to play guitar or harmonica or piano. Used to play sort of boogie woogie-ish type of stuff, played with rock and roll songs. Never knew the names of the songs . . . twelve bar blues, played along with them. A few coffeehouses refused to let me play when I came to New York. Bob Shelton helped by writing an article—talked around . . . someone from Elektra came down but nothing happened. Bob Shelton's been a friend for a long time. Friends are pretty hard to come by in New York. Dave Van Ronk has helped me along in card games because he's always losing. I've been with Jack Elliott—we have an Island upstate New York—we saw the island out in the lake—we named it Elliott Isle and swam back. Jack hasn't taught me any songs. Jack doesn't know that many songs. He's had a lot of chances. I went out to the Gleasons in New Jersey and stayed out there for a while in East Orange. They have a lot of [Woody] tapes—his VD songs. Learned a bunch of those—sung them to Woody. Should get the rest from Leventhal. Met Jesse Fuller in Denver at the Exodus. Bob was playing in a stripper place, the Gilded Garter in Central City, a little mining town. Came down to Denver two summers ago—Jesse was playing downstairs and upstairs was Don Crawford. Learned the way [Jesse] does songs—mixed his style in with mine at the time. Before that there was a farmhand in Sioux Falls, South Dakota, who played the autoharp. Picked up Wilbur's way of singing—never remembered his last name. Cowboys' styles I learned from real cowboys. Can't remember their names. Met some in Cheyenne. Cowboys nowadays go to Cowboy movies and sit there and criticize. Wear their hat this way or that—pick up their way of walking from the movies. Denver . . . The Tropics . . . owner has Gilded Garter in Central City . . . played twenty minutes, strippers worked for forty minutes with rock and roll band. I'd play for twenty minutes again. Never stopped. One night I was about ready to strip myself. Only lasted a week and a half. Worst place I ever played. A full drag. I have different ideas about folk music now. There's been no one around to cut records like the old Leadbelly, Houston and Guthrie. There are young people that are singing like that—but are being held back by commercial singers. People who have radio programs don't play them. Jim Kweskin, Luke Faust aren't appreciated by enough people. Folkways is the only company that would record such stuff. . . . Went up to Folkways. I had written some songs. I says, "Howdy, I've written some songs." Wouldn't even look at them. I heard Folkways was good. Irwin Silber didn't even talk to me. Never got to see Moe Asch. They just about said GO and I heard that *Sing Out!* was supposed to be helpful and friendly, big heart, charitable. I thought it was the wrong place. Must have been in the wrong place and *Sing Out!* was on the door. Whoever told me that was wrong. It seems ironic. I'm on a big label. The [*New York Times*] article came out on Thursday night . . . showed the article to John Hammond . . . and he's recording me. He asked me what I do. I've got about twenty songs I want to record. Some stuff I've discovered and some stuff I stole. That's about it. Used to see girls from the Bronx at Chicago, Antioch, with their gut string guitars singing "Pastures of Plenty," no lipstick, brotherhood songs. Struck me funny, not clowns, opened up a whole new world of people. I like New York kind of girl now, can't remember what the old kind was like. Can always tell a New Yorker out of town—wants everyone to know they're from New York. I've seen it happen—first four or five days people just stare at me. Down South it's bad to say you're from New York City. . . . Beatniks. Ten years ago a guy would get on a bus with a beard, long sideburns, a hat and people would say, "Look at the rabbi." Same guy gets on a bus today. The same people say, "Look at the Beatnik." Played the Fifth Avenue Hotel for the Kiwanis—for no money. A lot of different acts that night—dressed up like clowns—when someone would sing the clowns would perform. The clowns were paid but not the performers. Couldn't hear myself. A clown rolled up to pinch my cheek—kicked him in the nuts and no one saw—rest of the clowns left him alone. OK, but don't care for classical music. Don't go for any foreign music. I really like Irish music, and Scottish music, too. Colleges are the best audiences, much better than nightclubs. New York is the best place for music. Lived on the Mississippi River—about ten feet away under a great bridge. I took some theater courses. Said I had to take Science. I enrolled with 26 credits. Narrowed it down to 20. Then down to nine. Couldn't even make that. Carnivals and fraternities so much crap. So much phooey stuff. You might as well get out and live with some other people. A big hoax. Flunked out of anthropology. Read a little, went to see the movies. One time I flunked out of English for teacher said I couldn't talk. We had to read poetry, had to think about it for a long time. Poem should reach as many people as possible. I spent more time in Kansas City about 400 miles away. A girl-friend was there. Went to High School in Upper Minnesota [Hibbing] a nothing little town. Fargo, in North Dakota, a lumberjack and mining town. Used to hop trains. Big open pit. Lots of strikes there, lots of political stuff, a real mining town. It's easy to criticize big money makers like Belafonte, Kingston Trio. Stuff he does is really like a popular singer—criticized by Jazz, Folk and Calypso and he's making all the money. Won't criticize him until he sings one of my songs—but then he'll make a lot of money for me. I liked Belafonte on the TV show. Folk music is wide open for good voices. Instead of starting at the bottom in Opera or Show or Jazz they start at the top in folk music. . . . Read *Bound for Glory* twice. Book should be taught to college kids—his poetry should be taught in English classes.

February 1, 1962

Wrote a song the other night. "Ballad of Emmet Till." After I wrote it someone said another song was written but not like it. I wrote it for CORE—I'm playing it February 23. I think it's the best thing I've ever written. Only song I play with a capo. Stole the melody from Len Chandler—a song he wrote about a Colorado bus driver. . . . I went to Brooklyn Hospital [Woody]. Seeing him steady for a year. I met him when I was thirteen. He likes my songs. . . . Never figured I'd play with Belafonte. . . . Next album I'll play piano, guitar and harmonica—dub piano in. Writing a song called "The Death of Robert Johnson." His

Columbia LP is the greatest of his work. Don't like to go up to see John Hammond. Ivy League kids treat me like a king. At first I liked it. It gets sickening after a while. I took Len Chandler just to see what would happen. He couldn't believe it. . . . Hammond isn't a manager—more an adviser. I'm sort of disconnecting myself from the folk music scene. . . . Too many guys want to make a big entertainment out of it—with jazz and comedians. Can't see the future. I hate to think about it. It's a drag to think about it.

February 7, 1962

"Strange Rain" written while Gil Turner and I were in Toronto in December 1961. I set out to say something about fall out and bombtesting but I didn't want it to be a slogan song. Too many of the protest songs are bad music. Exceptions being "Which Side Are You On?" Most of the mining songs are good. The bomb songs, especially, are usually awkward and with bad music. Came to NYC in 1960—back to Oklahoma several times. Disastrous trip to California—no one liked me. Felt pretty low when I left. [Wrote] more than 20 songs.

February 22, 1962

Bob Dylan just rolled in and wants to sing a new song about fallout shelters. . . . Let me die in my footsteps before I die underground. Paxton's songs? "They're good, I guess." *Broadside* magazine? "I think it's a good magazine. Can't hardly tell from one issue. Sure need songs like that." I wanted to write a song about 1½ years ago on fallout shelters to tune of "So Long, It's Been Good to Know You." Song I wrote isn't like the rest of them. . . . John Hammond called Mitch Miller to hear some of Bob's songs. Mitch wanted them for Frankie Lane . . . telling of how Jimmy Driftwood sang on the "Battle of New Orleans" didn't get as much money as he could have. . . . I like Johnny Cash's songs. Because he's not trying to cover up. Writes real stuff. He writes a lot of songs. I think Woody Guthrie wrote better songs. I've seen some songs he never recorded. Favorite Woody Guthrie Songs: "Jack Hammer John" / "At The Mound of Your Grave" / "Slip Knot" / "Hard Traveling." I like them all really. Except some of them are absurd. . . . I just pick the melody out of the air sometimes. Prestige Records says if Columbia doesn't [record Dylan] give them a call. Folkways asked me for contemporary songs for an album of my own songs. . . . I heard Big Joe Williams when I was nine or ten in Chicago. I really didn't play so much. I just followed him around. I sung

With Doug Sahm recording *Doug Sahm and Band*, 1972. *Photo copyright © David Gahr.*

then. I got a cousin living in Chicago. He lives on the South Side. Funny thing. Big Joe Williams remembers it. . . . I think Paul Anka is the worst songwriter. Saw some of his songs in the Hit Parade book. I think Johnny Cash is the best songwriter.

March 14, 1962

If I wrote to sell, I could do twenty a day. I'm just not. Can't see anything in it. Some of the songs passed off as songs! These [songs of mine] are contemporary songs [referring to his new song "Life and Death of Don White"].

ROBERT SHELTON

BOB DYLAN: A DISTINCTIVE FOLK-SONG STYLIST (1961)

New York Times, September 29, 1961

This review by the highly influential New York Times *pop music critic did much to launch Dylan's career. Shelton is perceptive both about Dylan's ability in "sopping up influences like a sponge" and also about his tendency to turn his own life into myth. Shelton would later write a biography of Dylan based on his friendship with the singer in his early years.—CB*

A bright new face in folk music is appearing at Gerde's Folk City. Although only 20 years old, Bob Dylan is one of the most distinctive stylists to play in a Manhattan cabaret in months.

Resembling a cross between a choir boy and a beatnik, Mr. Dylan has a cherubic look and a mop of tousled hair he partly covers with a Huck Finn black corduroy cap. His clothes may need a bit of tailoring, but when he works his guitar, harmonica or piano and composes new songs faster than he can remember them, there is no doubt that he is bursting at the seams with talent.

Mr. Dylan's voice is anything but pretty. He is consciously trying to recapture the rude beauty of a Southern field hand musing in melody on his porch. All the "husk and bark" are left on his notes and searing intensities pervade his songs.

Mr. Dylan is both comedian and tragedian. Like a vaudeville actor on

At Columbia studios recording his first album, 1962. *Photo courtesy of UPI/Corbis-Bettmann.*

the rural circuit, he offers a variety of droll musical monologues: "Talking Bear Mountain" lampoons the overcrowding of an excursion boat, "Talkin' New York" satirizes his troubles in gaining recognition and "Talking Havah Nageilah" burlesques the folk-music craze and the singer himself.

In his serious vein, Mr. Dylan seems to be performing in a slow-motion film. Elasticized phrases are drawn out until you think they may snap. He rocks his head and body, closes his eyes in reverie and seems to be groping for a word or a mood, then resolves the tension benevolently by finding the word and the mood.

Mr. Dylan's highly personalized approach toward folk song is still evolving. He has been sopping up influences like a sponge. At times, the drama he aims at is off-target melodrama and his stylization threatens to topple over as a mannered excess.

But if not for every taste, his music-making has the mask of originality and inspiration, all the more noteworthy for his youth. Mr. Dylan is vague about his antecedents and birthplace, but it matters less where he has been than where he is going, and that would seem to be straight up.

J. R. GODDARD

RECORDS: BOBBY DYLAN (1962)

Village Voice, April 26, 1962

Soon after his arrival in New York, Dylan made several appearances that were enthusiastically reviewed by the New York Times *pop music critic Robert Shelton. This led to John Hammond's hearing the young singer and signing him to Columbia Records, despite the fact that most of the label's executives were less than enthusiastic about Dylan's musicianship. His first album, titled* Bob Dylan, *was produced by Hammond and was well received in the local press, as is shown by this* Village Voice *review.—CB*

A little over a year ago a rather short, peripatetic young man, his beardless, aqualine face crowned by an old cap, wandered into Izzy Young's Folklore Center on MacDougal Street. Picking up an autoharp, he began mumbling a song about some bloke named Captain Gray. People looked on in amusement as he began hopping around a bit. He was funny to watch and anybody with half an ear could tell he had a unique style. But few could have guessed on that wintry Sunday morning that a real enfant terrible had arrived on the folk music scene—or that within a single year he would emerge as one of the most gifted and unusual entertainers in the whole country.

The singer is Bobby Dylan. Ample proof of his talent can be heard in an LP just issued by Columbia Records under the direction of the famed John Hammond.

Right off the bat this reviewer has to say that the record seems one of the best to come from the boiling folk pot in a long, long time. One reason is that Dylan is blessed with a gift of style—individual, dynamic STYLE! Singing country and folk blues in a sometimes wavering, sometimes cacophonous voice to his own driving guitar (harmonica alternates with voice), he displays a sense of rhythm and timing as good as the old-time singers he's learned from. And Dylan, who is still but a downy-cheeked 20, can also muster a growling, grumbling force backed up by flailing guitar which can drive you wild.

His first LP shows his wide range. Moribund songs like "Man of Constant Sorrow" or "See That My Grave Is Kept Clean" are splendidly, refreshingly done. Then come comic numbers like "Talkin' New York" in which Dylan tells how he was cheated-mistreated by Village coffee-house and cabaret owners on landing here. But Dylan remains a masterful pace-changer. No sooner has he finished a driving "Gospel Plow" than he's turning to beautiful counterpoint in the swinging "Baby Let Me Follow You Down."

One of the most notable jobs, however, is on the classic "House of the Rising Sun." It's a version learned from Dave Van Ronk; he wrings the same rare, almost surrealistic sense of life and death from it that has marked Van Ronk's rendering in recent years.

The remainder of the album only reinforces this explosive country-blues debut. It's a collector's item already.

R. GILBERT

TOMORROW'S TOP TWENTY? (1963)

Scene No. 17, January 26, 1963

This is an early notice of Bob Dylan in London. Dylan had arrived in London on December 17 or 18, 1962, brought over by the BBC to appear as a folksinger in a TV play called Madhouse on Castle Street. *During this visit, he met and befriended English folksinger Martin Carthy, as well as American expatriate Richard Fariña. He recorded some backing vocals and harmonica parts on Fariña's and Eric von Schmidt's self-named album for the tiny Dobel's music shop label in mid-January, just before returning to the states.*

In this article, the author muses on the success of folk music and how pop music might be changed by it, both in England and in America. Dylan comes across as very brash and more than a little overbearing. The author takes an appropriately skeptical attitude toward both Dylan and his Svengali-promoter, Albert Grossman.—CB

It really would be a test of the assimilatory powers of Tin Pan Alley if folk music suddenly hit the charts in a big way. How, for instance, would the men in sharp suits deal with Bob Dylan, the shambling boy genius of American folk music?

Dylan does his very best to talk, act, dress and behave as much like a Tennessee mountain man as he can.

When I first met him he was talking vaguely about heading off for Rome, Paris or maybe New York. It worried him very little that he was halfway through the tele-recording of the BBC play, *Madhouse on Castle Street*, and that high-level conferences were being held all over London because of an overtime squabble at the BBC which threatened to take the production time of the play some weeks beyond the time stipulated in Dylan's contract.

"They're payin' me two thousand dollars to do this play," said Dylan. "If I got to stay another three weeks to finish it they'll probably have to pay the same money all over again.

"But to me two thousand, four thousand, I can't imagine the difference. It's too much money. And what's the money for three whole weeks of time? Three weeks is too long to lose."

Dylan is one of the biggest stars on the American folk circuit, other members of which include Joan Baez, who has sold a million records and has two LPs in the best-selling charts, Peter, Paul and Mary, a trio who sold 290,000 copies of a recent record, and Odetta, a tall, handsome Negress who started a late-night season at the Leicester Square Prince Charles Theatre on January 10.

Despite the pessimism of British record company executives, folk music is now one of the likeliest outside bets in the race to provide the next popular music boom.

There is a boom in folk music clubs: straws in the wind have been provided by Robin Hall and Jimmie MacGregor, who sold almost 30,000 copies of their *Football Crazy* EP, against the average folk record sales of around 2,000. The anti-romantic songs of artists like Mike Sarne and Bernard Cribbins have a relationship with folk music that, however slender to the purists, seem to indicate that a simpler, earthier form of folk music is in demand.

Which may put the twenty-two-year-old Dylan in the category of stars-of-the-immediate-future. And as there is no one in show business simpler or earthier than Dylan, the near future may give the commercial experts a few problems—even experts in the art of molding any kind of music to suit mass record-buying tastes. . . .

It was a lunchtime dawn for the tousled boy who opened the door, on which hung a Do Not Disturb notice. Thin-faced, with about a week's growth of boyish hair on his chin, he rubbed a floppy mass of hair out of his eyes and perched on his bed, feet bare, legs crossed tailor fashion.

His guitar case stood in the center of the floor, a pile of rolled-up shirts erupted from an open suitcase and a large sheepskin jacket in dire need of cleaning lay beside the bed, where it had obviously been dropped the night before.

Dylan is the most exciting white folk and blues singer, the experts say, America has produced. He writes many of his own songs, sings them "consciously trying to recapture the rude beauty of a Southern farmhand musing in melody on his porch," and accompanies himself on guitar and harmonica (fixed round his neck).

Dylan talked like Brando imitating that Southern farmhand. "I'm not in show business," he said. "Money? I don't know how much I make. Sometimes I ask, sometimes I don't. I don't know what I spend it on, it just falls through holes in my pockets."

The curtains were still drawn in his room and they remained that way for the next three hours.

"I don't like singing to anybody but Americans. My songs say things. I sing them for people who know what I'm saying."

While it is true that on his CBS long-player now available over here Dylan's songs are, at first, unintelligible to anyone, perhaps, who isn't a Southern farmhand, he makes an exciting sound—and the unintelligibility of vocals hardly affected the commercial success of rock singers.

"Nowadays I just play at concerts," he said. "Clubs I don't play at. A few years ago when I needed the money they wouldn't pay me. Now they're writing all the time asking me to play. Sometimes I write back and tell them no, sometimes I just don't answer. But they keep right on asking, offering me percentages of the house and all."

Dylan dressed to go out to a local cafeteria for lunch with his manager, Mr. Albert Grossman. Grossman Enterprises manages the fortunes of many of America's best folk singers.

Mr. Grossman, a bear-like man from New York, is the kind of manager who fights hard for his stable and their right to treatment suited to the activities as true artistes, rather than box office commodities.

It's unlikely that Dylan or Grossman could be persuaded to sweeten their product to suit the immediate demands of The Charts.

As Dylan shambled through the chromium and neon hotel lounge in tartan shirt, denims and battered boots, many people stared, none harder than the middle-class Americans who form the bulk of that particular establishment's clientele.

Women stared hardest of all. The receptionist, the waitress and the chambermaid all seemed to enjoy conversing with Dylan, in itself an omen of popularity.

Later that afternoon Mr. Grossman and Dylan decided they would finish the TV play, in which Dylan played a guitar-playing hobo.

A week or so after that I caught up with Mr. Grossman and Dylan in London again. Dylan was now wearing a black hat with a colored band and a curvy brim.

With two of his biggest names in London at the same time, Mr. Grossman found time between long phone discussions, conferences and taxi journeys to talk about himself and folk music.

He started Chicago's first folk club, the Gate of Horn, about six or seven years ago ("I'm terrible on dates") and went on presenting folk concerts, realizing that there was no one else around who would take folk "from cellars into the more general area of show business."

The famous 1963 Newport Folk Festival finale where Peter, Paul, and Mary; Joan Baez; Dylan; the Freedom Singers (with Berniece Reagon); and Pete Seeger sang "Blowin' in the Wind." *Photo copyright © David Gahr.*

"I'm just giving it a nudge towards a permanent and major place in the pop and serious music of America," he says. "In Britain I don't think folk has found its identity yet. All it needs is someone with a sense of tradition, who knows what it is all about, and yet is living in 1963, sensing everything that is going on today.

"Folk is more popular in universities and colleges than rock and is almost equally popular among other young people. When they grow up it will go with them into places of the highest level.

"It's just a matter of time."

I asked an executive of one of the big four record companies whether he thought folk music would boom here.

"Maybe in the States, not here. We've got more folk singers on our lists than we have buyers."

This may prove that record companies start pushing when the boom is on. Radio Luxembourg has a record show that is laughingly called Folk Music, being to the ear no more than one semitone away from rock.

This may prove that Radio Luxembourg is Radio Luxembourg.

Asked for details about Bob Dylan's LP, the CBS publicity department girl said nobody knew very much about it.

A lot of heads are going to be scratched if and when the folk brigade break through into the bigtime. Perhaps it is the very extent of the difficulties they'll have fitting men like Mr. Grossman and Bob Dylan into the preordained scheme of things that is making Tin Pan Alley so slow in getting with the folk scene.

NEW YORK TIMES

NORTHERN FOLK SINGERS HELP OUT AT NEGRO FESTIVAL IN MISSISSIPPI (1963)

July 7, 1963

This spot news article on the civil rights movement shows that not all New York Times reporters read Robert Shelton's reviews. "Bobby Dillon" is identified as a local singer, and his song "Only a Pawn in Their Game" is identified as one of the most popular of those performed that night.—CB

Greenwood, Mississippi, July 6—Three northern folk singers led by Pete Seeger brought a folk-song festival to the Deep South this evening. They sang in the yard of a Negro farm home on the edge of a cotton patch three miles south of here. The song festival, or hootenanny, was sponsored by the Student Nonviolent Coordinating Committee, which has been conducting a voter registration drive among Negroes in Mississippi delta towns for more than a year. The festival was attended by 250 to 300 persons. Most of them were Negroes. There were a score or more of young white people, plus several white newsmen and a television camera crew of four white men from New York. Three cars with white men in them were parked in a lane across the highway from the scene of the sing. There was also a highway patrol car with two policemen sitting along the road. There were no incidents. Joining Mr. Seeger in leading the songfest, in which most of the audience joined at one time or another, were Theodore Bikel and Bobby Dillon, who, like Mr. Seeger, are white. There was also a Negro trio, the Freedom Singers, from Albany, Georgia. All paid their own expenses for the trip and sang without a fee. One of the more popular songs presented by a local singer was one dedicated to Medgar W. Evers, the Mississippi field secretary of the National Association for the Advancement of Colored People, who was slain last month in Jackson, Mississippi. A Greenwood man, Byron de La Beckwith, has been indicted in the shooting. The refrain of the song was that the man who shot Mr. Evers didn't know what he was doing and should be forgiven, "He's only a pawn in their game." The sing was to have begun at 10 A.M., but it was a blistering hot day, with a high of 97 degrees. So it was postponed until the sun had almost gone down, and it proceeded into the night.

VARIETY

BOB DYLAN, 22, A FOLKNIK HERO (1963)

September 1963

This unattributed piece from the trade journal Variety *is full of hip business lingo, noting Dylan's unexpected success on the New York scene.—CB*

Bob Dylan is emerging as the big wheel in the current folknik spin. He's scoring in the recording, songwriting and concert field and is considered by many guitar-hooters as the single most important creative force on the folk scene.

In addition to clicking in the pop field with the authorship of "Blowin' in the Wind," the 22-year-old singer from the Midwest is also in the vanguard of the Negro protest movement with his composition "Only a Pawn in Their Game," a song saga of Medgar Evers. As a disker, he's now clicking with his Columbia Records LP, *The Freewheelin' Bob Dylan*, which Columbia sales execs report to be selling at the rate of about 10,000 copies a week.

Dylan also appears to be shaping as the folksingers' folksinger. He's being championed by such folkniks as Peter, Paul and Mary, Pete Seeger, Joan Baez, Odetta, among others. At the recent Newport Folk Festival,

Peter Yarrow, who was to sing "Blowin' in the Wind" with Peter, Paul and Mary, said, "This song was written by the most important folk artist in America today." Miss Baez called him on stage to share her concert and at the conclusion of Dylan's own performance, every major star at the Festival joined him on stage for a "We Shall Overcome" finale.

Since Newport, Dylan has been appearing, unannounced, as part of Miss Baez's concerts. At the recent Forest Hills [N.Y.] concert, Miss Baez devoted the first half of her program to several of Dylan's songs, and then she introduced him in the second half, in which he performed solo and did duets with her. In October, he starts his own concertizing with one-man shows in New York (Carnegie Hall), Philadelphia, Boston, and Chicago, Plans are also being made for a college tour.

Dylan started his professional career a little over a year ago singing in Greenwich Village clubs after coming to New York to see veteran folk writer Woodie Guthrie, who is ailing in a local hospital. He was signed to a long-term disk deal by John Hammond of Columbia's artist and repertoire department.

The label has released two albums: *Bob Dylan* and *The Freewheelin' Bob Dylan*. In the first album, only two selections were written by him; on his second, only one was not written by him.

His song catalog was recently put into folio form by M. Witmark and Sons under the publication title *The Bob Dylan Song Book*.

PAUL NELSON AND JON PANKAKE

FLAT TIRE (1963)

Little Sandy Review, June 1963

The Little Sandy Review *was a mimeographed, small "magazine" published out of Dylan's home state of Minnesota by local folkniks John Pankake and Paul Nelson. Nelson and Pankake represented the younger generation of folk fans and knew Dylan "back when" he was just a struggling would-be folksinger. After giving a rave review to his first album, they were disapointed by his second. Their critique showed their knowledge of the source material that Dylan borrowed (stole?) to create his own songs, making for an unusually perceptive review. Nonetheless, they shortchange many classic songs, perhaps an early indication of the folk movement's disenchantment with their erstwhile hero.—CB*

"With my thumb out, my eyes asleep, my hat turned up an' my head turned on, I's driftin' and learnin' new lessons," Bob Dylan was quoted as saying in *Time*, May 31, 1963. Unfortunately, about half of his eagerly awaited second album suggests that both his eyes and his head were asleep.

Frankly, *The Freewheelin' Bob Dylan* is a great disappointment. That such a creative energy and driving force as Dylan would ever be satisfied with some of the material issued here is a great mystery. The virtues of the first album were an electrifying and mercurial inventiveness (both as a songwriter and as an interpreter) and a natural gift for genuine directness and simplicity in the finest folk-derived sense; those virtues barely exist here. As a songwriter, he has become melodramatic and maudlin, lacking all Guthriesque economy; his melodies bear more relation now to popular music than folk music. As a performer, he is at times affected and pretentious, although his harmonica technique has greatly improved. The main trouble now seems to be that he has no foundation or base for his songs; they seem to float vaguely above the ground in amorphous hazes; the talent is still apparent, but all the parts and working mechanisms seem to have broken down or gone out of control. Like Chaplin's feeding machine in *Modern Times*, the functions have gotten all mixed up, and the result is a mess.

"Blowin' in the Wind," Dylan's "This Land Is Your Land," gets the album off to a fine start; Bob sings and plays it well, and the song should be with us at least as long as the folk revival (and probably a lot longer). "Girl From the North Country" and "Bob Dylan's Dream" are examples of what the liner notes (by Nat Hentoff) describes as Dylan's "particular kind of lyricism." The latter is so mawkish and slushy that one wonders if he meant it as a joke, while the former, despite a pretty melody, is marred by a strangely foppish manner of singing. "Masters of War," Dylan's epic Protest song, is dull and monotonous both in text and performance; its total effect suggests a manufactured rather than a real anger. "A Hard Rain's A-Gonna Fall," being proclaimed by some as Dylan's masterpiece, seems far more a poem than a song (although Dylan says in the notes: "Anything I can sing I call a song"). Some of the images are striking and apt ("ten thousand talkers whose tongues were all broken"); others merely akin to bad beatnik poetry. The cut is, however, one of the most interesting on the record. "Oxford Town," about James Meredith, is a pleasant surprise: a protest song that ironically implies its "grimness" through common sense and good humor rather than baldly stating it.

Dylan wrote "Down the Highway" when his girl went to Italy for a few months. In it, he attempts to utilize Charlie Pickett's beautiful guitar run on an unrelated song of the same title that appears on *The Rural Blues* (RBF 202); the result is practically pure folknik, and Dylan has missed Pickett's point altogether. "Don't Think Twice, It's All Right," according to reports, is the next Dylan song that will be given the pop treatment by groups like the Chad Mitchell Trio and the Limeliters; it has a certain bittersweet charm to it. "Corrina, Corrina" makes feeble and cautious use of piano, bass, and drums in a pallid attempt at rhythm-and-blues. "Honey, Just Allow Me One More Chance" (from *Henry Thomas Sings the Texas Blues!* Origin Jazz Library OJL-3) gets the same treatment from Dylan as did Jesse Fuller's "You're No Good" on the first album; perhaps it was a leftover cut from then, since its style is far more frantic and pell-mell than anything else on this record.

Undoubtedly the strangest, loosest, funniest, and least worked out pieces on the album are the three long nonsense and talking songs: "Bob Dylan's Blues," "Talking World War III," and "I Shall Be Free." All are by turns engaging and futile, and all eventually fail because there is no logical continuity or point to them. Dylan is brilliantly funny or touching one moment, then floundering hopelessly in arid and embarrassing improvisation the next. His imagery falls far short of Guthrie's magic, and his wacky verses don't quite have that flash of humanitarian genius that marked Woody's as the work of a true folk poet. Instead, they stumble and stagger along, going nowhere, and not always with much style. There is, however, a great jugband harmonica on "Talking World War III." "I Shall Be Free" uses roughly the same tune and form that Woody and Leadbelly used on their recordings of "We Shall Be Free" for Folkways (2483 and 2488), although Dylan's verses are completely different.

A fine local singer recently made a most perceptive remark about the urban folk scene in general, not particularly about Dylan. He said, "Some singers are 98 percent personality and only 2 percent folk music, but that two percent is a whole lot better than most of the people in folk music today." It seems a good summation of *The Freewheelin' Bob Dylan*, an album that, like Arthur Miller's salesman, is "way out there in the blue, riding on a smile and a shoeshine," and nothing else. Dylan bases every-

His first motorcycle ride, at the 1964 Newport Folk Festival. *Photo copyright © David Gahr.*

thing here almost 100 percent on his own personality; there is hardly any traditional material, and most of the original material is not particularly folk-derived. It is pure Bob Dylan (Bob Dylan's dream, as it were), with its foundations in nothing that isn't constantly shifting, searching, and changing. What Dylan needs to do is to square the percentages between traditional and original back to 50–50 (as in his first album) to give some anchor of solidarity to his work; his absurd concoctions and blendings miss their mark here (whereas before they landed dead center), and the album floats away into never-never land, a failure, but a most interesting one. Don't make the mistake of crossing off Bob Dylan yet, however; he still remains one of our most promising songwriters and performers. As it stands, he'll merely have a first and a third album.

J. R. GODDARD

TIMES THEY ARE A-CHANGIN' (1964)

HiFi-Stereo Review, May 1964

Goddard, the same critic who lauded Dylan's first album in the Village Voice, *returns with his view of the bard's third disc. Already Dylan's bristly personality and his willingness to attack the press have begun to color the reaction to his performances. Goddard's discomfort with Dylan's growing resentment of any criticism is balanced by his still obvious fan's admiration for the singer/songwriter in this fascinating period review.*—CB

Interest: **Dylan the prophet**
Performance: **Mannered**
Recording: **Very good**
Stereo quality: **Good**

Bob Dylan the brilliant folksinger, who began to give way on his second album to Bob Dylan the brilliant polemicist, is now, with his third album, Bob Dylan the tortured bearer of visions. It is difficult for me to report on this latest record, having had part of my review of Dylan's second disc taken exception to by Dylan himself on the Carnegie Hall stage and I feel some small involvement in his career and also, as Norman Mailer now must, a hesitancy to comment too quickly on the achievements of public figures.

All the songs on this album are by Dylan, and many are in the vein he has made familiar. "Ballad of Hollis Brown," whose melody owes much to Woody Guthrie's "Pastures of Plenty," and "The Lonesome Death of Hattie Carroll," are two more reflections of Dylan's now familiar sense of outrage at the more obvious kinds of social injustice. "North Country Blues," a miner's song, has, like the as-yet-unreleased "Walls of Redwing," a fine feel for folk-like melody and a superb sense of place. "Boots of Spanish Leather" is a mourning, ruminative companion piece to "Girl from the North Country." "Only a Pawn in Their Game," like "Masters of War," is a broadside, this time about Medgar Evers and his assassin. "One Too Many Mornings," like "Bob Dylan's Dream," is a rare instance of completely personal feelings converted into communicable poetry. "With God on Our Side," a running chronicle of our country's wars, is brilliant and angry, one of the best things Dylan has done, until a confusing (and possibly confused) reference to Judas Iscariot is rung in at the last minute. I have commented on Dylan's singing previously, being especially taken with what I consider to be a harsh honesty, a vital excitement, an authentic, personal style in the tradition of Woody Guthrie. One wants to believe Dylan.

So far, Dylan's appeal has been mainly to the college set and to critics; the general public, as yet, has little knowledge of him. But Dylan has begun to act—in performance, in interviews and in private—as though his battle for recognition were already won. His main interest now, he says, is his message—his concern with such unexceptional causes as the Negro rights movement and nuclear disarmament—and he tends to interpret any criticism directed at him as being an attack on the cause.

What troubles me most about this new record are the three songs called "Restless Farewell," "The Times They Are A-Changin'" and "When the Ship Comes In," and Dylan's self-conscious on-the-road poetry that serves as liner notes. Together, they point out the peculiarly defensive tone of this entire production.

"Restless Farewell" is an unremitting "apologia pro vita sua" consisting of Dylan's oblique answers to the "dust of rumors" that he claims have been visited on him by those who do not understand his message. But his message, rather than being transformed into art, is turned into sulky mannerism. This criticism is disconcertingly true of the album as a whole, and if one listens to the vague threats of a new order that make up "The Times They Are A-Changin'" and "When the Ship Comes In," it becomes possible to speculate on how much freedom of dissent there would be if Dylan, the angry dissenter, were ever in authority.

Budd Schulberg once wrote a short story, which was later made into a film, called *A Face in the Crowd*, about a hillbilly singer with a fabricated past who began to consider himself a political force. Lonesome Rhodes, the protagonist of that piece, destroyed himself when he began to collect and bleed over his own press notices. It would be a great shame if Bob Dylan, who I once thought—and would still like to think—was the most important folksinger and writer we have had since Woody Guthrie, were to become only a mannered apologist for his own wounded self-esteem.

IRWIN SILBER

AN OPEN LETTER TO BOB DYLAN (1964)

Sing Out! 14(5), 1964

Irwin Silber was one of the grand old leftists of the folk movement. Long-time editor of the leading folk magazine Sing Out!, *Silber was an early champion of Dylan's who, like many others, was disturbed by his early commercial success. Before the famous 1965 Newport Folk Festival "incident," Silber was already worrying that Dylan was becoming too popular and forgetting his topical song roots. This "open letter" was his attempt to pull Dylan back into the fold.—CB*

With his manager, Albert Grossman, at Newport, 1965. *Photo copyright © David Gahr.*

Dear Bob:

It seems as though lots of people are thinking and talking about you these days. I read about you in *Life* and *Newsweek* and *Time* and the *Saturday Evening Post* and *Madamoiselle* [*sic*] and *Cavalier* and all such, and I realize that, all of a sudden, you have become a pheenom, a VIP, a celebrity. A lot has happened to you in these past two years, Bob—a lot more than most of us thought possible.

I'm writing this letter now because some of what has happened is troubling me. And not me alone. Many other good friends of yours as well.

I don't have to tell you how we at *Sing Out!* feel about you—about your work as a writer and an artist—or how we feel about you as a person. *Sing Out!* was among the first to respond to the new ideas, new images, and new sounds that you are creating. By last count, thirteen of your songs had appeared in these pages. Maybe more of Woody's songs were printed here over the years, but, if so, he's the only one. Not that we were doing you any favors, Bob. Far from it. We believed—and still believe—that these have been among some of the best new songs to appear in America in more than a decade. "Blowin' in the Wind," "Don't Think Twice," "Hattie Carroll," "Restless Farewell," "Masters of War"—these have been inspired contributions which have already had a significant impact on American consciousness and style.

As with anyone who ventures down uncharted paths, you've aroused a growing number of petty critics. Some don't like the way you wear your hair or your clothes. Some don't like the way you sing. Some don't like the fact that you've chosen your name and recast your past. But all of that, in the long run, is trivial. We both know that many of these criticisms are simply cover-ups for embarrassment at hearing songs that speak directly, personally, and urgently about where it's all really at.

But—and this is the reason for this letter, Bob—I think that the times they are a-changing. You seem to be in a different kind of bag now, Bob—and I'm worried about it. I saw at Newport how you had somehow lost contact with people. It seemed to me that some of the paraphernalia of fame were getting in your way. You travel with an entourage now—with good buddies, who are going to laugh when you need laughing and drink wine with you and insure your privacy—and never challenge you to face everyone else's reality again.

I thought (and so did you) of Jimmy Dean when I saw you last—and I cried a little inside me for that awful potential for self-destruction which lies hidden in all of us and which can emerge so easily and so uninvited.

I think it begins to show up in your songs, now, Bob. You said you weren't a writer of "protest" songs—or any other category, for that matter—but you just wrote songs. Well, okay, call it anything you want. But any songwriter who tries to deal honestly with reality in this world is bound to write "protest" songs. How can he help himself?

Your new songs seem to be all inner-directed now, inner-probing, self-conscious—maybe even a little maudlin or a little cruel on occasion. And it's happening on stage, too. You seem to be relating to a handful of cronies behind the scenes now—rather than to the rest of us out front.

Now, that's all okay—if that's the way you want it, Bob. But then you're a different Bob Dylan from the one we knew. The old one never wasted our precious time.

Perhaps this letter has been long overdue. I think, in a sense, that we are all responsible for what's happening to you—and to many other fine young artists. The American Success Machinery chews up geniuses at a rate of one a day and still hungers for more. Unable to produce real art on its own, the Establishment breaks creativity in protest against any non-conformity to the System. And then, through notoriety, fast money, and status, it makes it almost impossible for the artist to function and grow. It is a process that must be constantly guarded against and fought.

Give it some thought, Bob. Believe me when I say that this letter is written out of love and deep concern. I wouldn't be sticking my neck out like this otherwise.

SING OUT!

REPLIES TO SILBER'S OPEN LETTER (1964)

Sing Out! *received many letters both pro and con after running Silber's "open letter." Here are the excerpts that they ran, showing the division in the folk community over Dylan's recent success. A footnote to history: correspondent John Sinclair later became famous because of his far-left writings and association with Detroit's radical rock band, the MC5.—CB*

Dear Editor:

It's rather amusing to note that Dylan's most-requested song at Newport was one of those "inner probing and self-conscious" ones entitled "Hey, Mister Tambourine Man."

Neil Alan Marks
Forest Hills, N.Y.

—

. . . Dylan was never the run-of-the-mill folksinger the hippies seem to want. . . . Even his "committed" songs had a deeper irony and a more profound intelligence to them than any other of the worker-war-bomb polemics everyone sings. . . . Anyone with a simple awareness, an elementary grasp of what's going on in this world, can talk about the obvious evil around him, [but this is just] superficial. Dylan has begun to go beneath the surface. . . .

John Sinclair
Detroit, Mich.

—

Your last issue disturbed me somewhat. It seems to me that Mr. Silber's criticisms may prove premature: all artists go through phases of development. It is ridiculous to pounce upon an artist of twenty-three and denounce him for a new trend, in particular, for introspection, which is only natural in a person's early years and these times. It also seems quite evident that he has enough character to know what he's doing and to survive the American Success Machinery. As to Newport, I did not see him "lose contact with people."
. . . It seems inevitable that a real artist will produce both very bad and very good, and as long as he is unique, he will be very controversial. . . . We get the idea: *Sing Out!* will reendorse Bob Dylan when and if he returns to his old song topics.

Carol Sheffield
Cambridge, Mass.

—

It took much courage for Mr. Silber to "stick his neck out" in writing the truth about Bob Dylan now. The "open letter" is a respected and highly effective form of journalism, and there is no reason why he shouldn't have used it, but I would hate to see the letters I imagine he will get because of it. Bob Dylan is a public figure; it is good to see such concerned criticism about him. Praise or criticism—it doesn't matter as long as it is honest.

Roger De Lino
Pittsburgh, Penn.

BERNARD KLEINMAN

DYLAN ON DYLAN (1984)

Westwood One (Radio Station Discs), November 17, 1984

In this portion of a 1984 interview, Dylan talks candidly about his early career—unlike his early interviews, in which he was known to stretch a fact or two. He also comments on his recording philosophy and why he tours. Besides interviewer Kleinman, Artie Mogull, who worked for Witmark & Sons music publishers in 1962 and signed the fledgling songwriter to that firm, was also on hand.—CB

B.K.: *Is it true that you taught yourself guitar and harmonica?*

Dylan: Well, nobody really teaches themselves guitar and harmonica, you know, when you don't know anything first of all you get yourself a book or something. What I remember is learning a couple of chords from some books and then going out to watch people, you know, to see how they're doing it. You don't go so much to hear 'em . . . you just go to see how they do what they do, get as close as you can, see what their fingers are doing. In those early stages it's more like a learning thing, and that can sometimes take . . . years, many years. But to me I kind of picked it up fairly quickly, I didn't really play with that much technique. And people really didn't take to me because of that, because I didn't go out of my way to learn as much technique as other people. . . . I mean, I know people who spent their whole lives learning John Lee Hooker chords, just hammering on, you know, on the E string, and that was all. But they could play it in such a beautiful way it looked like a ballet dancer. Everybody had a different style, they had styles and techniques, especially in folk-music, you know, there was your southern mountain banjo, then flat picking, then your finger picking techniques, and just all of these different runs, you know, different styles of ballads. Folk-music was a world that was very split-up . . . and there was a purist side to it. Folk people didn't want to hear it if you couldn't play the song exactly the way that . . . Aunt Molly Jackson played it. And I just kind of blazed my way through all that stuff [laughter]. I would hear somebody do something and it would get to a certain point that you'd say, what do you want from that, you'd want to see what style they were playing . . . I don't know, I just stayed up day and night just barnstorming my way though all that stuff. And then I heard Woody Guthrie, and then it all came together for me. . . .

B.K.: Do you remember the first Woody Guthrie record you heard?

Dylan: Yeah, I think the first Woody Guthrie song I heard was "Pastures of Plenty." And "Pretty Boy Floyd" and another song . . . he used to write a lot of his songs from existing melodies, you know, "Grand Coulee Dam." They just impressed me.

B.K.: Got to you?

Dylan: Oh, yeah. Because they were original, they just had a mark of originality on them, well the lyrics did. I just heard all those songs and I learned them all off the records. All the songs of Woody Guthrie that I could find, anybody that had a Woody Guthrie record or that knew a Woody Guthrie song. And in St. Paul at the time, where I was, there were some people around who not only had his records but who knew his songs. So I just learned them all, some of the best records that I heard him make were these records that he made on the Stinson label, with Cisco Houston and Sonny Terry. I don't know if Leadbelly was on there too, I learned a bunch of Leadbelly's stuff too and learned how to play like that. But one of the biggest thrills I ever actually had was when I reached New York, whenever it was, and I got to play with Cisco Houston, I think I got to play with him at a party someplace. But I used to watch him, he used to play at Folk City. He was an amazing looking guy, he looked like Clark Gable, like a movie star.

Mogull: He reminded me a little of Tennessee Ernie, actually.

Dylan: Yeah.

Mogull: Also very unheralded.

Dylan: Oh, completely. He was one of the great unsung heroes. One of the great American figures of all time, and no one . . . you know you can ask people about him and nobody knows anything about him.

B.K.: *When do you think you started to develop something that was uniquely yours? You were talking about playing Woody Guthrie . . .*

Dylan: Well, when I came to New York that's all I played—Woody Guthrie songs. Then about six months after that I'd stopped playing all Woody Guthrie songs. I used to play in a place called Cafe Wha?, and it always used to open at noon, and closed at six in the morning. It was just a nonstop flow of people, usually they were tourists who were looking for beatniks in the Village. There'd be maybe five groups that played there. I used to play with a guy called Fred Neil, who wrote the song "Everybody's Talking" that was in the film *Midnight Cowboy*. Fred was from Florida I think, from Coconut Grove, Florida, and he used to make that scene, from Coconut Grove to Nashville to New York. And he had a strong powerful voice, almost a bass voice. And a powerful sense of rhythm. . . . And he used to play mostly these types of songs that Josh White might sing. I would play harmonica for him, and then once in a while get to sing a song. You know, when he was taking a break or something. It was his show, he would be on for about half an hour, then a conga group would get on, called Los Congeros, with twenty conga drummers and bongos and steel drums. And they would sing and play maybe half an hour. And then this girl, I think she was called Judy Rainey, used to play sweet Southern Mountain Appalachian ballads, with electric guitar and small amplifier. And then another guy named Hal Waters used to sing, he used to be a sort of crooner. Then there'd be a comedian, then an impersonator, and that'd be the whole show, and this whole unit would go around nonstop. And you get fed there, which was actually the best thing about the place.

Mogull: *How long a set would you do?*

Dylan: I'd do . . . oh, about half an hour. If they didn't like you back then you couldn't play, you'd get hooted off. If they liked you, you played more, if they didn't like you, you didn't play at all. You'd play one or two songs and people would just boo or hiss. . . .

B.K.: *This wasn't your own stuff you were singing there?*

Dylan: No, I didn't start playing my own stuff until . . . much later

B.K.: *Well, when did you start to perform your own stuff?*

Dylan: Well, I just drifted into it, you know, I just started writing. Well I'd always kinda written my own songs but I never played them. Nobody played their own songs then. The only person that did that was Woody Guthrie. And then one day I just wrote a song, and the first song I ever wrote that I performed in public was the song I wrote to Woody Guthrie. And I just felt like playing it one night—and so I played it.

B.K.: *Was writing something that you'd always wanted to do?*

Dylan: No, not really. It wasn't a thing I wanted to do ever. I wanted just a song to sing, and there came a certain point where I couldn't sing anything. So I had to write what I wanted to sing 'cos nobody else was writing what I wanted to sing. I couldn't find it anywhere. If I could, I probably would have never started writing.

B.K.: *Was the writing something that came easy to you? Because it is a craft that you do very well and you talk about it so causally.*

Dylan: Well, yeah, it does come easy. But then . . . after so many records sometimes you just don't know anymore whether . . . am I doing this because I want to do it or because you think it's expected of you. Do you know what I mean? So you'd start saying, well, it's time to write a song—I'll write a song. And you'll try to do something but sometimes it just won't come out right. At those kind of times it's best just to go sing somebody's songs.

B.K.: *Was it a lot of work, writing? Was it a labor?*

Dylan: No. It was just something I'd kinda do. You'd just sit up all night and write a song, or . . . in those days I used to write a lot of songs in cafes. Or at somebody's house with the typewriter. "A Hard Rain's A-Gonna Fall" . . . I wrote that in the basement of the Village Gate. All of it, at Chip Monck's, he used to have a place down there in the boiler room, an apartment that he slept in . . . next to the Greenwich Hotel. And I wrote "A Hard Rain's A-Gonna Fall" down there. I'd write songs at people's houses, people's apartments, wherever I was.

B.K.: *Were you much of a polisher, I mean did you write it and then pore over it?*

Dylan: Pretty much I'd just leave them the way they were. . . .

~

Dylan: Well, I don't know why I walked off that show [*Ed Sullivan*, 1963]. I could have done something else but we'd rehearsed the song so many times and everybody had heard it. They'd run through the show, you know, and they'd put you on and you'd run through your number, and it always got a good response and I was looking forward to singing it. Even Ed Sullivan seemed to really like it. I don't know who objected to it, but just before I was going to sing it they came in, and this was show time, you know. They came in, there was this big huddle, I could see people talking about something. I was just getting ready to play, you know . . . and then someone stepped up and said I couldn't sing that song. They wanted me to sing a Clancy Brother's song, and it just didn't make sense to me to sing a Clancy Brother's song on nationwide TV at that time. So . . . I just left.

Mogull: *Do you remember that time you were down in San Juan, Puerto Rico, at the CBS convention. And . . . it was being held at the San Juan Hilton, I guess . . . this huge record convention, and it was just as Bob was beginning to hit. And the President of CBS at the time was a fabulous man named Goddard Lieberson. And . . . they wouldn't let Bob in the hotel, because he was not wearing a tie or a jacket. . . .*

Dylan: Yeah, or a shirt.

Mogull: *And Lieberson, to his credit, told the hotel manager either he comes in the hotel or I'm pulling the whole convention out of here. Have I told the story right?*

Dylan: Yeah, he was a big supporter of mine. Goddard Lieberson, as was John Hammond. Without those people like that I don't think anything would have happened for me. If I was to come along now, in this day, with the kind of people that are running record companies now, they would . . . you know . . . bar the doors, I think. But you had people back then who were more entrenched in individuality.

Mogull: *And also not as insecure in their jobs.*

Dylan: No, they ran things, you know, they made decisions and it stuck. Now, I mean, it seems like everybody chats with somebody else, it's like, well, I'll tell you tomorrow, call me back later, yeah, we almost got a deal, stuff like that.

B.K.: *Did you get along with Lieberson okay . . . ?*

Dylan: Oh, yeah, he was great . . . he even used to come to some sessions of mine. He'd stop in and say hello, you know. . . .

B.K.: *Was there ever any pressure on you? I mean, some people considered your music almost subversive. Although I always considered it very American.*

Dylan: I guess they did . . . I don't know. But, like I said, they seemed to run things. You know, other people may have been talking under their breath or something, behind their back, and things like that. But at this time their big acts were Mitch Miller, Andy Williams, Johnny Mathis. I didn't really begin to sell many records until the second record . . . and the "Subterranean Homesick Blues" that made the charts.

B.K.: *That was an amazing single when you think of what the singles were like at the time.*

Dylan: They made some good records then, that, you know, were good pop records. Not on Columbia though. Phil Spector was doing a lot of stuff at the time, and Jerry Lieber and Mike Stoller. . . .

B.K.: *Were you listening to a lot of pop stuff at the time?*

Dylan: Yeah, I listened to a lot of pop stuff, but it never influenced what I was doing. At least to any great degree. It had earlier, like the really earlier stuff, when rock 'n' roll came in, after Elvis, Carl Perkins, Buddy Holly, those people. Chuck Berry, Little Richard, that stuff influenced me. . . . You know, nostalgia to me isn't really rock 'n' roll. Because when I was a youngster the music I heard was Frankie Laine, Rosemary Clooney, Dennis . . . what's his name? Dennis Day? And, you know, Dorothy Collins . . . the Mills Brothers, all that stuff. When I hear stuff like that it always strikes a different chord than all the rock 'n' roll stuff. The rock 'n' roll stuff, I had a conscious mind at that time, but ten years before that it was like "Mule Train" and . . . Johnny Ray knocked me out. Johnny Ray was the first person to actually really knock me out.

B.K.: What was it? What do you think it was about Johnny Ray?

Dylan: Well, he was just so emotional, wasn't he? I ran into him in an elevator in Australia . . . he was like one of my idols, you know. I mean, I was speechless, there I was in an elevator with Johnny Ray! I mean what do you say?

B.K.: When you started to move from the pure folk style into a more electric style, was that a tough one?

Dylan: We're getting into a touchy subject [laughter].

B.K.: Well, I mean, today you go on stage and both of those things coexist. Nobody thinks twice.

Dylan: Yeah, they always did coexist. . . .

B.K.: I'm not talking so much about that, but at least what it seemed like from the outside was that people were trying to tell you how to make your music.

Dylan: Oh . . . there's always people trying to tell you how to do everything in your life. If you really don't know what to do and you don't care what to do—then just ask somebody's opinion. You'll get a million different opinions. If you don't want to do something, ask someone's opinion and they'll just verify it for you. The easiest way to do something is to just not ask anybody's opinion. I mean, if you really believe in what you're doing. . . . I've just asked people's opinion and it's been a great mistake, in different areas. In my personal life, I've asked people what do you think about doing this and they've said . . . Oh Wow! . . . You know, and you end up not using it or else using it wrong.

Mogull: As a matter of fact, I think the artist has to make the innate decision about their . . .

Dylan: Yeah, you know what's right. When those things come you know what's right. A lot of times you might be farting around and not knowing what's right and you might do something dumb, but that's only because you don't know what to do in the first place. But if you know what's right and it strikes you at a certain time then you can usually believe that instinct. And if you act on it, then you'll be successful at it. Whatever it is.

B.K.: *Recording is a whole other thing from being on stage. And you, from what I've read, try and record as spontaneously as possible . . . ?*

Dylan: I have, yeah, I have, but I don't do that so often anymore. I used to do that . . . because recording a song bores me, you know, it's like working in a coal mine. Well, I mean, it's not really as serious as that, you're not completely that far underground! Maybe not in a literal sense, but . . . you could be indoors for months. And then what you think is real is just not anymore, you're just listening to sounds and your whole world is just working with tapes and things. I'm not . . . I've never liked that side of things. Plus I've never gotten into it on that level, when I first recorded I just went in and recorded the songs I had. That's the way people recorded then. But people don't record that way now, and I shouldn't record that way either because they can't even get it down that way any-more. To do what I used to do, or to do what anybody used to do you have to stay in the studio a longer time to get that right. Because, you know, technology has messed everything up so much.

B.K.: *It's messed it up?*

Dylan: Yeah, it's messed it up. Technology is giving a false picture. Like if you listen to any of the records that are done now they're all done in a technology sort of way. Which is a conniving kind of way, you can dream up what you want to do and just go in and dream it up! But you go see some of that stuff live and you're gonna be very disappointed, because . . . er . . . I mean, if you want to see some of it live. You may not want to know. Well, I think it's messed it up, but that's progress, you know. You can't go back to the way it used to be. For a lot of people it's messed things up, but then for a lot of other people it's a great advantage. In other words, you can get something right now, it doesn't have to be right but you can get it right. You know, it can be totally wrong but you can get it right! And it can be done just with sound and . . . We were just recording something the other night and we were gonna put some hand-claps on it. And the guy sitting behind the board, he was saying "Well do you guys wanna go out there and actually clap . . . ? I got a machine right here that can do that." And the name of this thing was Roland or something [laughter]. So we went out and clapped instead. It wasn't any big deal, we could have had some machine do it. . . . But that's just a small example of how everything is just machine-oriented, you know.

B.K.: You talk almost like . . . I don't really know how to put it . . . like the world's gone here and you're old-fashioned.

Dylan: Well, I feel I'm old-fashioned, but I don't believe I'm old-fashioned in the way that I'm not modern-fashioned. You know, on a certain level there is no old-fashioned and there's no new-fashioned . . . really nothing has changed. I don't think I'm old-fashioned in the kind of way that I feel I'm a passe person that's sitting somewhere . . . you know, out in Montana . . . just watching it snow. But even if I was, I'm sure that would be okay.

Mogull: Yeah, Bob, but you can't go to a concert like Wembley and get that kind of . . .

Dylan: Yeah, okay . . . but life is like that, you don't get that many years to live, right? So how long can you manage to keep up with things . . . ? And when you're keeping up with things what are you keeping up with? Who buys most of the records nowadays? twelve-year-old kids? Who buys Michael Jackson's records? twelve-year-olds. Fourteen-year-olds. Sixteen, twenty . . . I don't know who buys fifty million records of somebody. You know, you can't compete with a market that's geared for a market for twelve-year-olds. You know, you have rock 'n' roll critics that are forty years old writing about records that are geared for people that are ten years old! And making an intellectual philosophy out of it.

B.K.: But you don't listen to that stuff?

Dylan: No, I don't listen to that stuff, and I don't listen to those critics. I've come up with a lot of people who should know a whole lot better, who have made a career about writing about rock 'n' roll. Writing about rock 'n' roll . . . ! I mean . . . you know, how indecent can you be? Well, I'm not saying that it's all bad, people have to express themselves. So rock 'n' roll gives them a thrill, or did give them a thrill. Well, most of the people that I can think of as rock 'n' roll authorities are people who have documented down what I remember growing up with as it started . . . right? So everybody knows where the roots of rock 'n' roll are. Everybody knows who does what, but to make such an intellectual game out of it is beside the point, you know, it's not really going to add anything to the history of popular music. It's just going to feed a lot of cynical people and self-righteous people who think they've got a claim on a rock 'n' roll goldmine . . . or whatever. So I find that very distasteful.

B.K.: *Do you have . . . I'm not going to ask you which ones . . . but are there any things that you look back on and say "Jesus, that was a good one" . . . ?*

Dylan: Oh, yeah. Some of the songs you're talking about, you know, I can't write those songs today. No way. But I look at those songs, 'cos I sing 'em all the time, I wonder where they came from and how they came . . . how it's constructed. Even the simpler songs, I look at them that way. I couldn't do them now, and I don't even try, I'd be a fool to try. I think there are a lot of good songwriters though, what I've done I've done all alone, but there's a lot of other good songwriters . . . of my era.

Mogull: *Like who, Bob?*

Dylan: Randy Newman writes good songs, Paul Simon's written some good songs, I think "America" is a good song, I think "The Boxer" is a good song. I think "Bridge over Troubled Water" is a good song. I mean, he's written a lot of bad songs too, but everybody's done that. Let's see . . . some of the Nashville writers . . . Shel Silverstein writes great songs. Really. Like he's one of my favorite songwriters. You know, whatever, you're expressing it out of the amount of knowledge and light and inspiration you're giving on it. If you're just given an inch, you know . . . well you've just got to make of that as much as you can.

B.K.: *Have you ever tried your hand at any of the other arts?*

Dylan: Yeah, painting.

B.K.: *Really, do you do much of it?*

Dylan: Yeah, well, not so much in recent years, but it's something that I would like to do if I could . . . you've got to be in the right place to do it, you have to commit a lot of time . . . because one thing leads to another and you tend to discover new things as you go along. So it takes time to develop it, but I know how to do it fundamentally so once I get into the rhythm of it, and if I can hang with it long enough. . . .

B.K.: Do you take time for yourself?

Dylan: Oh, yeah, I take time for myself. I don't have any public time. People think I do but that's my time.

B.K.: That's a great place to be.

Dylan: Well, that's the place you were at when you were born. That's the place you should be. I mean, what's there to make you not be in that place? Do you have to be part of the machine . . . so what if you're not part of the machine?

Part Two

DON'T LOOK BACK
1965–1967

O. B. BRUMMEL

ANOTHER SIDE OF BOB DYLAN (1965)

High Fidelity, January 1965

This amusing review written in the style of Dylan's "poetic" liner notes shows a mainstream journalist's reaction to the more pretentious side of Mr. D.—CB

now i been listenin
like a reviewer gotta
t bob dylan records
for about two years
n he writes his own material
just like edgar guest
n uncle
   josh
      billings used t
n that's creditable

some o bob's early ballads
are pretty good
like blowin in the wind
n with god on our side
but these new ones
ain't much
in fact most o them
sound like he wrote em fast
maybe three
   or four
      per day
includin bad days

still they come from the north
n they come from the south
from the mountains o
the grand concourse
n the prairies o

greenwich village
for t listen t bob's ballads
even though bob don't carry
much of a tune
n joan n judy
n even peter
paul n mary
sing em dutifully
cause bob is the laureate o the cause
god help it

n now
whenever you buy one o
bob's releases
columbia don't bother with
no album notes
they jus fill the sleeve
with bob's leftover verse
n man that's culture
   with a capital
      cull

but bob
he got two problems
small ones
the language he writes in
aint english
the measures he beats out
aint song

n this kind o
inverted intellectuality
jus bores
   the hell
      out o me

J. R. GODDARD AND BOB DYLAN

DYLAN MEETS THE PRESS (1965)

Village Voice, March 25, 1965

Dylan quickly earned a reputation for his absurdist answers to the often absurd questions of newspaper interviewers. Here, friendly critic Goddard and Dylan together have some fun making up a totally absurd interview. Phil Ochs, of course, was the prominent folk/protest singer; Al Aronowitz was an early champion of New York's Beat writers.—CB

Q: Bobby, We know you changed your name. Come on now, what's your real name?

B.D.: Philip Ochs. I'm gonna change it back when I see it pays.

Q: Was Woody Guthrie your greatest influence?

B.D.: I don't know that I'd say that, but for a spell, the idea of him affected me quite much.

Q: How about Brecht? Read much of him?

B.D.: No. But I've read him.

Q: Rimbaud?

B.D.: I've read his tiny little book *Evil Flowers* too.

Q: How about Hank Williams? Do you consider him an influence?

B.D.: Hey look, I consider Hank Williams, Captain Marvel, Marlon Brando, the Tennessee Stud, Clark Kent, Walter Cronkite and J. Carrol Naish all influences. Now what is it—please—what is it exactly you people want to know?

Q: Tell us about your movie.

B.D.: It's gonna be in black and white.

Q: Will it be in the Andy Warhol style?

B.D.: Who's Andy Warhol? Listen, my movie will be—I can say definitely—it will be in the style of the early Puerto Rican films.

Q: Who's writing it?

B.D.: Allen Ginsberg. I'm going to rewrite it.

Q: Who will you play in the film?

B.D.: The hero.

Q: Who is it that you're going to be?

B.D.: My mother.

Q: What about your friends the Beatles? Did you see them when you were there?

B.D.: John Lennon and I came down to the Village early one morning. They wouldn't let us in the Figaro or the Hip Bagel or the Feenjon. This time I'm going to England. This April. I'll see 'em if they're there.

Q: Bob, what about the situation of American poets? Kenneth Rexroth has estimated that since 1900 about thirty American poets have committed suicide.

B.D.: Thirty poets! What about American housewifes, mailmen, street cleaners, miners? Jesus Christ, what's so special about thirty people that are called poets? I've known some very good people that have committed suicide. One didn't do nothing but work in a gas station all his life. Nobody referred to him as poet, but if you're gonna call people like Robert Frost a poet, then I got to say this gas station boy was a poet too.

Q: Bob, to sum up—don't you have any important philosophy for the world?

Rehearsing for the famous electric concert at the 1965 Newport Folk Festival with members of the Paul Butterfield Blues Band, including Mike Bloomfield, bassist Jerome Arnold, drummer Sam Lay (*obscured*) and Al Kooper on keyboards. *Photo copyright © David Gahr.*

B.D.: Are you kidding? The world don't need me. Christ, I'm only five feet ten. The world could get along fine without me. Don'cha know, everybody dies. It don't matter how important you think you are. Look at Shakespeare, Napoleon, Edgar Allan Poe, for that matter. They are all dead, right?

Q: Well, Bob, in your opinion, then, is there one man who can save the world?

B.D.: Al Aronowitz.

PAUL J. ROBBINS

BOB DYLAN IN HIS OWN WORDS (1965)

Los Angeles Free Press, September 17, September 24, 1965

An unusually serious and thoughtful interview from Dylan. In it, he discusses his current relation to the folk movement and his attitude toward his older social-protest songs. Dylan had appeared at the Hollywood Bowl on September 3; the following day, he gave a typically absurdist performance at a press conference. This interview was probably given sometime during those days. Note: Blind Boy Grunt *was a name Dylan used on some recordings, particularly of his topical songs, to mask his identity.—CB*

P.R.: *I don't know whether to do a serious interview or carry on in that absurdist way we talked last night.*

B.D.: It'll be the same thing anyway, man.

P.R.: *Yeah, okay. . . . If you are a poet and write words arranged in some sort of rhythm, why do you switch at some point and write lyrics in a song so that you're singing the words as part of a Gestalt presence?*

B.D.: Well, I can't define that word, poetry, I wouldn't even attempt it. At one time I thought that Robert Frost was poetry, other times I thought that Allen Ginsberg was poetry, sometimes I thought François Villon was poetry—but poetry isn't really confined to the printed page. Hey, then again, I don't believe in saying "Look at that girl walking! Isn't that poetry?" I'm not going to get insane about it. The lyrics to the songs . . . just so happens that it might be a little stranger than in most songs. I find it easy to write songs. I been writing songs for a long time and the words to the songs aren't written out just for the paper; they're written as you can read it, you dig. If you take whatever there is to the song away—the beat, the melody—I could still recite it. I see nothing wrong with songs you can't do that with either—songs that, if you took the beat and the melody away, they wouldn't stand up. Because they're not supposed to do that, you know. Songs are songs. . . . I don't believe in expecting too much out of any one thing.

P.R.: Whatever happened to Blind Boy Grunt?

B.D.: I was doing that four years ago. Now there's a lot of people writing songs on protest subjects. But it's taken some kind of a weird step. Hey, I'd rather listen to Jimmy Reed or Howlin' Wolf, man, or the Beatles, or François Hardy, than I would listen to any protest song singers—although I haven't heard all the protest song singers there are. But the ones I've heard—there's this very emptiness which is like a song written "Let's hold hands and everything will be grand." I see no more to it than that. Just because someone mentions the word "bomb," I'm not going to go "Aalee!" and start clapping.

P.R.: Is it that they just don't work anymore?

B.D.: It's not that it don't work, it's that there are a lot of people afraid of the bomb, right. But there are a lot of other people who're afraid to be seen carrying a *Modern Screen* magazine down the street, you know. Lot of people afraid to admit that they like Marlon Brando movies. . . . Hey, it's not that they don't work anymore but have you ever thought of a place where they do work? What exactly does work?

P.R.: They give a groovy feeling to the people who sing them, I guess that's about it. But what does work is the attitude, not the song. And there's just another attitude called for.

B.D.: Yeah, but you have to be very hip to the fact about that attitude—you have to be hip to communication. Sure, you can make all sorts of protest songs and put them on a Folkways record. But who hears them? The people that do hear them are going to be agreeing with you anyway. You aren't going to get somebody to hear it who doesn't dig it. People don't listen to things they don't dig. If you can find a cat that can actually say "Okay, I'm a changed man because I heard this one thing—or I just saw this one thing. . . ." Hey it don't necessarily happen that way all the time. It happens with a collage of experience which somebody can actually know by instinct what's right and wrong for him to do. Where he doesn't actually have to feel guilty about anything. A lot of people can act out of guilt. They act because they think somebody's looking at them. No matter what it is. There's people who do anything because of guilt. . . .

P.R.: And you don't want to be guilty?

B.D.: It's not that I'm NOT guilty. I'm not any more guilty than you are. Like, I don't consider any elder generation guilty. I mean, they're having these trials at Nuremberg, right? Look at that and you can place it out. Cats say "I had to kill all those people or else they'd kill me." Now, who's to try them for that? Who are these judges that have got the right to try a cat? How do you know they wouldn't do the same thing?

P.R.: This may be a side trip, but this thing about the statute of limitations running out and everybody wants to extend it? You remember, in Animal Farm, *what they wrote on the wall? "All animals are equal." But later they added "but some are more equal than others." It's the same thing in reverse. That some are less equal than others. Like Nazis are really criminals, so let's really get them; change any law just to nail them all.*

B.D.: Yeah, all that shit runs in the same category. Nobody digs revenge, right? But you have these cats from Israel who, after twenty years, are still trying to catch these cats, who're old cats, man, who have escaped. God knows they aren't going to go anywhere, they're not going to do anything. And you have these cats from Israel running around catching them. Spending twenty years out of their lives. You take that job away from them and they're no more or less than a baker. He's got his whole life tied up in one thing. It's a one-thought thing, without anything between: "That's what it is, and I'm going to get it." Anything between gets wiped all away. I can't make that, but I can't really put it down. Hey: I can't put anything down, because I don't have to be around any of it. I don't have to put people down which I don't like, because I don't have to be around any of those people. Of course there is the giant great contradiction of What Do You Do. Hey, I don't know what you do, but all I can do is cast aside all the things not to do. I don't know where it's at once in a while, all I know is where it's not at. And as long as I know that, I don't really have to know, myself, where's it at. Everybody knows where it's at once in a while, but nobody can walk around all the time in a complete Utopia. Dig poetry. You were asking about poetry? Man, poetry is just bullshit, you know? I don't know about other countries, but in this one it's a total massacre. It's not poetry at all. People don't read poetry in this country—if they do, it offends them; they don't dig it. You go to school, man, and what kind of poetry do you read? You read Robert Frost's "The Two Roads," you read T. S. Eliot—you read all that bullshit and that's just bad, man, it's not good. It's not anything hard, it's just soft-boiled egg shit. And then, on top of it, they throw Shakespeare at some kid who can't read Shakespeare in high school, right? Who digs reading *Hamlet*, man? All they give you is *Ivanhoe, Silas Marner, Tale of Two Cities*—and they keep you away from things which you should do. You shouldn't even be there in school. You should find out from people. Dig! That's where it all starts. In the beginning—like from 13 to 19—that's where all the corruption is. These people all just overlook it, right? There's more V.D. in people 13 to 19 than there is in any other group, but they ain't ever going to say so. They're never going to go into the schools and give shots. But that's where it's at. It's all a hype, man.

P.R.: Relating all this: if you put it in lyrics instead of poetry, you have a higher chance of hitting the people who have to be hit?

B.D.: I do, but I don't expect anything from it, you dig? All I can do is be me—whoever that is—for those people that I do play to, and not come on with them, tell them I'm something I'm not. I'm not going to tell them I'm the Great Cause Fighter or the Great Lover or the Great Boy Genius or whatever. Because I'm not, man. Why mislead them? That's all just Madison Avenue selling me, but it's not really selling me, 'cause I was hip to it before I got there.

P.R.: Which brings up another thing. All the folk magazines and many folk people are down on you. Do they put you down because you changed or . . .

B.D.: It's that I'm successful and they want to be successful, man. It's jealousy. Hey, anybody with any kind of knowledge at all would know by instinct what's happening here. Somebody who doesn't know that is still hung up with success and failure and good and bad . . . maybe he doesn't have a chick all the time . . . stuff like that. But I can't use comments, man. I don't take nothing like that seriously. If somebody praises me and say "How groovy you are!" it doesn't mean nothing to me, because I can usually sense where that person's at. And it's no compliment if someone who's a total freak comes up and says "How groovy you are!" And it's the same if they don't dig me. Other kinds of people don't have to say anything because, when you come down to it, it's all what's happening in the moment which counts. Who cares about tomorrow and yesterday? People don't live there, they live now.

P.R.: *I have a theory, which I've been picking up and shaking out every so often. When I spoke with the Byrds, they were saying the same thing as I am saying—a lot of people are saying—you're talking it. It's why we have a new so-called rock and roll sound emerging, it's a synthesis of all things, a . . .*

B.D.: It's further than that, man. People know nowadays more than before. They've had so much to look at by now and know the bullshit of everything. People now don't even care about going to jail. So what? You're still with yourself as much as if you're out on the streets. There's still those who don't care about anything, but I got to think that anybody who doesn't hurt anybody, you can't put that person down, you dig, if that person's happy doing that.

P.R.: *But what if they freeze themselves into apathy? What if they don't care about anything at all anymore?*

B.D.: Whose problem is that? Your problem or theirs? No, it's not that, it's that nobody can learn by somebody else showing them or teaching them. People got to learn by themselves, going through something which relates. Sure, you say how do you make somebody know something . . . people know it by themselves; they can go through some kind of scene with other people and themselves which somehow will come out somewhere and it's grind into them and be them. And all that just comes out of them somehow when they're faced up to the next thing.

P.R.: *It's like taking in until the time comes to put out, right. But people who don't care don't put anything out. It's a whole frozen thing where nothing's happening anywhere; it's just like the maintenance of status quo, of existing circumstances, whatever they are. . . .*

B.D.: People who don't care? Are you talking about gas station attendants or a Zen doctor, man? Hey, there's a lot of people who don't care; a lot don't care for different reasons. A lot care about some things and not about others, and some who don't care about anything—it's just up to me not to let them bring me down and not to bring them down. It's like the whole world has a little thing: it's being taught that when you get up in the morning, you have to go out and bring somebody down. You walk down the street and, unless you've brought somebody down, don't come home today, right? It's a circus world.

P.R.: So who is it that you write and sing for?

B.D.: Not writing and singing for anybody, to tell you the truth. Hey, really, I don't care what people say. I don't care what they make me seem to be or what they tell other people I am. If I did care about that, I'd tell you; I really have no concern with it. I don't even come in contact with these people. Hey, I dig people, though. But if somebody's going to come up to me and ask me some questions which have been on his mind for such a long time, all I can think of is "Wow, man, what else can be in that person's head besides me? Am I that important, man, to be in a person's head for such a long time he's got to know this answer?" I mean, can that really straighten him out—if I tell him something? Hey, come on. . . .

P.R.: A local disc jockey, Les Claypool, went through a whole thing on you one night, just couldn't get out of it. For maybe 45 minutes, he'd play a side of yours and then an ethnic side in which it was demonstrated that both melodies were the same. After each pair he'd say, "Well, you see what's happening. . . . This kid is taking other people's melodies; he's not all that original. Not only that," he'd say, "but his songs are totally depressing and have no hope."

B.D.: Who's Les Claypool?

P.R.: A folk jockey out here who has a long talk show on Saturday nights and an hour on each night, during which he plays highly ethnic sides.

B.D.: He played those songs? He didn't play something hopeful?

P.R.: No, he was loading it to make his point. Anyway, it brings up an expected question: why do you use melodies that are already written?

B.D.: I used to do that when I was more or less in folk. I knew the melodies; they were already there. I did it because I liked the melodies. I did it when I really wasn't that popular and the songs weren't reaching that many people, and everybody around dug it. Man. I never introduced a song, "Here's the song I've stole the melody from, someplace." For me it wasn't that important; still isn't that important. I don't care about the melodies, man, the melodies are all traditional anyway. And if anybody wants to pick that out and say "That's Bob Dylan," that's their thing, not mine. I mean, if they want to think that. Anybody with any sense at all, man, he says that I haven't any hope. . . . Hey, I got faith. I know that there are people who're going to know that's total bullshit. I know the cat is just uptight. He hasn't really gotten into a good day and he has to pick on something. Groovy. He has to pick on me? Hey, if he can't pick on me, he picks on someone else, it don't matter. He doesn't step on me, 'cause I don't care. He's not coming up to me on the street and stepping on my head, man. Hey, I've only done that with very few of my songs, anyway. And then when I don't do it, everybody's [saying] they're rock and roll melodies. You can't satisfy the people—you just can't. You got to know, man; they just don't care about it.

P.R.: Why is rock and roll coming in and folk music going out?

B.D.: Folk music destroyed itself. Nobody destroyed it. Folk music is still here, if you want to dig it. It's not that it's going in or out. It's all the soft mellow shit, man, that's just being replaced by something that people know there is now. Hey, you must've heard rock and roll long before the Beatles, you must've discarded rock and roll around 1960. I did that in 1957. I couldn't make it as a rock and roll singer then. There were too many groups. I used to play piano. I made some records, too.

P.R.: Okay, you got a lot of bread now. And your way of life isn't like it was four or five years ago. It's much grander. Does that kind of thing tend to throw you off?

B.D.: Well, the transition never came from working at it. I left where I'm from because there's nothing there. I come from Minnesota, there was nothing there. I'm not going to fake it and say I went out to see the world. Hey, when I left there, man, I knew one thing: I had to get out of there and not come back. Just from my senses I knew there was something more than Walt Disney movies. I was never turned on or off by money. I never considered the fact of money as really that important. I could always play the guitar, you dig, and make friends—or fake friends. A lot of other people do other things and get to eat and sleep that way. Lot of people do a lot of things just to get around. You can find cats who get very scared, right? Who get married and settle down. But, after some-body's got something and sees it all around him, so he doesn't have to sleep out in the cold at night, that's all. The only thing is he don't die. But is he happy? There's nowhere to go. Okay, so I get the money, right? First of all, I had to move out of New York. Because everybody was coming down to see me—people which I didn't really dig. People coming in from weird-ass places. And I would think, for some reason, that I had to give them someplace to stay and all that. I found myself not really being by myself but just staying out of things I wanted to go to because people I knew would go there.

P.R.: *Do you find friends—real friends—are they recognizable anymore?*

B.D.: Oh, sure, man, I can tell somebody I dig right away. I don't have to go through anything with anybody. I'm just lucky that way.

P.R.: *Back to protest songs. The IWW's work is over now and the unions are pretty well established. What about the civil rights movement?*

B.D.: Well, it's okay. It's proper. It's not "Commie" anymore. *Harper's Bazaar* can feature it, you can find it on the cover of *Life*. But when you get beneath it, like anything, you find there's bullshit tied up in it. The Negro civil rights movement is proper now, but there's more to it than what's in *Harper's Bazaar*. There's more to it than picketing in Selma, right? There's people living in utter poverty in New York. And then again, you have this big Right to Vote. Which is groovy. You want all these Negroes to vote? Okay, I can't go over the boat and shout "Hallelujah" only because they want to vote. Who are they going to vote for? Just politicians; same as the white people put in their politicians. Anybody that gets into politics is a little freaky anyway. Hey, they're just going to vote, that's all they're going to do. I hate to say it like that, make it sound hard, but it's going to boil down to that.

P.R.: *What about the drive for education?*

B.D.: Education? They're going to school and learn about all the things the white private schools teach. The catechism, the whole thing. What're they going to learn? What's this education? Hey, the cat's much better off never going to school. The only thing against him is he can't be a doctor or a judge. Or he can't get a good job with the salesman's company. But that's the only thing wrong. If you want to say it's good that he gets an education and goes out and gets a job like that, groovy. I'm not going to do it.

P.R.: *In other words, the formal intake of factual knowledge . . .*

B.D.: Hey, I have no respect for factual knowledge, man. I don't care what anybody knows, I don't care if somebody's a walking encyclopedia. Does that make him nice to talk to? Who cares if Washington was even the first president of the United States? You think anybody has actually ever been helped with this kind of knowledge?

P.R.: Maybe through a test. Well, what's the answer?

B.D.: There aren't any answers, man. Or any questions. You must read my book . . . there's a little part in there about that. It evolves into a thing where it mentions words like "Answer." I couldn't possibly rattle off the words for these, because you'd have to read the whole book to see these specific words or Question and Answer. We'll have another interview after you read the book.

P.R.: Yeah, you have a book coming out. What about it? The title?

B.D.: Tentatively, "Bob Dylan off the Record." But they tell me there's already books out with that "off the record" title. The book can't really be titled, that's the kind of book it is. I'm also going to write the reviews for it.

P.R.: Why write a book instead of lyrics?

B.D.: I've written some songs which are kind of far out, a long continuation of verses, stuff like that—but I haven't really gotten into writing a completely free song. Hey, you dig something like cut-ups? I mean, like William Burroughs?

P.R.: Yeah, there's a cat in Paris who published a book with no pagination. The book comes in a box and you throw it in the air and, however it lands, you read it like that.

B.D.: Yeah, that's where it's at. Because that's what it means, anyway. Okay, I wrote the book because there's a lot of stuff in there I can't possibly sing . . . all the collages. I can't sing it because it gets too long or it goes too far out. I can only do it around a few people who would know. Because the majority of the audience—I don't care where they're from, how hip they are—I think it would just get totally lost. Something that had no rhyme, all cut up, no nothing, except something happening, which is words.

P.R.: *You wrote the book to say something?*

B.D.: Yeah, but certainly not any kind of profound statement. The book don't begin or end.

P.R.: *But you had something to say. And you wanted to say it to somebody.*

B.D.: Yeah, I said it to myself. Only, I'm lucky, because I could put it into a book. Now somebody else is going to be allowed to see what I said to myself.

P.R.: *You have four albums out now, with a fifth any day. Are these albums sequential in the way that you composed and sung them?*

B.D.: Yeah, I've got about two or three albums that I've never recorded, which are lost songs. They're old songs; I'll never record them. Some very groovy songs. Some old songs which I've written and sung maybe once in a concert and nobody else ever heard them. There are a lot of songs which would fill in between the records. It was growing from the first record to the second, then a head change on the third. And the fourth. The fifth I can't even tell you about.

P.R.: *So if I started with Album One, Side One, Band One, I could truthfully watch Bob Dylan grow?*

B.D.: No, you could watch Bob Dylan laughing to himself. Or you could see Bob Dylan going through changes. That's really the most.

P.R.: *What do you think of the Byrds? Do you think they're doing something different?*

B.D.: Yeah, they could. They're doing something really new now. It's like a danceable Bach sound. Like "Bells of Rhymney." They're cutting across all kinds of barriers which most people who sing aren't even hip to. They know it all. If they don't close their minds, they'll come up with something pretty fantastic.

BEVERLEY HILLS PRESS CONFERENCE (1965)

September 4, 1965

This is a transcript of the press conference Dylan held after performing at the Hollywood Bowl. In comparison with the interview he gave to P. J. Robbins at about the same time, it reveals "another side" of Bob Dylan. The press conference was held in a bungalow at the Beverly Hills Hotel. Dylan arrived with David Crosby of the Byrds, a Columbia executive, and a barefoot woman. The conference lasts about an hour, and Dylan again plays his word games with the press, much to mass bemusement.—CB

Q: What do you think of your teenage fans?

B.D.: What do you mean when you say "teenager"? I don't know what you mean. I have no picture of a teenager in my mind. Name me a teenager. I have no recollection of ever being a teenager.

Q: Then you feel no responsibility toward your fans?

B.D.: I didn't make them my fans. They're my fans because I do what I do. I do what I want to do the way I want to do it. That's all I've ever done. People who call themselves my old fans mean like for two years they've been my fans. I've been recording for five years.

Q: What do you think of the new folk music?

B.D.: Everyone sounds incompetent.

Q: Will your increasingly large number of teenage fans influence your future work or plans?

B.D.: No. Just have to hire secretaries for the fan mail.

Q: What about your old protest songs?

B.D.: I'm not a preacher. Songs can't save the world, I know that. Whatever you have to give, you give. That's the way it is.

Q: How do you feel about the power grabbers, the people who can influence directly and indirectly what you do?

B.D.: They can't hurt me. Sure they can crush you and kill you. They can lay you out on 42nd and Broadway and put the hoses on you and flush you in the sewers and put you on the subway and carry you out to Coney Island and bury you on the Ferris wheel. But I refuse to sit here and worry about dying.

Q: Have you written anything besides songs?

B.D. Yes, a book will come out in December. It's called *Tarantula* but that title isn't definite yet.

Q: Is it a book of poetry?

B.D.: Some people might call it poetry. It's a book of words.

Q: Do you prefer writing poetry or songs?

B.D.: Poems. I don't have to condense or restrict my thoughts into a song pattern.

Q: Are you interested in television appearances?

B.D.: Yes, I wouldn't mind doing specials.

Q: Any other ambitions?

B.D.: I've always wanted to be Gary Cooper in *High Noon*.

Q: Are you interested in actively communicating your songs; in getting through to your audience?

B.D.: I don't have to prove anything to anyone. Those people who dig me know where I'm at—I don't have to come on to them. I'm not a ballroom singer.

Q: What about those in the audience who aren't grooving with you?

B.D.: I'm not interested in them.

Q: Do you feel you're using more "urban imagery" than in the past; that your lyrics are becoming more sophisticated?

B.D.: Well, I watch too much TV, I guess.

Q: What about Donovan?

B.D.: I like everybody. I don't want to be petty.

Q: A word for your fans?

B.D.: The lamp post stands with folded arms.

Q: What do you think of the new Bob Dylan?

B.D.: What's your name?

Q: Dave Moberg.

B.D.: Okay. What would you think if someone asked you, What do you think of the new Dave Moberg? What new Dave Moberg?

Q: Is Joan Baez still relevant?

B.D.: She's one of the most relevant people I know.

Q: Do you feel you're living a real life?

B.D.: No. I don't have any responsibility to the people who are hung up on me. I'm only responsible for what I create—I didn't create them.

Q: Has your success infringed on your personal life?

B.D.: What personal life? Hey, I have none.

Q: About your conversion to folk-rock . . .

B.D.: I had this thing called "Subterranean Homesick Blues." It just didn't sound right by myself. I tried the piano, the harpsichord. I tried it as blues. I tried it on the pipe-organ, the kazoo. But it fit right in with the band. I haven't changed a bit. I just got tired of playing the guitar by myself.

Q: What is the most important thing in your life these days?

B.D.: Well, I've got a monkey-wrench collection and I'm very interested in that.

Q: Do you think that anything of consequence happens at these things?

B.D.: Interviewers will write my scene and words from their own bags anyway, no matter what I say. I accept writers and photographers. I don't think it's necessary at all, but it happens anyway. I am not really involved.

The famous *Don't Look Back* tour, London, 1965, with Joan Baez. *Photo courtesy of Hulton-Deutsch Collection/Corbis.*

LAURIE HENSHAW

MR. SEND-UP (1965)

Disc Weekly, May 22, 1965

Dylan is extremely uncooperative in this interview, conducted on May 12 during his famous Don't Look Back *tour of England. In early interviews, Dylan had fabricated a believable life story; now he doesn't even bother, making up facts willy-nilly, perhaps as a sendup of the gullibility of the earlier interviewers or (more likely) a sendup of his own propensity to invent.—CB*

L.H.: *Can you tell me when and where you were born?*

B.D.: No, you can go and find out. There's many biographies and you can look to that. You don't ask me where I was born, where I lived. Don't ask me those questions. You find out from other papers.

L.H.: *I'd rather hear it from you.*

B.D.: I'm not going to tell you.

L.H.: *Can you tell me exactly when you entered the profession? When you first started writing songs?*

B.D.: When I was 12.

L.H.: *And you were writing poetry at the time? And you are writing a book now?*

B.D.: I've got a book done.

L.H.: *Is it already published?*

B.D.: It's going to be published in the fall.

L.H.: *What's it called?*

B.D.: I'm not going to tell you.

L.H.: Can you give me an idea what it is about?

B.D.: No.

L.H.: Can you tell me your favorite song among the ones you've written?

B.D.: I don't have any. I've no personal songs that I wouldn't consider apart from any other.

L.H.: You must obviously make a lot of money nowadays?

B.D.: I spend it all. I have six Cadillacs. I have four houses. I have a plantation in Georgia. Oh, I'm also working on a rocket. A little rocket. Not a big rocket. Not the kind of rocket they have in Cape Canaveral. I don't know about those kind of rockets.

L.H.: Do you have personal things—cameras, watches and that sort of thing?

B.D.: No, I don't. I buy cars. I have a lot of cars, the Cadillacs. I also have a few Oldsmobiles, about three.

L.H.: Do you have fears about anything political.

B.D.: No.

L.H.: Of course, your songs have a very strong content. . . .

B.D.: Have you heard my songs?

L.H.: I have. "Masters of War." "Blowin' in the Wind."

B.D.: What about "Spanish Lover"? [*sic*] Have you heard that? Why don't you listen to that? Listen, I couldn't care less what your paper writes about me. Your paper can write anything, don't you realize? The people that listen to me don't read your paper, you know, to listen to me. I'm not going to be known from your paper.

L.H.: You're already known. Why be so hostile?

B.D.: Because you're hostile to me. You're using me. I'm an object to you. I went through this before in the United States, you know. There's nothing personal. I've nothing against you at all. I just don't want to be bothered with your paper, that's all. I just don't want to be a part of it. Why should I have to go along with something just so that somebody else can eat? Why don't you just say that my name is Kissenovitch. You know, and I, er, come from Acapulco, Mexico. That my father was an escaped thief from South Africa. OK. You can say anything you want to say.

L.H.: Let's talk about you. Your clothes, for instance. Are your tastes in clothes changing at all?

B.D.: I like clothes. I don't have any particular interests at all. I like to wear drapes, umbrellas, hats.

L.H.: You're not going to tell me you carry an umbrella.

B.D.: I most certainly do carry an umbrella. Where I come from everybody carries an umbrella. Have you ever been to South Dakota? Well, I come from South Dakota, and in South Dakota people carry umbrellas.

L.H.: What would you say has been the greatest influence in your life?

B.D.: You! Your paper happens to influence me a lot. I'm going to go out and write a song after I've seen you—you know—what I'm used for. I feel what I'm doing and I feel what your paper does. And you have the nerve and gall to ask me what influences me and why do I think I'm so accepted. I don't want to be interviewed by your paper. I don't need it. You don't need it either. You can build up your own star. Why don't you just get a lot of money and bring some kid out here from the north of England and say "We're gonna make you a star! You just comply with everything, everything we do. Every time you want an interview you can just sign a paper that means we can have an interview and write what we want to write. And you'll be a star and make money!" Why don't you just do that? I'm not going to do it for you.

L.H.: Why should we bother to interview you if we didn't think you were worth interviewing?

B.D.: Because I'm news. That's why I don't blame you, you have a job to do. I know that. There's nothing personal here. But don't try to pick up too much, you know.

L.H.: *When did you start making records?*

B.D.: I started making records in 1947, that was my first recording. A race record. I made it down South. Actually the first record I made was in 1935. John Hammond came and recorded me. Discovered me in 1935, sitting on a farm. The man who discovered Benny Goodman saw me down the street. He had me in to do a session. It happened just like that. Otherwise I wouldn't be here.

L.H.: *Do you have a favorite guitar?*

B.D.: Favorite guitar? I have 33 guitars! How can you have one favorite? I'm going to quit playing the guitar anyway. I'm playing the banjo.

L.H.: *Have you heard Manfred Mann doing "With God on Our Side"?*

B.D.: No, I haven't heard it. I've only heard about it.

L.H.: *It was sung on* Ready Steady Goes Live *and it made quite an impact.*

B.D.: I would like to have seen it.

L.H.: *How do you feel about other groups doing your songs?*

B.D.: Well, how would you feel about other groups doing your songs?

L.H.: *I'd be complimented.*

B.D.: I'd feel the same as you.

L.H.: *What sort of people do you like? What type do you cultivate?*

B.D.: I would cultivate the kind of person that sticks to his job. Sticks to his job and gets his job done. And is not too nervous. But nervous enough not to come back!

L.H.: *What kind of people do you take an instant dislike to?*

B.D.: I take an instant dislike to people that shake a lot. An instant dislike—wham! Most of the time I throw them against a wall. I have a bodyguard, Toppo. [Dylan here puts his hands to his mouth and calls to the next room] TOPPO! Is Toppo in there? I have a bodyguard to get rid of people like that. He comes out and wipes them out. He wiped out three people last week.

L.H.: *Do you paint?*

B.D.: Yeah, sure.

L.H.: *What sort of painting?*

B.D.: I painted my house.

HENRIETTA YURCHENCO
FOLK-ROT: IN DEFENSE (1966)
Sound & Fury, April 1966

This author gives an overview of both the academic scene's disdain for Dylan and the folk scene's growing disillusion with him. Sympathetic to the singer, Yurchenco still can't get over the "clang clang" of the electrified Dylan. Still, this is an interesting defense of Dylan-the-bard versus his critics, and an early discussion of the virtues and vices of "folk-rot."—CB

In our age of overexposure it is apparently not enough to excel in one's field; one must be articulate about it and about one's self and be available and responsive to public and critical demand and instruction. I suspect that even our astronauts are selected not only for scientific qualifications and physical endurance, but also, to some degree, for their effectiveness before a microphone.

The controversy over Bob Dylan as a poet extends beyond the minor points mentioned above. Literary academicians also have their say. The publication *Books* conducted a poll of professors, critics and poets, which brought the following responses: Said Howard Nemerov, "Mr. Dylan is not known to me. Regrets." An English professor at the University of Vermont commented: "Anyone who calls Bob Dylan 'the greatest poet in the United States today' has rocks in his head. . . . Dylan is for the birds and the bird-brained," or, "His poetry sounds like a very self-conscious imitation of Kerouac, and for an English teacher this is pretty feeble praise. My students . . . have lost respect for Dylan, for they think he is after publicity and the nearest buck." John Ciardi wrote: "My nephew (a drummer) would agree that Bob Dylan is a poet, but like all Bob Dylan fans I have met, he knows nothing about poetry. Neither does Bob Dylan." A few, like John Clellan Holmes, went to his defense: "He has the authentic mark of the bard on him, and I think it's safe to say that no one, years hence, will be able to understand just what it was like to live in this time without attending to what this astonishingly gifted young man has already achieved." All shades of opinion were represented—from blind hostility to unqualified praise, and also the indifference of an older generation forgetful of its own rebellious youth.

If Dylan has done nothing else, he is responsible for the present widespread interest in poetry. He has taken it away from the academicians, off the dusty library shelves, and put it where it can be heard by countless thousands of young people. In our unpoetic age where an audience of a few hundred people at a poetry reading is unusual, Dylan's feat is quite remarkable.

From the start Dylan's poetry was characterized not only by the acuteness and individuality of his vision but by his gift for words and imagery. His poetic tools have been sharpened, particularly in his recent album *Highway 61 Revisited*. Virtuosity for its own sake, which sometimes needlessly halted the poetic flow, is now not so pronounced. Though still stunning and often startling, his images are more related to the central theme; therefore his construction is more disciplined, less erratic.

Dylan may be a popular poet, but he is not a simpleton, as some of his critics imply. He is very well read—and a poet of his time. Stanley Kunitz, quoted in Thomas Meehan's *New York Times* article, says: ". . . and popular art is the foundation on which fine art rests. Thus, the higher the level of taste there is in the popular arts, the more promising is the hope for the evolution of great fine art." But even more to the point is Kunitz' statement "there is no reason why popular art and a more selective, esoteric art can't cheerfully coexist."

The folk music community has been shaken to its very roots ever since Dylan appeared at the Newport Folk Festival in the summer of 1965 with

Paul Butterfield's Blues Band. Writing in *Sing Out!*, the nation's leading folk music magazine, Paul Nelson stated that Newport 1965 split apart the two biggest names in folk music, Pete Seeger (who had the backing of the crowd) and Bob Dylan (who was booed off the stage). He writes, "They [the audience] might have believed they were choosing humanity over a reckless me-for-me attitude, but they weren't. They were choosing suffocation over invention and adventure, backwards over forwards, a dead band instead of a live one." For Nelson also it seems only a matter of Seeger versus Dylan, whether to accept Pete's quest for a better, more brotherly world—or Bob's, "where things aren't often pretty, where there isn't often hope, where man isn't always noble, but where, most importantly, there exists a reality that coincides with that of this planet. Was it to be marshmallows and cotton candy or meat and potatoes?" The choice (continues Mr. Nelson) is between "a nice guy who has subjugated and weakened his art through his constant insistence on a world that never was and never can be, or an angry passionate poet who demands his art to be all, who demands not to be owned, not to be restricted. . . ."

This oversimplification does gross injustice to Seeger, Dylan, and the audience. It underestimates the great range of Seeger's seasoned understanding and overestimates the profundity of young Dylan's insights. It reflects a recurrent (and regrettable) need of both aficionados and critics—the need for "variety" in their diet of hero-worship; which partly explains why they periodically provide their heroes with a pedestal and just as regularly yank it from under them—pedestal their heroes never asked for in the first place, by the way. Why in the name of good folk music should anyone have to "choose between" two such authentic (and different) artists as Seeger and Dylan? Cannot we "choose" both?

Mr. Nelson makes more sense on the subject of the artist's freedom to write when and how he pleases. Even before Newport, Dylan's free wheeling wandering from the topical song field had kicked up a storm in folk-song circles. What a blow it was to have the most gifted songwriter since Guthrie not only "desert" the ranks, but disassociate himself from the "movement" entirely! The fact that Bob has never pretended to be solely a protest song writer has not stopped his critics from either condemning him or preaching the path of righteousness to him, or warning him of the dire pitfalls of commercial success.

In one of my talks with Bob at the outset of his career, he described the early months in New York: "I wrote wherever I happened to be. Sometimes I'd spend a whole day sitting at a corner table in a coffee house just writing whatever came into my head . . . just anything. I'd look at people for hours and I'd make up things about them, or I'd think, what kind of songs would they like to hear and I'd make one up." Hardly the words of a young writer concerned only with the hot issues of the outer world.

If it were only a question of entertainment criteria, if Dylan were only another Rudy Vallee, Frank Sinatra, Eddie Fisher, or Bing Crosby (all great performers in the popular field), we would have nothing to talk about. But Dylan is different from them all; he is a creator, and he has his literary finger on the pulse of the perplexing problems that beset young people today. His subjects, whether they concern (as they did until recently) political and social issues or whether they reflect inner problems (his current preoccupations), are all germane to our times and his life.

Whether Dylan is a great poet, history will have to decide, but he is unquestionably our most popular. He has given poetry a significance and stature which it has never had in American life. Furthermore, he is a bard—a singing poet in an ancient but thoroughly neglected tradition.

European, Near and Far Eastern and African epic poets have for thousands of years sung their national chronicles. Today, epic poetry (sung poetry) is an important factor in the national culture and has passed into the literary traditions of other lands. Not even such fine poets as Walt Whitman and Robert Frost—among our greatest—were truly popular poets; they were known mainly to intellectuals. This is not of course to imply that all popular poets are great, nor that the stature of the others is diminished.

In his latest albums, *Bringing It All Back Home* and *Highway 61 Revisited*, Dylan sings of the chaos and the absurdities of our changing world, the lack of understanding between adults and the young. He ridicules the dullness, the inadequacies and pointlessness of academic life. He chides those of his own generation who would settle for a comfortable, protected world, who let others make decisions for them, who prefer status and security to adventure in life. Of the fearful he says, "They're some people terrified of the bomb, but there are other people terrified to be seen carrying a *Modern Screen* magazine." He speaks out frankly about love and sex. His poetry reflects a positive attitude; it seems to urge: live as fully and purposefully as possible, intellectually and emotionally. Obviously Dylan is still a protest writer: what else could he be called?

The subjects of Dylan's songs, the substance of his thoughts, are neither startling nor new. The "sexual revolution" which began after World War I is still growing, this present generation has already reaped some advantage from it. (At least teenagers can talk about it at the dinner table.) As for the academic world, when has it not been under fire from hot youth? What makes Dylan's poetic themes relevant today—in short, what is "new"—is today's frame of reference. Never before has mankind been threatened, as we are today, with total destruction; that is why attitudes toward pleasure for its own sake, the absurdity of life, the desire to escape (or to stand fast and accomplish), are all proper grist for his poetic mill. Because he is a poet, and young, Dylan is frequently impatient, disgusted, intolerant. But one thing is certain: for the young people, whose passionate challenge to the world and its values has not yet been "tempered" by the wear-and-tear of the years, or by the weary cynicism that too often passes for wisdom, and who seem to sense, even when they cannot always critically evaluate, the meaning of his poetry, Bob Dylan is the most popular, the most powerful figure of our time.

The music in Dylan's first albums was in the mainstream of American folk music of the early 1960s. The sources of his musical settings were blues, Southern Appalachian country music, traditional ballads, Woody Guthrie, and early Elvis Presley (before his snake-hipping era). Accompanying himself on guitar and harmonica, Bob emulated country rather than city style. His singing was crude, direct, unembellished, and very appropriate to his material. Then came the switch to rock-and-roll, or folk-rock, as the combination of folk tune and electrified instruments is called. On the basis of this development (hardly new, for Dylan has been playing popular piano for a long time), he has been roundly condemned by folk music fans.

Duane Eddy, the well-known R&R man, has recently recorded Dylan's tunes in instrumental arrangements—and it is quite surprising how good they really are. While it is true that the engineering on *Highway 61 Revisited*, all folk-rock, makes it almost impossible to hear the words over the metallic clang of the instrumental backing, it should not obscure the fact that the album has some great tunes. Some of it is very exciting, but an entire LP of clang, clang, heard at top volume (a necessary condition of listening), is exhausting. What I find unpardonable is the lack of song texts. It has long been practice of many recording companies to include the words on the album jacket. Why not on Dylan's, where the words are absolutely necessary? Most listeners I know rehear each song a dozen times, writing the words out as best they can. A book of lyrics of *Highway 61* is now in the music stores, so if you want to get the maximum benefit, another investment—a book—is necessary.

Time will tell whether Dylan is a flash in the pan or of lasting importance. I hope Bob will decide for himself what his next move will be, without the "advice" of either his doting admirers or his critics. He has a basic honesty which should see him through. When his first album appeared, my review in *The American Record Guide* was unfavorable. When we met for the first time, Bob looked me squarely in the eye and said, "I read your review. . . ." "I'm sorry," I said, "I didn't like the record!" "Oh, that's all right," he said, smiling shyly. "It *was* terrible, and you were the only one who said so. Thanks!"

His present disassociation from the issues of war, integration, and nuclear destruction may only be temporary. Part of his irritation may undoubtedly be attributed to the pontifical and patronizing hounding of the people in the topical song field. But nothing is forever. Dylan has shown his ability to express contemporary life on many levels, all of them valid and pertinent to our time. If he chooses to ignore the political scene today, that is his privilege; but no one can accuse him of hiding in an ivory tower. No one denies the urgency of such issues as war and peace, integration, and the war on poverty, but this hardly justifies anyone setting himself up as censor. Will success corrupt him? That remains to be seen. For the present, in this time of dreary conformity and intellectual cowardice in the face of a world gone mad, Dylan's words and music are fresh and alive, and deserve to be heard.

ADRIAN RAWLINS

WHAT'S HAPPENING, MR. JONES? (1966)

Farrago, April 29, 1966

In this discussion of Dylan's 1966 Australian tour, his Bobness is favorably compared to poets modern and ancient.—CB

Largely unacknowledged by English Departments, Ezra Pound has been waging a single-handed campaign for the preservation of the "dead art" of poetry, the sublime in its original sense.

What *is* usually acknowledged by academic critics, however, is the fact that he failed. At least for the majority of people and universities.

Speaking briefly, what Pound aimed at was a restitution of poetry's place among the natural and daily life activities of a community.

Those with a sense of history must know that English poetry has not properly occupied this place since the Elizabethans. It would certainly seem an impossibility in today's world of mass media and standardized attitudes, to say the least.

And yet, over the past two years poetry of an often sublime magnitude has found its way into the very core of mass media banality, the hit parades, in the guise of "folk songs" or "contemporary protest songs," written and performed by Bob Dylan.

I say "guise," because Dylan's songs, to him, were neither of these things. They were tests of his own poetic ability, severe technical disciplines and an engagement of his talents which assured him of an audience because the form in which he cast it was popular.

Incidentally, from his point of view, almost without wanting to, he made the most creative contribution to real folk music since Leadbelly (with whom he is qualitatively equal though, of course, different) and, in the process, defined the conscience, assayed the world-sensibility, of his generation.

But this, for Dylan, was an artistic apprenticeship, not his one and only style.

An originator in the absolute sense, Dylan is the supreme iconoclast and cultural renewer. Like Picasso, he must move on to the next phase of his genius's stern dictation to him. And his (artistic) word is law because he and no one else is rewriting the rules (as a legion of imitators is currently substantiating).

Bob Dylan is rescuing the art of poetry from oblivion in a way that neither Eliot nor Pound nor the American poetry and jazz movement ever could.

To elucidate: Poetry, on the printed page, is a little like eggs before they're fried—the "taste," the "guts," is latent, not yet in existence. Worse, the meaning is open to drastic misinterpretation (given the gross misuses of language in the normal communications media).

Dylan, who uses language as did Villon, Rimbaud, Breton, Eluard and Cocteau, assures the inviolability of his art by being its interpreter—this is the only true and enduring meaning of his troubadour phase ("The Times They Are A-Changin'," "Hard Rain," etc.).

It is still true, however different is the overall sound. Dylan has solved, to his own satisfaction, the conundrum that sent Pound mad (the relationship in poetry of speech and song) by making songs that contain the rhythm and texture of speech and the imaginistic intensity of the most elevated poetry at once. The music of his current phase, his "Stone" period, adds an ancient quality of ecstasy in its only possible contemporary form.

His lyrics now are no less poetic than hitherto; if anything they are more so, but they are also more of a piece with the day-to-day texture and color of American vernacular speech. His music—which can be called Rockabilly, Razzamatazz or Juking Music more accurately than it can be called Rock 'n' Roll—aims at absolute sound, filling up the spaces left by the Beatles or Rolling Stones, and other commercial r&r groups.

I mean this quite seriously. The English groups have borrowed inspiration from an American tradition they cannot fully comprehend (simply because it is not their own). Commercial r&r might be a gas to dance to, but it is not as serious an expression of American life as, say, Ma Rainey's blues were, which were also popular in their day.

Dylan and his band (actually Canadian in origin) are producing a song and sound unit which is better organized, more genuinely exciting, more uplifting, better emotionally balanced, more absolute than any other sound in the general "beat" genre. Its aim, which should be successful, is to give you a happy jolt, a joyous charge, to obliterate totally the smell of everyday (but not with fairy floss: with magic talismans) and place in its stead the heady stuff of wonderment. A combination of poesy, cold fact and artistic distortion—in a word, an imaginary experience evoking that reality which never surrenders to the usual commands.

At a news conference in Stockholm, Sweden, April 29, 1966. *Photo courtesy of UPI/Corbis-Bettmann.*

There you are! Like artists, particularly poets, since the beginning of time, Bob Dylan is singing about freedom, the freedom of the individual soul.

His two Melbourne concerts at Festival Hall were not successful on his terms (which alone obtain) because the audience in the main could not grasp the meaning of his words and were unfamiliar with this particular sound (though he has issued two LPs in this mode).

Dylan, I know painfully, took this as rejection; it was simply nonculpable ignorance. But the audience which could have simply let the exciting, fresh, stimulating sound wash over it and thereby gotten what Dylan's liberating art is all about, preferred to, as it were, hold back, stand back and frown. And this is an act of nonlove, that is to say, a sin.

Of course, it is not the people's fault that it knows not what joy is, but it is surely a sad and bitter indictment of a land which calls itself free.

Dylan will not be back again. If you judged him on these concerts, might I ask you to suspend that decisive act till his next LP appears. There you will find the proof of what I have said about his qualitative significance within the tradition of American music—that is, of course, if you have any real knowledge of that tradition (Mr. Jones!).

VARIETY

BOB DYLAN DESTROYS HIS LEGEND IN MELBOURNE: CONCERT STRICTLY DULLSVILLE (1966)

April 27, 1966

Here is a typical review from the Australian tour, taking Dylan to task for his lackadaisical performing style. Surprisingly, this critic preferred the electric half to the acoustic part of the concert.—CB

Melbourne, Australia. Over the last two years every overseas folksinger coming Down Under has included a Bob Dylan song in his repertoire, talked of him in tones of awe, and always the response from the Aussie audiences has been overwhelming.

Therefore there's been great anticipation over the first Aussie tour of Dylan himself. And it was expected his concerts would be a quick sellout as has always happened with Peter, Paul and Mary.

But from the very start Dylan blotted his image in Australia. His fans were shocked to read press reports of his arrival in Sydney that he "wouldn't write for Negroes if you paid me $1,000," and to the implicit belief that he was shocked at the "horror of young boys being killed in wars," his glib reply was "this doesn't disturb me at all," adding "in fact I'm quite happy about the state of the world. I don't want to change it."

Undoubtedly these news reports kept some of his fans away from his concerts, as here in Melbourne the Festival Hall has been about 60 percent full. And of those fans who did brave his concerts, quite a few were disappointed. Some walked out in disgust before the end.

Alone on stage for an hour duration of the first half—which incidentally was over a quarter of an hour late in commencing—Dylan monotonously and untunefully slowly belted out his numbers, accompanying himself on a guitar and harmonica. The harmonica playing was the best part of his art.

His manner toward his audience bordered on insolence. More than once he had a fit of spluttering and coughing, which he seemed to delight in doing right into the mike.

In the second half Dylan was accompanied by an unprogrammed quintet—a pianist, drummer, two guitar players and a fifth member who played an electric organ. The sound of the organ lent a sweetness to the music, that made pleasurable listening. And Dylan's voice, half drowned by the backing, didn't seem as bad. And one could also hear the words.

But he annoyed the audience by taking time to tune up on the guitar so that on two occasions he received a slow handclap. Unlike any other artist who has appeared at the Festival Hall, Dylan made no attempt to introduce his musicians to the audience.

Throughout his performance, considering the number of people present, the applause was lukewarm, and there were no requests for encores at the end. In fact, Dylan left the stage without taking a bow—and no one seemed bothered about this. The performance I caught was on the second night. It's understood that at the opening performance there was considerable booing from the audience.

On the basis of this concert, Dylan would be advised to remain in the background and let other more seasoned performers with more personality and stage appeal interpret his work.

MAYFAIR HOTEL PRESS CONFERENCE, LONDON (1966)

May 3, 1966

Dylan gives his fifteenth press conference in a year. Again the press is totally bemused, leading to headlines like "At Least in His Songs Mr. Dylan Has Something to Say" and "Cliff Richard Was Never Like This." The questions are all fairly obvious, which may account for Dylan's flippant responses. Excerpts from this conference are included in Eat the Document. *After the conference, Dylan climbed out onto the balcony of the Mayfair so that he could be photographed, shades in hand, peering down upon the people.—CB*

Q: Will you be playing an amplified guitar in your concerts?

B.D.: I'm not sure if I will or not.

Q: Does the term "folk-rock" mean anything to you?

B.D.: Folk-rot?

Q: No, folk-rock. It's sometimes applied to the kind of music you make.

B.D.: No. Well, they say a lot of things about me. I'm a folk-singer. A protest singer. A protest folk-singer—no more and no less.

Q: Are you still making up as many songs as you used to?

B.D.: Yes. I'm making up as many words as I used to do. I'm only interested in writing songs. I don't want to make singles anymore.

Q: Who do you think is the best folk-singer in the world?

B.D.: Oh, Peter Lorre.

Q: Will you be doing TV shows for the BBC again this year?

B.D.: Yes, I'll do anything. But I don't know if I'll do them or not. I just get the word from other people to turn up somewhere, and I'm there.

Q: You've been influenced by many blues singers—Bukka White, Son House, Big Joe Williams, for example—do you still listen to such people?

B.D.: I know Big Joe, of course, but I've never listened to these men on records too much. Lately I've been listening to Bartók and Vivaldi and that sort of thing, so I wouldn't know what's happening.

Q: How many people are there in your backing group?

B.D.: Oh, fourteen, fifteen.

Q: What? All here?

B.D.: Yes, they're all here.

Q: Who are they?

B.D.: Oh, George, Harry, Red, Jason, Gus, Frank, Mitch.

Q: What is the name of your group?

B.D.: I don't know. I don't believe they have a name.

Q: How much money do you make?

B.D.: I don't know. I don't know anything. People just phone me and tell me to turn up somewhere at a certain time and I turn up. I never knew when I was poor till I was rich.

Q: Why don't you write protest songs anymore?

B.D.: All my songs are protest songs. You name something, I'll protest about it.

Q: Why do some of your songs bear no relation to their titles?

B.D.: Give me an example.

Q: "*Rainy Day Women No. 12 & 35.*"

B.D.: Have you ever been to North Mexico for six straight months?

Q: Not recently.

B.D.: Well, I can't explain it to you then. If you had, you'd understand what the song's about.

Q: What are these film people doing here?

B.D.: I don't know.

Q: Who's the guy with the top hat?

B.D.: I don't know. I thought he was with you. I sometimes wear a top hat in the bathroom.

Q: Will you be meeting the Beatles?

B.D.: I don't know.

Q: What about the book you've just completed?

B.D.: It's called *Tarantula*, it's about spiders. It's an insect book. Took about a week to write, off and on. There are three hundred and sixty pages. My next book is a collection of epitaphs.

Q: Is it true you're now married?

B.D.: [Pointing to Jones Alk] That's my wife.

Jones Alk: I'm the cameraman's wife.

B.D.: It would be very misleading if I said, yes, I was married, and I would be a fool if I said no. It would be very misleading if I said no, I wasn't married, and I'd be a fool if I said yes. I'm not going to answer that because I don't want to lie to you. I might be married, I might not. It's hard to explain really.

Q: May we assume that you are married?

B.D.: You can assume anything you like. I was born married—forty-five years ago.

Q: Are you married to Joan Baez?

B.D.: Joan Baez was an accident.

Q: A mistake?

B.D.: No, an accident. I brought my wife over last time and nobody took any notice of her.

Q: So you are married then?

B.D.: I'd be a liar if I answered that.

Q: But you just said you had a wife.

B.D.: That depends on what you mean by "married."

Q: Is she a common-law wife?

B.D.: I don't know what you mean by "common-law."

Q: Do you have any children?

B.D.: Every man with medical problems has children.

Q: What are your medical problems?

B.D.: Well, there's glass in the back of my head. I'm a very sick person. I can't see too well on Tuesdays. These dark glasses are prescribed. I'm not trying to be a beatnik. I have very mercuryesque eyes. And another thing—my toenails don't fit.

Q: Are you still in touch with Dana Gillespie?

B.D.: Yeah! Where is Dana? Come on out, Dana! I've got some baskets for her. Put your clothes on.

Q: What do you think about Paul Simon? Or Bob Lind?

B.D.: Never heard of them.

Q: Bob, your hair has got me worried. How do you get it like that?

B.D.: How do I get it like that? I comb it like that.

Q: What do you think of England?

B.D.: England is OK, but I prefer America. America is what I know. It's all there for me.

Q: How do you account for your success?

B.D.: What I did, I did because there was nobody else around at the time to do it, that's all. At the time I started there was no folk-scene in America. There was Frankie Avalon and Fabian. Before that we were eleven and twelve and we played rock and roll. Then when I was about sixteen or seventeen, along came Odetta. When the Beatles came along there was nobody in the U.S.A. They'd all become too old. And folk-music as you know it came along to fill up the gap in American music, that's all.

Q: Were you affected by growing up poor?

B.D.: Being poor when I was young didn't have a terrific influence on me. Where I came from, everyone was the same, so you didn't know you were poor, because you had nothing to compare with.

Part Three

PITY THE POOR IMMIGRANT
1967–1974

With Rick Danko and Robbie Robertson of the Band, Carnegie Hall, 1968. *Photo copyright ©*
David Gahr.

PETER EGAN

THE GREAT DYLAN CRASH (1998)

Cycle World, February 1998

Dylan's mythic motorcycle ride in 1966—that led to several months of seclusion at his Woodstock home—continues to haunt and fascinate members of his generation. This article from Cycle World *takes us back to the legendary spot, with some interesting commentary on it both from a cyclist's and a boomer's perspective.—CB*

Just last week I found myself on a cross-country trip in my ancient 356 Porsche, driving along the southern edge of the Catskill Mountains in New York, right through the famous village of Woodstock. Sharing the driving with me for a few days of the trip was my old motorcycle touring buddy, Mike Cecchini, from Bethesda, Maryland.

Woodstock, of course, is best known for the great rock festival of 1969, which actually took place on a farm near Bethel, New York, about 35 miles away. The Woodstock title stuck, however, because (a) that's where the festival was originally planned to be; and (b) the name had a certain magic.

Why magic?

Well, mainly because Bob Dylan lived there, having discovered the place while visiting the country retreat of his manager, Albert Grossman.

Also, Dylan's backup band (who later named themselves, simply, the Band), rented a little pink-shingled house nearby, a place they christened "Big Pink," composing the songs there for their first album: *Music from Big Pink*. With the Band and Dylan in town, lots of other musicians moved into the area, so the place became a kind of counterculture hotbed.

But, besides its abundance of famous residents, Woodstock was also known for another event in pop-culture lore: The Dylan motorcycle crash.

As every reasonably hip high school and college student knew in those days, Bob rode a Triumph. He was pictured on the cover of his *Highway 61 Revisited* album in a Triumph T-shirt, and he'd been photographed sitting astride his Triumph 500. I still have this photo in a book, and the bike looks to me (on close inspection with a magnifying glass) to be a 1964 Speed Tiger T100SR. Or maybe a '63. In any case, you can see that the left front fork is drooling oil from the upper seal, just as my own

'68 Triumph 500 is doing at this very moment. Nice to know nothing ever changes.

I was working that summer on a railroad section crew, just about to start my freshman year at the University of Wisconsin, when news came over the radio of Dylan's crash on July 29, 1966. My friends and I were both stunned and not surprised at all, in equal measure. This, after all, was the Age of Disasters. Assassinations, the war in Vietnam, race riots, drug overdoses and motorcycle crashes seemed to be claiming lives of the famous and nonfamous at a rate almost too fast to calculate. None of us, in fact, thought we would live to be very old.

Still, Dylan's motorcycle accident was sad news. I think I can say without contradiction that he was simply the man, the music legend of the era. He was held in the same high artistic regard as the Beatles, but with all of it poured into a single individual. If nothing else, he wrote more songs that I took the trouble to learn on my own guitar than any other songwriter before or since.

Anyway, he crashed his motorcycle, and the underground rumor mill went wild: Dylan is paralyzed; Dylan is so badly disfigured he will never appear in public again; Dylan has a head injury and cannot speak, etc., etc.

Then in 1968, he came out with a new album, *John Wesley Harding*, and we all examined his photo on the cover for signs of damage. Scars? Stitches? He appeared to be standing upright under his own power. The album sounded good. Apparently he was okay.

The accident is still somewhat shrouded in mystery, but biographers seem to agree that he indeed had a motorcycle accident, locking up his back brake while swinging into a corner just south of Highway 212 on Zena Road, about a mile east of Woodstock, where the road takes a tight S-bend near the site of an old mill. Some visitors to his home reported him wearing an arm sling and a neckbrace. In any case, the accident seems not to have been too terrible, and it appears Dylan used the mishap as an opportunity to quit touring for a while, stay at home with his family and get some much-needed rest.

So, against this background, Mike and I came driving into Woodstock on Highway 212, on a late fall afternoon, 31 years later. And there, just out of town, was Zena Road. We turned off and, sure enough, found a severe S-curve just past the site of an old mill. I got out and walked around in the late afternoon sunlight.

Bad curve, all right. Beautiful spot, right next to the mill creek, with yellow autumn leaves falling lazily onto the water and whirling downstream. But easily a place where you could go in a little too fast. Maybe brake too hard too late, lose confidence, fail to countersteer or just plain run out of traction. I walked through the corner and thought, "Yes, I could crash here myself. No problem."

Mike, who is not so steeped in rock lore as I, smoked a cigarette patiently and leaned on the car, soaking up the sun rays while I walked around. I hoped he didn't mind the little detour, my dragging him here for some kind of quiet contemplation of historical vibes and private meaning. He kindly left me alone and said nothing, as he had two days before, when we visited the Vietnam War Memorial.

Hard to explain what brings us to these places. What are we looking for? My friend George Allez has visited at least three times the Iowa base-ball diamond where *Field of Dreams* was filmed. He can't explain the allure, but every time he drives west, he stops there for a while and just

Performing with Pete Seeger, Judy Collins, and Arlo Guthrie at the Woody Guthrie Memorial concert, Dylan's first public appearance after his motorcycle accident, Carnegie Hall, 1968. *Photo copyright © David Gahr.*

At the Concert for Bangladesh accompanied by Leon Russell on bass, Madison Square Garden, 1971. *Photo courtesy of UPI/Corbis-Bettmann.*

takes it all in, as though the ghost of Shoeless Joe might still walk out of the cornfield.

We all have our own ghosts, I guess, and we like to pay them homage. Triumphs and the songs of Bob Dylan meant a lot to me at the time of his crash, and they still do. So it was just a place I had to go, to see for myself, as if to visit an incident from my own past at which I had somehow failed to be present. Such is the power of music—and motorcycles—to move us around in time. Pure transportation.

After a while, we got back in the Porsche and drove off in search of Big Pink. As we headed up the road, a line from a Band song ran though my head: "If I thought it'd do any good, I'd stand on the rock where Moses Stood. . . .

JEAN STROUSE.

BOB DYLAN'S GENTLE ANARCHY (1967)

Commonweal, 1968

*After Dylan's motorcycle accident, he withdrew for months, inspir-
ing rumors of his death or tragic disfigurement. He returned with
a new album and new sound. This is one of the more perceptive
reviews of that (first) comeback album.—CB*

Bob Dylan's new album, *John Wesley Harding*, is like the feeling left long
after seeing *Bonnie and Clyde*; gently anarchic. It is the anarchy of everyone doing his own thing, assuming that freedom can exist only outside the
laws and layers of society. The outsiders—outlaw, hobo, immigrant, joker,
thief, girl in chains, drifter, saint—form an existential community simply
in reaction to "them." But Dylan is hardly simplistic: the album is a collection of narratives in precise moods and voices, and its affirmation lies
in the community between artist and audience, in the poet's certainty that
his vision is shared by those capable of understanding it.

Musically, *John Wesley Harding* is Dylan's return to where he started,
knowing the place for the first time. After his famous experiments with
electronic sound the backgrounds for these songs seem deceptively simple.
The easy mingling of folk, rock, country-western, and blues is unobtrusive
but superb; Dylan's voice has mellowed and lost its earlier plaintive tone;
the beat and instrumentation (including electric bass, drums, steel guitar)
of each song are perfectly fitted to the quality of the individual narrative.

The lyrics combine various formal conventions—ballad structures,
allegorical characterizations, the epic distance of moral tales—with enigmatic Dylanisms. He is the master of the put-on as he sings narratives with
no dramatic action, eluding meaning-seekers while drawing attention to
the tone, imagery, and assumptions of the voice he adopts. For example,
"John Wesley Harding" is about an American Robin Hood, friend to the
poor, who "never hurt an honest man." Dylan sings of the "time they talk
about"—but skips the expected climax and we learn only that "he took a
stand" and soon the situation was "all but straightened out." The only
quality making Harding the hero of the song (and, as it is the title song, of
the album) is his lawless goodness: he carries a gun in "every" hand but
his virtues are gentle, even Christian. The song's assumptions are that

Harding is an outlaw and a good guy, and that "they" are out to get him: "No charge against him could be proved . . . No man could rag or chain him down." Dylan's playful use of syntax here ("a gun in every hand") and of rhyme and pronunciation elsewhere (in "The Ballad of Frankie Lee and Judas Priest," fright is pronounced "freight" to rhyme with sight pronounced "sate") contrasts with clichés like "always lend a helping hand," trite rhymes like "moon . . . spoon," and tortured word orders for the sake of rhyme. Is Dylan mocking the rules and limitations of language, using them to move beyond convention—or is he simply hung up trying to find rhymes and meters for his thoughts so they will somehow become songs? There is no reason why he would have to use rhymes if he felt they were only hanging him up. The rest of his verbal games are so sophisticated that this ineptitude seems to be part of a colossal and maybe defensive put-on. The attractive thing about put-ons is that you can wait for others' reactions before deciding how straight you want to play.

Dylan plays high on a tightrope strung out between richly religious, allusive moralizing, and an arch tone of complete put-on. The Christian metaphors in "I Dreamed I Saw St. Augustine" are used straight, without undercutting; but beyond the timely "sad complaint" of St. Augustine:

No martyr is among ye now
Whom you can call your own
But go your way accordingly
And know you're not alone.

is the guilty dream of the speaker ("I was amongst the ones / That put him out to death,"), his terrified awakening, and unstated questions of sin and redemption. The final image of the speaker ("I put my fingers against the glass / And bowed my head and cried") leaves a very real but mysterious sense of fear, guilt, and aloneness: the old symbols work in vague emotional evocation, but any precise "interpretation" must follow the jaunty mockery of the harmonica's coda to a different end.

The sense of vague secular apocalypse is strongest in "All Along the Watchtower," a song that gets better all the time; indeed it condenses and reflects much of the rest of the album. Roughly paraphrased: society is a total assault on jokers and thieves (Shakespeare's fools, biblical outcasts, the outsiders-as-social critic) but rather than bitter invective, the reaction here is a casual certainty of revolution. "We" out here just have to get ourselves together and it will happen; "they" (princes, their women and bare-

Making his major motion picture debut in *Pat Garrett and Billy the Kid*, 1973. *Photo courtesy of UPI/Corbis-Bettmann.*

foot servants) in there are doomed. The magnificent vagueness of "the wind began to howl," which could be the beginning of the song, is totally unlike the lack of climax in "John Wesley Harding." The title song is in the past tense, and we are assured by the narrative voice that everything came out all right, and that the specific action is irrelevant where the style of the hero becomes morality and affirmation. But here the issue is a kind of religious belief—hippie faith in the drug revolution, political faith in the third world and guerilla warfare—a hope for radical change in the future-present that becomes apocalyptic as one becomes increasingly committed to it. Still, the belief that "it" will happen is tempered here by the frozen imminence of apocalypse, and it remains as accessible to doubts and hopes as the present.

The moral seriousness of these reflections is offset by "The Ballad of Frankie Lee and Judas Priest" and other put-ons. "The Ballad" is the longest cut on the album, and the richest in religious allusion: Judas Priest as tempter, the whore house ("that's not a house it's a home") called Eternity ("though you might call it Paradise"), Frankie Lee dying of thirst in the moral desert, and the little neighbor boy who carried him to rest, walking along "with his guilt so well concealed." There is a frightening delight in meaninglessness: drawled words (inviting avid listeners to turn one speaker all the way down and the other to full volume, playing the same line over and over to hear every syllable and decide whether the foot-stool is above the "cloudy" or "plotted" plain, or whether for sixteen nights and days he "laid" or "made" or "raved"), irrelevant details, and non sequiturs. The essence of the song, if there is one, seems to be in the neighbor boy's muttering, "Nothing is revealed." But these words are buried in the heavy and irrelevant moralizing:

> . . . one should never be where one does not belong,
> So when you see your neighbor carrying something,
> And don't go mistaking paradise
> For that home across the road

The important thing about this kind of put-on—and the main way in which the album is so different from Dylan's earlier work—is the quality of the distance it keeps. Dylan, even after the long-awaited pseudo-revelation of *Don't Look Back*, is no more familiar than he was three years ago. But his style is more dramatic now, in the sense that he seems to have more control of his imagination: his personality—hidden before behind a come-on of mysterious masks—is no longer the tangible center of his work, but is at once within and beyond it.

The final brilliance of the album is in the slow rock irony of "I'll Be Your Baby Tonight." The song is one last flung comment on the possibilities of doing your own thing. It poses a safe, romantic retreat against the world "out there" in heavy, sleepy imperatives ("Close your eyes, close the door . . . Shut the light, shut the shade"). The strung-out slurring of "that mocking bird's gonna sail awaaaay," the nursery-rhyme quality of moon/spoon, the incredible "Bring that bottle over here," and the picture of love as a simple pastoral escape from worry and fear (especially coming as it does right after the tight, cool, bluesy celebration of love in "Down Along the Cove"—the only other love-themed song in the album) laugh at easy solutions. So does the album cover, a surreal parable about three broken kings searching for the key to Bob Dylan's new album—which turns out to be neither faith nor froth but Frank, who opens it up by taking them just far enough so they can say they've been there. He gooses himself all over the room instead of simply telling them he is a moderate man: annunciation, like everything else, depends on the way you feel that you live.

GRAHAM TAYLOR

TRAPEZE KING OF ROCK AND ROLE (1974)

Let It Rock, March 1974

Dylan's much-maligned Self Portrait *album here is reevaluated by critic Taylor, who sees in it both the ultimate put-on and the ultimate self-revelation.*—CB

"There is no eye," Dylan said in 1965, "there is only a series of mouths—long live the mouths." It's a useful comment to remember in considering any of his albums, but is particularly relevant to an appreciation of *Self Portrait*. No eye is no I, and *Self Portrait* is the least personal of Dylan's albums, the only one on which he doesn't appear as "himself." Not that the selves on previous albums were real (Dylan, unlike some of his fans, has always recognized the difference between artistic integrity and personal sincerity; the latter concept being largely irrelevant to any discussion of his—perhaps all—art), but at least each role was usually maintained throughout an LP. On *Self Portrait* this is not so, and all those people who were deceived by the title into thinking that the album would disclose the "real" Dylan were very disappointed and hung up by the result. Not that the title is only a trick—like the rest of the album, it is both humorous and serious. For *Self Portrait* is Dylan playing at being himself, or rather his selves, since he reminds us of so many of his previous roles (all the tired horses?); and this too, he knows, is just another role (come on, you don't think he wasn't aware that the painting on the cover looks nothing like him, do you? Blind Boy Grunt was a joke too).

Everything passes, everything changes. If *Self Portrait* is about anything, then it is about the relationship between music, time and identity, though to put it in such heavy terms is misleading, for the keynotes of the album are its delicacy, its subtlety and its playfulness. In one way it's reminiscent of his very first album: Dylan approaching a body of traditional material with humour and affection. But whereas *Bob Dylan* is noteble for its exuberance, its absurdly youthful enthusiasm for the blues, *Self Portrait* is relaxed, the humour far more measured, and the execution extremely sophisticated. On the first album, Dylan adapts the songs to this role of that time; on *Self Portrait*, he changes his roles to fit in with the songs. At the same time, too, he transforms them—not via a "personal" interpretation, a coopting of the song to establish a Dylan persona which would subordinate the music to a "self," but by a commitment to the song that at once breathes new life and opens up new life within it. He's not always successful but is frequently enough to make *Self Portrait* a remarkable achievement.

Time and identity? Well, the album presents numerous kinds of songs and those that are of the same kind are performed in totally different ways. The implication seems to be that there can be no finally definitive versions; that a song will continually change its meaning through time and the identity of the performer, and that this identity will itself be shifting in time and according to the demands of the song. So we have two "Alberta"s, one sober, one joyful; two versions of "Little Sadie," one searching, one settled; two voices on "The Boxer," one Dylan's old (young) voice, the other his new (old) one! There are two contrasting views of the rock star—"The Mighty Quinn" and "Minstrel Boy"—and two replays of old Dylan hits—"Like a Rolling Stone" and "She Belongs to Me"—chosen perhaps as representatives of his two best known emotional poses. His new songs invoke old musical traditions: the archaic language of "Belle Isle" recalls the Gallic folk ballad, while "Living the Blues" updates a style of music reminiscent of the fifties.

As a contrast, "Blue Moon" is a gentle parody of another type of fifties music, which firmly places it in its historical context. "Let It Be Me," one Everly Brothers song, is given a quiet, respectful treatment that is similar to the original; "Take a Message to Mary," another Everly hit, is transformed by a wholly fresh treatment which, by returning it—as Bill Damon has shown—to the Code of the West, also makes it older. One performance takes us back to the original, reminding us of the roots of our culture; the other extends the song through time, making it both new and mythical.

A similar change occurs on "Copper Kettle," which is turned from an old folk number into something beyond time and category: so that even when Dylan sings "we ain't paid no whiskey tax since 1792" it doesn't date the song. The performance effortlessly suspends the listener's sense of time—it will always be happening now, and the now is timeless. The effect is achieved through the conviction and immediacy of Dylan's vocal—it takes you right there—and by the use of chorus and strings, which lift the song out of the folk genre (and the past) without fixing it anywhere else, so that it becomes a thing in itself, indefinable and lovely. The chorus and strings also remind you that this is a performance; they act as a distancing, or alienation, technique which ensures the song is not "taken over" by Dylan's singing and the listener's involvement in that.

The mere presence of the backing on "Copper Kettle" brings this off: on "Blue Moon," where the style is not so obviously out of place, the Chorus' singing becomes slightly exaggerated—that elongated "ooo ooo wooooooooh"—(as does Dylan's: witness the lurch in "you saw me standing al-lone"), and we are again being reminded that this is a performance, and a humorous one, the comedy being underlined by the self-conscious romanticism of Doug Kershaw's violin. Dylan must have been aware of the absurdity of his singing "Blue Moon," much as he must have seen the absurdity of his singing "Man of Constant Sorrow" or "See That My Grave Is Kept Clean" on the first album. He pulls it off, though, each time; through different means, but always, I'm sure, with a smile to himself. And I can't help smiling with him.

Self Portrait then is a tour de force of performance. Dylan's singing is immaculate throughout; if you don't believe me, check out the analyses of individual songs in Bill Damon's *Rolling Stone* article (No. 65), which I've borrowed from freely.

For now, I'll use the single example of "The Boxer," the most maligned track on the album. The use of two voices on this track is a touch of genius; Dylan's young voice and his more recent Nashville voice immediately bring to life the time gap between events at the beginning of the song and its conclusion, and the way in which each song re-creates the emotional changes which the character in the song has undergone. It is the new voice which leads; confident, almost slick at times (you can imagine a politician's grin on the last syllable of "promises") yet touched with world weariness: the young voice is more uncertain, hovering around the other like a ghostly reminder of his past. On the second chorus, the young voice sings an extra "lie, lie, lie," hinting perhaps at youthful exuberance, and the difference between early idealism and the compromises of later life—almost as if he's saying "no, these *are* lies, this couldn't happen to me." Its especially poignant coming, as it does, after the verse on loneliness. Bill Damon makes another useful observation on this verse: "My favorite moment follows the man's confession that he has been with the whores on Seventh Avenue. Dylan drifts into a solemn 'ooh lie lie' that becomes both a self-reproach and a consolation." In the final verse, there is another fascinating moment: on "I am leaving, I am leaving" the new voice almost stops, as if suddenly overcome by the emotional charge of the words, while the young one blithely carries on with the song, unaware of the significance of the lyric, which is still in his future.

The theme of "The Boxer" is thus acted out in Dylan's singing; by superimposing the two voices, he is able to suggest how the identity of one changes in time, and how his old and new identities approach differently the one song (which is the story of his life), and how that song itself is molded by the way it is sung. Another instance of Dylan's voice "becoming" the meaning of the song is "Early Morning Rain," where the emotional identification of the singing with the character described in the lyric is absolutely flawless.

Self Portrait explores the relationship between music, time and identity—how each is continually changing the others and being changed in turn. It is a celebration of variety beautifully performed, with great sympathy, humor, affection and intelligence. If it is not so impressive on achievement as *Highway 61 Revisited* or *Blonde on Blonde*, I still think it would be foolish to want Dylan to repeat that self over and over. "Desolation Row" has its limitations too, and the artist needs always to be moving on, opening up new horizons, taking risks. *Self Portrait* was a risk because it was so unpredictable, so totally against expectations; but I think it works, and that it's fun.

An interviewer once asked Dylan "So if I started with Album One, Side One, Band One, I could truthfully watch Bob Dylan grow?" The reply was, "No, you could watch Bob Dylan laughing to himself. Or you could see Bob Dylan going through changes. That's really the most." That's *Self Portrait* too; and enough from me, except to add that, naturally, none of the above is what I believe to be the real truth about the album. I just hope you'll listen to it again, and maybe enjoy it this time.

GREGG M. CAMPBELL

BOB DYLAN AND THE PASTORAL APOCALYPSE (1975)

Journal of Popular Culture, 1975

An academic critic relates Bob to the tradition of the great pastoral writers and philosophers, placing him in a long tradition of revolutionary poets.—CB

From the beginning of his life, Dylan, like so many other poets and visionaries, was an outsider, an alien. Born May 24, 1941, in Duluth, Minnesota, Dylan was raised in a middle-class Jewish home in Hibbing, a mining town in Minnesota's Iron Range country. But as Robert Allen Zimmerman, Dylan found little in the petite bourgeiosie milieu of his home town to sustain his imagination or nurture his inner promptings.

Robert Zimmerman was thus a stranger in a strange land, who, like so many other strangers, created a mask, a fictive persona—Bob Dylan— to shield what was most essential in himself from the stares, threats and scorn of a careless and hostile society. In the country-western music of Hank Williams, Dylan first found a voice with whom he could converse and feel kinship; as a first-found friendship, this underdog identity of the country-western tradition—from Jimmie Rodgers, through Woody Guthrie, to Johnny Cash—would be one of the deepest and most enduring strains of Dylan's life and art. He became a cowboy long before he recognized his own Jewishness.

But more than a mask, Bob Dylan was an extension of Robert Allen Zimmerman—a fantasy, a mythic persona that could be altered, expanded upon and perhaps abandoned as his vision of himself grew richer, fuller and more complete. Thus with the symbiotic fictional stance of the wry compassionate observer, Bob Dylan took to the road in the early 1960s seeking to resolve the riddle of his own identity and to affirm his destiny.

The fascinating thing about reviewing Dylan's career is that we have in his music and poetry a virtual moment by moment account not only of his own quest, but also of the quest of an entire generation of American and Western European youth toward a renewed vision of authenticity and human dignity. Music and poetry have often played an important, if not essential, role in a people's self-definition, especially when they are setting out on new historical or revolutionary roles. Thus primitive Christians created their own music, Luther wrote hymns for the Protestant Reformation, and the Puritan Revolution was fueled by the poetry and music of its visionaries. The youth of the 1960s, no less than primitive Christians, Lutheran reformers or Puritan revolutionaries, was on a quest for redemption and salvation—a quest individual, collective and communal that was heralded and reflected in the changing musical modes of that decade.

"Music, man, that's where it's at," Dylan has said, reverently quoting a line from a Truffaut movie. And another poet observes of our era: "Music is truly the sound of our time, since it is how we most deeply recognize the home we may not have."

We have all lost our home in the last twenty (or one hundred) years. The accepted verities, of ethics, of lifestyles, of spiritual values, that have guided and shaped the European imagination for the last five hundred, indeed, for the last two thousand years, no longer provide efficacious guides to thought, action or aspiration. As Friedrich Nietzsche observed in the 1880s, our "God is dead"; or as a contemporary historian notes, we stand once again at the edge of history. We are a people lost, a people searching for new values and new myths to once again give meaning and dignity to our lives.

The poets and prophets of the counterculture believed that new truths, or rather, old and timeless truths had been revealed to them, and they expressed this vision in their apocalyptic music. But the apocalyptic tradition has deep roots in the Indo-European and Judeo-Christian imagination, and there are at least three identifiable variants of this tradition— the black or cataclysmic, the red or revolutionary, and the green or pastoral.

The black or cataclysmic apocalyptic tradition finds expression in the Old Testament prophets—Isiah, Jeremiah, Ezekiel—and in the New Testament, "Revelation of St. John the Divine." It appears in the black mass and witchcraft cults of the Middle Ages, and in the twentieth century in the poetry of Bertolt Brecht and the politics of Nazi Germany. In our time, the black apocalyptic tradition appears in the music of the Rolling Stones, in the lifestyle of the Hell's Angels and culminates in the Altamont Festival, held in Northern California on December 6, 1969.

The red or revolutionary tradition is most finely articulated in Karl Marx's attempts to give ideological rationality and direction to the black and green apocalyptic traditions. Like them it is an essentially religious vision, promising vindication, justification and salvation to the oppressed. Its major spokesmen, following Marx, are Lenin, Trotsky and Mao Tse-Tung—Mao being a poet, pragmatist and visionary of the highest order of genius.

The green or pastoral tradition appears first in Judeo-Christian culture in the Eden of the Book of Genesis where God and Man walked and talked with one voice. It appears in the poetry of Homer and Hesiod, in primitive Chrsitianity, in the monastic lifestyles of the Middle Ages, and in certain strains of Lutheran thought and practice.

In modern times the pastoral vision appears as a reaction to industrialism, in the Levellers and Diggers of seventeenth-century England, and in the utopian communes of early nineteenth-century America. The pastoral vision appears in the Populist Party Platform of 1892, and in William Jennings Bryan's "Cross of Gold" speech. In our times it is most clearly expressed in the music of the Beatles and culminates in the Woodstock Festival, held in the summer of 1969 in upstate New York.

The pastoral apocalyptic tradition is a tradition of innocence. A populist tradition of those who have never had power, who have never coerced their fellows, and are therefore uncorrupted. It is a revivalistic revitalistic tradition that forms the essence of the Pilgrim and Puritan expeditions to the New World and recurs throughout American history in the Great Awakenings of the eighteenth century and the revivals of the nineteenth. Thus, in contradiction to the beliefs of the members of the counterculture and some of its major Pied Piper apologists, the counterculture imagination has deep roots in Indo-European and Anglo-American history.

The pastoral and cataclysmic traditions share many themes, but the degree of blackness or the extent of cataclysm in the black apocalyptic tradition is directly related to the degree to which a people feel themselves oppressed, alienated and without hope. Release, justification and salvation can only be achieved through the total destruction, not only of the oppressors, but of the entire society. This cataclysmic vision is succinctly expressed in the "Pirate Jenny" song of Bertolt Brecht's *Threepenny Opera*:

And a ship with eight sails and
With fifty great cannon
Sails into the quay

When folk ask: now just who has to die?
You will hear me say at that point: All of them!
And when their heads fall, I'll say: Whoopee!

And the ship with eight sails and
With fifty great cannon
Will sail off with me.

Contrast the black vision of the "Pirate Jenny Song" to the pastoral vision of an early Dylan song with the same motif—"When the Ship Comes In." There is a revolution under way here also, the unjust shall be brought down, but there is no rancor, no resentment:

Oh the fishes will laugh
As they swim out of the path
And the seagulls they'll be smiling

Then the sands will roll
Out a carpet of gold
For your weary toes to be a-touchin.

This pastoral vision was a vision that Dylan held from the beginning of his career, but that did not find musical expression for him and the counterculture until the late '60s and early '70s.

When Dylan came "ramblin' out of the Mid-west" into New York City in the winter of 1960–61 to visit Woody Guthrie and to seek fame and fortune, he did sound "like a hillbilly," but he quickly adapted the protest forms of Guthrie and Pete Seeger and the underdog point of view of Jimmie Rodgers and Hank Williams to the mood of the early '60s. With such songs as "Blowin' in the Wind," "The Times They Are A-Changin'," and "With God on Our Side," Dylan became the poet-prophet-philosopher of the civil-rights movement.

The folk protest movement provided Dylan with a sanctuary, a temporary resting place, a way-station on his quest. But he soon found the lack of humour and the arrogant self-righteousness of the protest coda too restrictive, and by 1965 he was on the road again, seeking a larger vision of himself and human possibility.

This larger vision found expression in the album *Bringing It All Back Home* (March 1965), where Dylan, with his tremendous integrative genius, transvalued the electric amplified music of Negro rhythm and blues and white country-western music into a new art-form—folk-rock. "Subterranean Homesick Blues," the opening cut of the album, lay bare the hypocrisy, paranoia, hostility, absurdity and vacuity of the dominant liberal-technocratic society. With its intense, electric, drug-induced, stroboscopic tempo, it became the folk anthem of an entire generation of young people; a generation that was challenging the values that had dominated the Western European investigation for the last five hundred years, perhaps longer.

Perhaps, as Nietzsche believed, Socrates the rational optimist first led Western man into error. Perhaps St. Thomas, with the belief that through Reason man came to know the mind of God and the laws of Nature, was the first liberal. But the man who truly initiates our modern era is certainly Martin Luther; for Luther's truly revolutionary act was to preach that secular work is as worthy as sacred work. Through the idea that all work is a holy calling, Luther began that Faustian process that would involve Western man in the ever-increasing and never-ending domination of self, fellows and nature; a daemonic process that would give birth to mustard gas, the hydrogen bomb and space exploration.

In the domestic realm, this same Faustian dynamic has resulted in our consumer societies. Societies in which the GNP is taken as a valid measure of national worth. Societies in which the individual is led to believe that through the acquisition of *more*—more credit cards, more automobiles, more wives and sexual partners—he can achieve not only status, but spiritual salvation.

In *Bringing It All Back Home*, Dylan rejects the GNP and *Playboy* ethic. He says, we ain't gonna go to your schools for twenty years, and when we get done not goin' to your schools, we ain't gonna work in your farms, factories and insane asylums. The song "Maggie's Farm" contains a visionary prophecy of the Bank of America's throughout the nation, of Telegraph Avenue and the Oakland Induction Center, and of Kent and Jackson States. Of Maggie's Pa, Dylan says, "He puts his cigar out in your face just for kicks / His bedroom window is made out of bricks / The National Guard stands around his door."

In his next album, *Highway 61 Revisited*, Dylan first turned his criti-

cal eye on an upper-middle-class refugee from the dominant society—
"Miss Lonely," who went "to the finest school, all right," but "only used
to get / Juiced in it." And in "The Ballad of a Thin Man," Dylan scorn-
fully observed a middle-class liberal entering the cocktail party/street theatre of the absurd in the mid-'60s. But if Dylan is scornful and critical of
Miss Lonely and Mr. Jones, he is not without sympathy for them also; for
them, and for all his fellow Americans and fellow man.

For by 1965, in contrast to the arrogance of his folkie years, Dylan
realized that the absurdities of technocratic society are much more complex and ubiquitous than anything that can obviously be labeled "capitalism" or "racism." In the song "Highway 61 Revisited," Dylan
comments on the total absurdity of a society in which hype, manipulation and cupidity are the norms. In such a society the human beings, the
Yossarians and the Little Big Men, will always be on the run—orphans,
hobos, drifter—while the Milo Mindbender's and the General Custers
will have their day in the sun. Promote World War III? "Yes, I think it can
be very easily done. We'll just put some bleachers out in the sun and have
it all on Highway 61."

Highway 61 is an actual highway in North America that begins in
Canada and runs down through Duluth, Minnesota, where Dylan was
born; down through St. Paul, Minnesota, where F. Scott Fitzgerald was
raised; down through Hannibal, Missouri; down past East St. Louis, the
home of Chuck Berry; down past Dyass, Arkansas, the home of Johnny
Cash; down past Memphis, Tennessee, the home of Riley B. King and Elvis
Presley; down past Meridian and Oxford, Mississippi, the homes of
Jimmie Rodgers and William Faulkner, to end in New Orleans, Louisiana.

In the Greek language, the word "poet" means "maker," and Dylan
in the albums *Bringing It All Back Home*, *Highway 61 Revisited*, and
Blonde on Blonde is about the process of remaking the weltanschauung—
the goals, aspirations and values—of an entire generation of American and
West European youth; a weltanschauung that is exemplified in the east-
west traverse of Route 66, which ends in the golden state of California.
"Eureka—I have found it!" The pilgrims and emigrants who left Europe
believed that they had found it in America—in New England, in Illinois,
in Colorado, in California. But the promised land of our forefathers, the
new Eden, has become in our time a wasteland, a valley of ashes, a desolation row.

Highway 61 ends in New Orleans, and the album *Highway 61
Revisited* will end for Dylan with the song "Desolation Row." Dylan's

next album, *Blonde on Blonde*, will take place almost entirely on desolation row—bad drug trips, loneliness, despair, an almost total lack of communication are its motifs. In "Visions of Johanna," Dylan says, "We sit here stranded. We all doin' our best to deny it."—certainly a most un-American sentiment for a people who have always believed that they were the vanguard of historical progress.

There have been other American artists who felt stranded—Poe, Melville, Mark Twain in his maturity—but they have been dismissed as neurotic vagaries, outside of the mainstream of the American tradition. What is remarkable about the folk-rock period of Dylan's career—the years 1965 to 1968—is that an entire generation of young Americans believed that we were a people stranded. To them the American Dream seemed bankrupt.

Seen from another perspective, what happened to Bob Dylan and the flower children as they trudged confidently down Highway 61 in search of their identity and salvation is that they became truly lost and imprisoned in drugs, electricity and the arrogance of their belief in their own uniqueness and innocence. Perhaps because of the tempo of his life, perhaps because of his hubris, Dylan suffered a motorcycle accident in July 1966 and hovered very near death for many days. Through the hours and weeks of recovery, through the hours and weeks of reflection and dependence on friends and loved ones, Dylan came to perceive a new reality, a new vision of the possibilities of individual and communal life in the ruined wastelands of technocratic society.

Life cannot be lived on desolation row, nor could the vision of the counterculture be fully realized in the cities of New York, Los Angeles, or New Orleans. Part of Dylan's vision thus found its existential and mythic areas in Chaynee County, the Black Hills of South Dakota and the mountains of Utah, just as part of the counterculture's vision found realization in the communes of California, Oregon and New Mexico. But the escape to the mountains and the communes was still an escape—the counterculture's analogue to the middle-class bomb shelters of the 1950s. Thus, following his motorcycle accident, Dylan came to realize that the ultimate ground of existential and spiritual reality is the self. It is within the self and in personal relations that the ultimate terrors, absurdities and contradictions of a truly human existence must be met and resolved.

In the movie *Easy Rider*, Captain America says to Billy the Kid as they leave New Orleans, "We blew it." Yes, we blew it from the beginning of our trip. We, as Americans, blew it when we left our homes in Europe believing that through an easy ride of manipulating space and symbols we could transcend Time and Pain. But more significantly, modern man blows it every time he attempts to deny the innate dignity of self and his fellow human beings. This would be the message of Dylan's next album—*John Wesley Harding*.

In *John Wesley Harding*, Dylan reveals a new facet of his persona. There is a new sound to this album—totally acoustic, it is at once an affirmation of Dylan's country-western roots and a meditation on traditional American cultural values. Totally autobiographical, *John Wesley Harding* is an album of cryptic clarity in which Dylan tells us in cut after cut of his release from neurotic self-doubt, of his escape from drugs, from politics and from the arrogance of false innocence. Apocalyptic, it is an album in which Dylan turns from despair to affirm and celebrate life.

In the title cut, Dylan first warns against categorizing him or ourselves—"There was no man around / Who could track or chain him down," and then, in "As I Went Out One Morning," tells us of his escape from drugs and politics. Remarking on the fact, in "I Dreamed I Saw St. Augustine," that in our pursuit of rationality, we have killed our gods and turned our backs on dreams and visions as a source of knowledge, Dylan reaffirms a cosmic presence—"But go your own way accordingly / And know you're not alone."

In "All Along the Watchtower" and "The Ballad of Frankie Lee and Judas Priest," Dylan reflects on the vacuity of his own career and on the careers of all those who see life as a hype and a rip-off; of all those who see in every human relationship only an opportunity to aggrandize their own empty and soulless existence.

In "Drifter's Escape" and "Dear Landlord," Dylan speaks out first against neurotic self-judgment, and then against being hyped and typed by the dominant bourgeois society. In both cuts, Dylan speaks not only of his own dignity as an artist, but of the dignity of all men, and of the respect we ought to hold for one another.

In "I Am a Lonesome Hobo," Dylan again comments on the arrogance of a man "who did not trust his brother," which leads into "I Pity the Poor Immigrant," his most incisive indictment of the vacuities and cruelties of the Western European weltanschauung. We Americans are all emigrants whose forebears left their homes in search of a New Eden, but who went on in the nineteenth and twentieth centuries to impose their particular vision of salvation on others. Commenting specifically on the Puritan genesis of the American world blitzkrieg, Dylan says,

I Pity the Poor Immigrant
Whose strength is spent in vain
Whose heaven is like Ironsides
Whose tears are like rain.

Of the modern migrants, constantly in search of self, success and salvation, Dylan says, "I Pity the Poor immigrant / Who wishes he would
have stayed home . . . Who passionately hates his life / And likewise fears
his death."

Many commentators and critics have pointed out that all the indexes
of status and success in our society—alcoholism, divorce, suicide, nervous
breakdowns—must be symptons of a neurotic if not psychotic society.
Many have pointed out that the inability to accept the fact of death is a
denial of life. And many are becoming aware that we may have reached
the limits of progress through linear-rational thinking.

Thus Dylan and other artists of the counterculture have drawn upon
non-middle-class, non-Anglo and non-liberal sources for their visions of
renewed possibility. Dylan like his forebears the Negro Bluesmen and the
country-western singers accepts the ultimate mystery and tragedy of life.
Like Huck Finn and Ishmael, he accepts daemons and death as integral
aspects of life. And like Hawthorne, and Melville, and Faulkner, Dylan
and other artists of the counterculture are telling us that if there is no
historical progress, if man cannot achieve salvation through the ever-
escalating domination of self, fellows and nature, then the important
thing, the essential thing, the only truly human and noble course is to
attempt to live a flawed life in communion and harmony with one's fellows
and one's natural enviroment.

John Wesley Harding is thus an apocalyptic album in which Dylan
realizes his pastoral vision. The opening cuts are recorded with a heavy,
dirge-like beat, and Dylan's harmonica blows like a chill wind through the
ruins of a desolate landscape. But the tone and mood lighten, and the last
three cuts of the album form a triptych celebration of life. In "The Wicked
Messenger," Dylan says "nay" to bringing bad news, while in the next to
last cut, "Down Along the Cove," he says "yea" to love and communion
as he runs to meet his lover in the most idyllic of pastoral settings. The last
cut, "I'll Be Your Baby Tonight," is a straight country-western tune in
which Dylan again affirms eros and personal communion.

It is now possible to see that in 1968, just as in 1961 and 1965, Bob
Dylan was the vanguard of the counterculture. Following the release of

John Wesley Harding, many other musicians (most notably Crosby, Stills, Nash and Young) would return to a mellower acoustic instrumentalization. The Band would get top air-time with its secular hymns and Joan Baez would hit the Top Ten with "The Night They Drove Old Dixie Down"—Robbie Robertson's memorial to the Civil War from a Southern poor-white point of view. "Sweet Baby" James Taylor, Carole King and Carly Simon would all follow, once Dylan made the acoustic sound, the concern for self and a bittersweet celebration of American possibility legitimate modes of the counterculture imagination.

Just as enough time has passed to allow a retrospective look at Bob Dylan, so we now have enough perspective to recognize that the much celebrated "counterculture" was in reality a subcultural variant of the dominant society. From the benign coopting of hippie fashions to the malignant exploitation of hard drugs; from the fact that the music and the musicians had to be packaged, produced and marketed to the knowledge that the flower children participated as narcissistically in self-destruction as their elders (though their style was different), one recognizes that the "counterculture" exemplified all the con, hype, aggression and hostility of the dominant liberal technocratic society.

Indeed, the naivete and youthful optimism of the counterculture rendered it more vulnerable to manipulation and exploitation than the more cynical and rationalized dominant society. This tendency toward self-delusion was a function of the self-fulfilling prophecy propogated first by gurus like Pete Seeger, Timothy Leary or Allen Ginsberg, and later by the seers of the underground press. When toward the end of the decade, the imprimatur of respectability was laid on by the academics, it was a sign not that all the prophecies had or would be fulfilled, but that the counterculture's vitality and magic had dissipated.

Someone has remarked that Charles Reich's "Consciousness III" is really only "Consciousness I" in drag. Everyone walked around in costume; as an Indian Princess, a Cowboy or Gypsy, longing to raise the dead, revive the past or be someone else without any sense of responsibility, reality or authenticity. It is possible now to see that nostalgia was one of the dominant modes of the counterculture and that the dreams and fantasies of the flower children were as much directed toward the past as Disneyland or Knott's Berry Farm.

Dylan certainly was the vanguard of the counterculture. But if the counterculture is only a subcultural variant of the dominant society, then

Dylan becomes something other than a revolutionary prophet or transcendent visionary. He becomes one of the leading or cutting edges of the dominant society.

It is difficult and perhaps unjust to draw a line between Bob Dylan and Archie Bunker, but when one assesses Dylan's material since *John Wesley Harding*—the aggressive maintenance of the status quo, the concern for the personal, the celebration of things past—one is left with an overwhelming sense of nostalgia. It is even possible to acknowledge now that "Watching the River Flow" no longer brings to mind images of Siddhartha, but is more akin to Louis Armstrong's "Gone Fishin'."

Certainly there is a consistent and important strain of mysticism in Dylan's music that becomes more pronounced with *John Wesley Harding* and completely dominates *New Morning*. Perhaps this mysticism is essentially Jewish and possibly even Hasidic as some have attempted to document. But one does not have to be Hasidic or even Jewish to employ Biblical metaphors and syntax—witness William Faulkner, Herman Melville or William Blake. When we assess Dylan's mysticism since 1968, however, we are left neither with a sense of Blakeian transcendence nor Job-like wisdom, but rather with a stoical acceptance if not affirmation of the status quo that has always been indigneous to both the blues and the country-western traditions. Dylan was a cowboy before he recognized his Jewishness, and perhaps like Elliot "Ramblin' Jack" Adnopoz, he will remain more a cowboy than a Jew.

All of which is not to say that Bob Dylan and the flower children of the 1960s did not make significant and lasting contributions to the American tradition. Before there was an America, there was an American Dream. But with the first generation of Puritans there arose a tradition of the Jeremiah-voices crying in the wilderness, calling the Chosen People back to Yahweh's true and holy work. From the Mathers on down— Cooper, Thoreau, Hawthorne, Melville, Twain, Fitzgerald, Faulkner— each generation of Americans has had its Jeremiahs. Voices crying out that pursuing material wealth and power, killing Indians, enslaving Black men, wantonly destroying our natural enviroment was not truly God's work. In the 1960s, however, an entire generation of Jeremiahs rose to challenge the dominant view of the good life; and because the American dream was no longer working, that challenge could not be ignored.

Spokesmen for an ethical position, whether referred to as "male milliners" or "nattering nabobs of negativism," have traditionally received short shrift in American history. For everything we did worked; we had the pragmatic sanction. If God had not wanted us to conquer the world, he would not have given us the Gatling gun and the atomic bomb.

But since the 1950s, God has begun to act rather peculiarly: China fell, the Russians got the Bomb, and although few would say it, by any traditional American standards, we lost the Korean War. By the end of the 1950s Americans were standing at the ragged end of history. All the old certitudes were shaken, but the majority chose to cling ever more hysterically to those certitudes.

It was at this point, when the disparity between the rhetoric and the reality of the American dream became so vast—in the domestic affairs of race relations or the foreign affairs of naked imperialism—that the flower children, like the young lad in "The Prince Who Had No Clothes," spoke up. An entire generation of Americans called their Elders back to the pastoral vision that had been the original inspiration of the American dream.

Friedrich Nietzsche observed, "Only an horizon ringed round with myth can truly unify a culture." Throughout the seventeenth, eighteenth, nineteenth and early twentieth centuries the ever-expanding American horizon was ringed round with the myth of American invincibility and righteousness. But we have come to see that our traditional values are dysfunctional in the last third of the twentieth century and will be disastrous in the twenty-first.

Clearly God is no longer on our side. We no longer enjoy the pragmatic sanction. We are thus in need, as so many have begun to recognize, of dreaming better dreams, of creating a new mythology. And this certainly was the function of Bob Dylan and the flower children—to cite the reality of power arrogantly misused, and to remind us that the high vision of America has always been the creation of an equitable and humane society.

Dylan's genius is now quiescent. The pastoral vision is now swamped in a malaise of complacency. But perhaps this is not only to acknowledge, as William Irwin Thompson has postulated, that historical development is more like a switchback than an escaltor. Perhaps this is only an incubation period; a time when we are generating and nurturing those values that will allow us to meet the challenge of the twenty-first century.

In all this conjecture, one thing is becoming increasingly clear. By challenging the dominant American style of power, arrogance and hubris in the 1950s and 1960s, Bob Dylan and the flower children called America back to that which was most worthy and essential in its tradition and left an artistic statement and an ethical legacy worthy of Melville, Twain or Faulkner. We ask no more of any individual nor of any generation.

PETER KNOBLER

BOB DYLAN: A GUT REACTION (1973)

Crawdaddy, September 1973

*Here is an overview of Dylan's career, occasioned by the issuing the
first edition of his* Writings and Drawings.—CB

It was Spring in Greenwich Village in 1964. Grass was growing up
through dog shit and concrete around the occasional MacDougal St. tree
and I was walking, hands thrust deep in my pockets, through the folk
music streets. High school was almost behind me now, with young man-
hood to go. I was close to home, only a few blocks out on my own, but
my thoughts were thumbing and I wasn't aware that I'd already seen this
done. I kicked a cigarette butt soccer-style, ran to follow it up and scored
between a No Parking sign and the street. It was a normal day.

It was, in fact, nighttime. Sweater weather. I looked up and saw a
familiar figure, pretty girl on his arm, taking the eight steps down to the
Gaslight Cafe. His collar was turned up against the breeze—Freewheelin',
all over. I looked at him as he passed, took the breathless pause of adoles-
cence, turned and caught him.

"Uh, hey," I said softly in my corduroy innocence. "You're Bob
Dylan."

He looked at me as he was going down. "Yeah, man," he said, and it
was that edge-of-insight voice off the record, and I just started a grin.
"Sometimes."

———

"Do not create anything," Dylan wrote in 1964, "it will be misinterpreted." It was tucked inside a Philharmonic Hall concert program note (if
memory serves), "Advice for Geraldine on her Miscellaneous Birthday," a
piece which found Dylan on the edge of the evasion he had begun to carry
on him like a razor. "It won't change," he insisted. It will "follow you the
rest of your life."

Dylan's creations continue to follow him. At first he had to drag them
around ("dollar a day's worth"), but before long he and they were scam-
pering side by side, and at places like the Newport Folk Festival and
Carnegie Hall in 1963 what was so affecting about the ragamuffin gunner

was that he and his words and music were in perfect sync. No one had sung so convincingly about himself before, and as a huge group of post-war babies boomed, here came a young man running, broken so free from the household that the hounds couldn't catch him, in intuitive step out front of a generation kicking for liberation.

But he outkicked them, and as his speed built his creations bit by bit began to drag him. It seemed innocent enough at first; his step from group freedom to personal freedom foreshadowed Tim Leary, and as his own liberty was being limited he seemed to let fewer and fewer people take liberties with him. He had always written about what was pressing on him; now he took a closer look at his immediate surroundings. As they began to spin so did his work.

Finally it began getting away from him, his creations dragging him not entirely unwillingly behind them like the Chicano bandit behind generals' horses in Peckinpah's *The Wild Bunch*. The times were incandescent, the work inspired, but the ride was hard and Dylan finally had to cut it loose.

When he decided to ride again the pace was slowed, deliberate. The breakneck speed was gone, the wild horses of manic inspiration seemed consciously shackled and after a while slowed of their own volition. Every once in a while he's tried to run them again, and one morning they ran well and showed their form. But they're rusty, somehow have lost their gait. They're still speedsters, they're just a little out of shape.

It's been over a year and a half since *Bob Dylan's Greatest Hits Vol. 2* was released, almost three years since *New Morning*, but now all of a sudden Dylan is back on the mind. It's a mark of his influence that he can go unheard of for such great lengths of time and still pick up where he left off in public interest. Over the course of little more than a month Dylan has acted in his first fiction film, released a soundtrack album of new material, and offered the public a written collection of his complete works. Of these, by far the most valuable and interesting is the book.

More than his albums, Dylan himself has been interpreted with every new release. *Writings and Drawings by Bob Dylan* (Alfred A. Knopf) contains all of the works, except *Tarantula*, which individually have comprised the whole of the public Dylan, and through it one can trace the development of a public figure and a private sensibility. Due to Dylan's initial sense of mystery and then his growing financial consideration, this is the first time his work has been completely assembled to be read. There were various songbooks with chording and guitar instructions, but Dylan has never been quite this available.

Dylan has also had a history of mysterious and occasionally revealing gestures, (one suspects) willful confusions which will both excite and perhaps mislead someone who "thinks they really found" him. *Writings and Drawings* has a number of those moments, and they are a delight. It also includes, arranged by the periods in which they were written, all of his own songs that Dylan could find—some of them familiar through versions by the Byrds, Manfred Mann, Joan Baez, Peter, Paul and Mary and the like, other word-of-mouth classics, and still other songs which have never before been released.

The sheer bulk of effort is impressive. It is a physically attractive book without being unapproachable. Thick, and at $8^1/2$" x $10^1/2$", it can be carried like a notebook. Each song is given its own page, often more, and there's plenty of room to scribble. There's no dustcover and it's not cloth-bound, which serves both to make the book less academic and keep the price down. It's a book you really shouldn't be without.

But why now? This is an important step; one doesn't collect his life's work on a whim. There is a stock-taking to such a collection: one can find the result satisfactory and complete; one can be disappointed; one can see it as a chapter in a larger work. One can judge the past by it, or the future. Is Dylan closing an era, in effect saying, "This is what it was when it was?" That wouldn't bode well for the future. He's become very interested in film, say people near him lately; maybe he's planning to concentrate there and leave music to his odd moments.

Possible, but not very likely. Writing, singing and playing music has been what he's done best. It would be hard to shelve your strength, no matter how interesting your weakness, and Dylan still hasn't painted his "masterpiece."

It could be a looking back to find how he arrived at the present before pressing forward. Dylan is no doubt at a crossroads now. He must have come close to accomplishing what drove him to his limits; he has been a known man, a celebrity, a Superstar, an international influence, a mover of men. There seems little doubt that on some level that's what he was after; and he got it. Long ago. At the same time he is young enough to remember individual insights, yet old enough to have the details blurred. The fact of retrieving all his work may have served to refreshen his memory, and either reinforce or temper his decisions.

The manuscript was over a year in the works. By January 1972, *Bob Dylan's Greatest Hits Vol. 2* had been widely discussed and well received by an audience much of which knew Dylan only from *Nashville Skyline* on. The album had been structured as a reintroduction, with Dylan of one era balanced against Dylan of another, the result being something of a refresher for those who had forgotten and a revelation for those who had never known. This book was apparently begun in the wake of that success, Dylan's fast-moving interest focused and his audience shown still to be there.

When Dylan and his people had brought together his songs and prose in exactly the form they wanted it, they contacted a publisher.

Bob Gottlieb, the editor-in-chief of Alfred A. Knopf, who has previously published John Lennon's *In His Own Write* and *A Spaniard in the Works*, and *The Paul Simon Songbook*, was asked if he was interested in this book, and of course he was.

"At the time that this came to me as a publishing project," says Gottlieb, "the manuscript was complete. Bob demanded, and had every right to have, complete artistic control over his book. No editorial changes were made in the text from that point on."

The book is organized chronologically, each album coming first, cuts arranged as on the records, followed by songs written in that general period. Also included are liner notes Dylan wrote for his own albums and some for Joan Baez, as well as concert program blurbs, poems and some unidentified prose.

"I know it wasn't a rushed, overnight piece of hysteria," notes Gottlieb, "because too many books happen that way and I recognize the signs. There was nothing sloppy or careless or rushed or hysterical about this. It seemed to me very carefully worked, and I imagine over quite a period of time.

"I saw my job as simply to make him a beautiful book that he would be happy with for a long time . . . a book that somebody ten years from now will be having and using. And I think Bob's book is that. Bob was involved in all its aspects and phases."

The book itself is fascinating. It gathers Dylan for the first time. The work and thought Dylan gave it are evident, and the almost unnoticeable gestures in which Dylan used to flirtingly reveal himself are delightfully present. From everything one knows about Dylan, nothing was done casually.

The book opens with an off-hand revelation. Where the first few pages of most books are blank, Dylan has offered two of his work sheets with typed and handwritten verses, choruses of unfinished songs, random phrases and rhymes. The pages are not dated, and there's no way to know just when they were written, but they begin to show how the man's mind operates. Verbal doodles flit from the banal to the sublime but are never consummated. And off in the lower left-hand corner, after three stanzas about a switchboard operator and the barest inkling of a catchy phrase, come two bombshells:

"Sing something safe"

and:

"Is it right to think about what one can do or is it right to think about what one has done?"

They can't be accidents—Dylan must have plenty of other papers lying around—and they set the tone for the entire book. The dangers and comforts of singing "something safe" have undoubtedly occupied Dylan's mind since after *Blonde on Blonde*—he has been criticized for precisely this—and any collection of his work brings both past and potential to play. Here one finds Dylan's thinking about it too. Right off we are told nothing is resolved. Can we, his audience, still have an effect? He is asking himself, but there is influencing to be done, a decision perhaps yet to be made.

But go lightly. It was fan madness that slowed him last time and he's not forgotten. If he can't please everybody, Dylan writes, "I might as well not please nobody at all." The people are so many and he "just can't please them all." It's a final, handwritten inscription before you enter his book of words. A double-negative and native ambiguity, want it or not. It will be misinterpreted.

The first song in *Writings and Drawings* is "Talkin' New York," and it is accompanied by an illustration (Dylan's drawings throughout the book are more representative illustrations of specific songs than graphics of their own) of a recognizable Greenwich Village scene. In fact, it is unmistakably the northwest corner of Washington Square Park, not far from Dylan's house. But the park has been remodeled recently, and it is a picture of the redone park Dylan has drawn. It could mean nothing, just an oversight which Dylan either didn't pick up or considered too insignificant to correct. But the new drawing could also be a conscious statement that those times, the "Talkin' New York" times, are gone and have been replaced. It's a subtle shade, but there were times when Dylan could be read in those shades and there's no reason to believe he can't still. At his best, Dylan embodied an intuitive precision which gave even his simplest actions depth of which he himself was only vaguely aware. It makes you watch your step, but it makes those steps important. I assume that intuition is still there, just dormant.

One way to approach *Writings and Drawings* is to listen to the records chronologically and hear the changes in the musical tone as the man grew. If the book serves no other purpose than to bring Dylan records back into extensive currency, it has served well. But there is so much more here. One can see the development of a writer, from the bald yet insistent pounding of the "Ballad of Emmett Till" to the slightly more sophisticated "Only a Pawn in Their Game" and then (and this is the marvel of the book, the availability of comparison) in an incredible yet fully evident quantum leap to the brilliance of "Mr. Tambourine Man." The meter tightens and the words fall instead of being placed, but you can "hear vague traces of skippin' reels of rhyme," and there is something to tracing a man's creative history which puts you in closer touch with his present and one's own hopes for the future.

The Dylan wit is very apparent throughout the book, strongest when Dylan is at his ambiguous best and fading when he tries too hard. *Don't Look Back* showed how he used it as a defense and a weapon, but on paper one can trace its growth from puppy dog snip to teething protest yowl to snarling amphetamine put-down to a final joke on himself. He had the presence of mind, for instance (and I missed this when the record came out), to follow "Chimes of Freedom," his densest, most complex and wondrous work to that date, with "I Shall Be Free No. 10," which starts, "I'm just average, common too. . . ." It was the pixie behind the prescience and it was part of Dylan's charm. Much of his appeal, in fact, was to join him (if you could) in his joke. Dylan fan cliques picked up on that right away and got pretty snooty at times. Right about then, around *Another Side*, when Dylan started putting young adult universals into enchanted language, was when people started tossing his phrases into their word-salad conversations like precious avocados. The Weathermen started as a gleam in Dylan's eye.

Dylan didn't change many lyrics when he first compiled the book. The most noticeable changes appeared at first to be in *Another Side of Bob Dylan*, which is considerably different on the page than it is as recorded. But checking back in Bob Dylan songbooks published when the record was released you find that Dylan either did a lot of ad libbing in the studio while recording, or a lot of rewriting directly afterwards, because almost all of the alterations stand corrected nine years ago. If a check of written versus spoken lyrics reveals anything it is that Dylan was consistently more concerned with form, seemingliness and grammar on the printed page than on record. "Gotta's" are regularly changed to "musts," choruses remain constant on paper where they varied insightfully when sung. In fact, Dylan resisted making many phrasing and word changes for the better even now when he had the chance, perhaps on the theory that works when finished should be allowed to stand, or that to change one he'd have to rework them all and then he'd never move forward. He played around with "I Shall Be Free" from *Freewheelin'*, adding a verse and getting Brigitte Bardot, Anita Eckberg and Sophia Loren in the same room with Ernest Borgnine for kicks. And the politician who was eating bagels, pizza and chitlins is now eating "bullshit" too. But for the most part this is the Dylan you've known and loved.

Or thought you've known and loved. There's a sociological side-effect going on here that you could hardly have expected. When Dylan's first albums came out, up to and including *Blonde on Blonde*, stereos were not the household staples they are today. It astounds me, but I listened to the first seven Dylan records in mono, on a record player vintage 1958, which was roughly equivalent to catching it on AM radio in an open-top convertible at 85 miles an hour in a windstorm on Pike's Peak. Not much detail. As a result, I found when reading through songs I thought I knew by heart, I had missed a good bit! I'm far enough removed from the eye of that particular hurricane now to enjoy my mistakes. They reveal more about me than about Dylan, but then that too was part of the Dylan appeal. You could match perceptions with a guy who, it seemed, was always going through it just before you.

Dylan's development is very graphically evident in *Writings and Drawings*. It is as if he is asking to be discovered, as he always halfway was. He was snide enough to those gross enough to claim "they really found" him. "Some French girl" was talking about him to Shakespeare and "says she knows me well." Once in a while he even gave in, saying, "You said you knew me and I believed you did." It was on his mind, but it always seemed to me that nobody could be right because, to that point, everybody had been wrong—leaving Dylan isolated, disappointed and more than a little angry. He obviously didn't welcome insight into him—it had to fight its way through a stockpile of mistrust—but the possibility persisted. As long as he knew what was going on maybe someone else could too, and when it started to get past him maybe someone could pick up parts of it. All any Dylan freak wanted was that one chance to give it a try. Dylan began to communicate on a gut level and when he added the best rock and roll around to the purest intuition, there was no step he could take that didn't seem somehow the only step to be taken.

Dylan's intuition ran deep. He became in touch (on many levels, often below the conscious) with a gut consistency that if you had to define it you couldn't feel. He began it as a wise-ass kid when his songs refused to come unstuck in their rambling detail. He was linear, a story-teller ("Hattie Carroll," "North Country Blues," "Boots of Spanish Leather" and many others are detailed narratives with a tone at the core), but he could turn a phrase like a bandit and was topical on exactly the right topics. When he grew less linear, when the tone came forth and the narrative became oblique, it was this consistency which unified even the most frenetic images. He could throw words around like spangles in a wind and they'd have to mean something. They couldn't miss. He was in touch.

I once made the mistake of writing a college paper on "Stuck Inside of Mobile with the Memphis Blues Again." I took apart each stanza and put it back together again. I pored over every image, trying to make each connect. The chaos I gloried in in my room I purged from the piece. My professor returned it to me, commenting that I was "ingenious" in inventing substance but that from one verse to the next there was little or no continuity. I argued with him, but I should have agreed. The continuity was not in linear images but in gut tone. Dylan was wailing from a high-quality urgency I could neither define nor deny. And I was certain he didn't know how deep it went. He may well have meant he was stuck inside of Mobile, Alabama, with the Memphis, Tennessee, blues again, but I knew he was stuck inside a mobile (one of those hanging things)—and if he was stuck inside a mobile he was one of the crucial balancing weights (every component in a mobile is indispensible), and if he left or shifted or did anything but just hang there the entire mobile universe would go out of kilter and it would be his fault. And that's some Memphis blues!

My friend, at the same time, was sure he was saying "stuck inside, immobile," which is something else again. Or maybe mobile like a car, or fancy-free. Dylan may not have known it but on every level imaginable that song held up! All of his electric albums did. Such was the power of his words, the intuition he was part of, his concrete sense. Incredible.

Blonde on Blonde was the apex of that fragmented vision. His songs were regularly shattered like mirrors into jagged sections, each with its own unique yet truly reflective viewpoint. But interpretations did get out of hand, and the gut magic reached people with twisted guts and distorted like never before.

It was getting pretty crazy. With every step somehow accepted, there were no standards. Dylan could have been sloppy or tight and largely have gotten away with either. He was the biggest individual superstar since Elvis and had none of the seered guidelines rock idols can follow today. Even in coping with epic lunacy, Dylan led the way.

When Dylan stepped back—his motorcycle accident enforcing a calm he might have come to anyway—he abandoned his manic appeal, though he didn't jump headlong into a consciously conceived tranquility, it seems. (There is a section in *Writings and Drawings* called "From *Blonde on Blonde* to *John Wesley Harding*" which includes 21 songs, many of them from the so-called "basement tapes," some of them still fairly frenzied. The follow-up album to *Blonde on Blonde*, it now appears, would have been quite an experience.) He rather ambled into it.

When he reemerged, there seemed a conscious denial of the past madness. Gone was the sardonic wit, replaced by an austere diction and entirely new symbol system which left many of his former devotees with no immediate grasp on excatly what he was saying. There were few concretes—no more honky-tonk lagoons or escapades out on the D train to latch on to. About the time you started wondering what all this meant, you realized your gut wasn't telling you. Dylan's magic gut consistency was gone.

John Wesley Harding was austere and deep like a quarry pool. It was a head album, Dylan's first. *Nashville Skyline* again steered clear of intuitive connections, Dylan preferring to sing about such universals as love and love's constancy without using concrete examples from anyone's life, including his own. As if to maintain the purity of his privacy, he offered no glimpse into his concrete world. *Nashville Skyline* could take place anywhere, or nowhere. *Self Portrait* was the same.

But there was a strange stirring, some forgotten shifting of stomach juices, when *New Morning* appeared unannounced one autumn afternoon. Dylan's voice seemed to rasp again, and there were some vaguely recognizable scenes set in language that brought sly grins to all my friends' faces. "Day of the Locusts" had a concrete base—you could feel Dylan's presence, his old ambivalence updated by the twin behemoths, security and maturity. The overtones were ominous—locusts buzzed alluringly throughout the song—but Dylan both braved them and escaped. Once again he was talking about a recognizable self and a personalized yet universal fear. Once again a head was exploding, but this time it wasn't his.

"One More Weekend" was a married man's "Pledging My Time" in which Dylan introduced his kids, if only to leave them for a while. That was a first. He seemed remarkably forthcoming with his details, relaxed as he let them fall. The gem of the album, the song which spoke for the entire year, was "Went to See the Gypsy," in which Dylan visited a figure I assumed to be Presley. The song has all the banter, the vague yet potentially decipherable phrasing of classic Dylan without the manic frightrush. In the song Dylan is again tempted, ambivalent. He admits implicitly to fear (of exposure? of a lunatic relapse?) and to the desire to break away from watching himself, to go "through the mirror." Ultimately he lets it ride, but he has to go all the way home to "that little Minnesota town" to do it. It seems he was feeling the stirrings too.

Not long after *New Morning*, Dylan rehearsed a band consisting of Al Kooper, Harvey Brooks and (I believe) Rick Marrotta, with an eye to going back on the road for a spell. "We were terrible," says Kooper, though he can't explain how or why. "We were just terrible." Again Dylan retreated and hasn't released an album of his new personal work since.

Writings and Drawings includes three songs after *New Morning*: "I'd Have You Anytime," "Watching the River Flow" and "When I Paint My Masterpiece." ("George Jackson," "Wallflower" and the new works on the *Pat Garrett and Billy the Kid* soundtrack are not included due, apparently, to convenience, political and business considerations. The new material is the opening work in a new publishing catalogue, Ram's Horn Music, and so was held off.)

"Any Time" is the George Harrison collaboration and infinitely dismissable. The final two pages of writing faces "Watching the River Flow" with "Masterpiece." It's essentially a repeat of an irony used on *Greatest Hits Vol. II*. This wide-ranging book which includes Dylan at his most publicly profound is almost made to end with "I don't have much to say. . . ." It's an irony not wasted on a man who has been criticized in his lifetime for saying both too little and too much, simultaneously.

But that tempting absurdity is flush against Dylan's statement that he's not finished. The masterpiece is not painted but not out of mind. Dylan wants it; he must or he wouldn't have called such final attention to it. But both of his latest works (each copyright 1971) are near parodies of that desire; they talk about tranquility and high art without ever achieving either. And no amount of joking will bring them closer. Dylan approached the peak of his powers during the madness of the amphetamine express. He can't be expected to return to those lunatic days, they almost did him in. But the thread which ran through *Another Side*, *Bringing It All Back Home*, *Highway 61 Revisited* and *Blonde on*

Blonde, and which resurfaced for a continuing, fascinating moment in *New Morning*, is still potentially reachable. The urgency has been dulled but the core of the man remains. His concretes vary, and some could well inspire him.

Dylan's soundtrack to *Pat Garrett* was not written about him (and so joins *Self Portrait* and *Bob Dylan* as his only other-directed works) but it offered him a tone to play with. Did he perhaps need that after such a long time between releases and public response? He is neither Garrett nor Billy (does he still feel like a Jesse James?) and so the work gave Dylan some practice without undue pressure. The album is all tone, Dylan proving he can not only write to order but conjure sense from nonsense; the music is 100 times better than the film. The most interesting aspect of the soundtrack album is Dylan's three takes of his "Billy" theme. All the Dylan mannerisms are here in what is really a minor work. You can hear, as lines within verses change at what seems like whim, how Dylan manipulates words, plugs them in and pulls them like literary transistors in a remarkably malleable encyclopaedic sound system. It is the unstated workings of the man's mind which are intriguing here, compelling when he's working on something of real substance.

So the question remains: will Dylan return to what he has done best? It has not always been kind to him. It has ground his gut. The pressure to produce, once only to come up with new songs for the same people the second time around the concert circuit, has escalated until the demand now is for perfection. Having asked himself when his masterpiece will be prepared, he has at the same time made it more difficult. The next one, the word now seems to be going, better be the Big One. That's patently absurd—genius rarely comes on demand—but intimidating in any case.

When Dylan was running, when he was in circulation and surrounded by some of the best musical minds of his generation, when he was invincible and in touch with the keenest perceptive edge of his own awareness, then he could do no wrong. But now, as well as being rusty, he must worry about his audience. All these tests and reintroductions point to the thought that perhaps Dylan isn't certain his audience is there; or if they are there, where they are, or whom they are. It's been a long time since he faced them. Will Alice Cooper freaks welcome Bob Dylan? Who should he direct himself towards? And if these questions are being asked, then he must realize that the gut doesn't know, and that could be frightening.

Another possibility is that he has said what he has to say in music. That whatever drove him to achieve overwhelming influence and success is now fulfilled. Maybe he is content to live a life of relative quiet and doesn't feel the necessity to create much further. There is no ballet dancer's discipline to the rock and roll star's art, no routine and so no guaranteed output. Maybe he's simply pleased to live a life.

But a man doesn't lose his core, or create from alternate sources. The intuition and craft which inspired *Blonde on Blonde* was alive in *New Morning* and was pursued. Dylan may well have let the edges round slightly, but at the same time that proves the mettle is still there to be honed. The overwhelming urgency seems more dormant now than lost. What's needed is an atmosphere of willingness, both from Dylan and from the people he can reach. Nobody is particularly in touch with his guts these days. The man who's put me most in touch with mine has been stirring of late. He can be received warmly, without excessive demands but at the same time without fawning, stultifying adoration. If he returns, the effect could be transcendent. There's a balance here, like a mobile, but this time everyone can be there to greet him when he walks inside. There's more than faith here; it's a feeling I've got in my gut.

MICHAEL MCCLURE

FOR BOB DYLAN (1974)

Written in Toronto in the early seventies after a sound check wherein I was asked to stand in at the microphone for Bob so that lighting crew could set levels. Later that day, I introduced Dylan and Marshall MacLuhan.—MM

For Bob Dylan

My eyes are wide explosions
in the field of nowhere.
My pocket watch burns air
and sprouts golden antlers.
I'm
the stand-in
for flaming stars;
my heart murmurs
are electric guitars
and
my hair
reflects in rainbows

and in aura glows
that radiate my brow.
The tinsel ice
does melt
beneath my feet—
my words are fleet—
and my songs
are an armada.
I see
the smiles of cherubs float
from the barranca.
The world with all its facets
is a whirling boat
of leopards and of mice
from which I hurl
the radiant dice
of my perceptions.
All conceptions
of boundaries
are lies!

LARRY SLOMAN

BLOOD ON THE TRACKS: DYLAN LOOKS BACK (1974)

Rolling Stone, November 21, 1974

This is a discussion of the original recording sessions for Dylan's Blood on the Tracks *album. Ultimately, many of these cuts were replaced by tracks Dylan made with some local Minneapolis-based musicians in late December after he listened to a mock-up acetate that engineer Phil Ramone had made for him.—CB*

It looked like old times at Columbia's A&R Studio September 16th. John Hammond Sr. was there, Phil Ramone was working the board. Eric Weissberg and Barry Kornfeld, two old Gaslight regulars, were unpacking their guitars. And sitting out in the cavernous studio, acoustic in hand and harmonica holder in place, practically hidden behind a battery of six microphones, Bob Dylan was creating another album. And it was almost as if Dylan were consciously conjuring up the ambience of the early Sixties, surrounding himself with the same familiar faces, attempting to exorcise, as he put it on *Planet Waves*, "the phantoms of my youth." And by all accounts, he was eminently successful.

"This is his first definitive LP in a long time, it's a return to 1965," Barry Kornfeld commented. "The songs are great—lyrically he's writing stories again, little vignettes about himself," says Weissberg. "I'm bereft of words to describe it, it's the best material I ever heard him do," added New Riders steel man Buddy Cage. "Is Dylan back?" chuckled a Columbia executive. "Where's he been?"

Hammond heard of the session the day it started "and I could hardly believe it," he said. "So I went over there. I said to Bob, 'This is a strange day to start recording,' because it was Rosh Hoshanna and it was hard to get musicians. And Bob said, 'Well why not today? It's the new year, isn't it?' I have never heard Bob so assured and so musically unsophisticated. There's folk and classical influences on the new stuff. He's got four or five incredible singles. I'm still absolutely stunned."

The album, scheduled for rush release November 1st, is tentatively titled *Blood on the Tracks* and judging from the cuts it appears that he has reimmersed himself in the world of carnival people, energy vampires, and karma hustlers and they're all out there, back on Highway 61. There are several opuses on this album, "Idiot Wind" for one ("Everytime you open your mouth / It's idiot winds / It's a wonder you breathe at all"), a nine-minute foray into the phenomenology of fame. There's "Jack of Hearts," a song that Dylan told Mick Jagger, who dropped by during the sessions, was unlike anything he'd ever heard, but then again unlike anything he'd ever written. It's murky, compressed, like a fourteenth-century narrative poem, really more like a show than a song as it unfolds an impressionistic tale of carnivals and saloons and those that live on the underside of life.

There are also love songs, cuts like "You're Gonna Make Me Lonesome (When You Go)," "If You See Her, Say Hello," "You're a Big Girl Now" and "All Tangled Up in Blue." Dylan also recorded titles like "Shelter from the Storm," "Buckets of Rain," "Meet Me in the Morning," "Twist of Fate" and "Up to Me."

The music is sparse, with a minimum of drums, a lot of bass, a bit of organ, some pedal steel and, of course, Bob's acoustic guitar and harmonica. The scheduled cover is a shot of a huge red rose on a white background. And Bob was reportedly hunting for old photos of himself performing at Gerde's Folk City for the back sleeve.

This album, like most of Dylan's previous sessions, was recorded with a minimum of preparation. According to Columbia sources, Dylan flew into New York around the middle of September, called up the company and said, "Let's do a record." On such short notice, engineer Ramone was unable to secure the New York studio musicians he routinely employs, people like Pretty Purdie, Kenny Ascher and David Spinozza. Ultimately, Eric Weissberg (half of the famous banjo duel) brought along his band Deliverance, but the scenario sounded like Weissberg's 115th Nightmare:

"I had seen Bob on the street about a year ago and we talked for a while and he said he wanted me to work with him but then I hadn't heard from him. All of a sudden, a year later, I get a call from his office saying what's your availability next week. Then I didn't hear anything for a while and on the following Monday I had one date, a jingle from 10 to 11 A.M., and I happened to be home at two in the afternoon, which is amazingly unusual and the phone rang and a woman says hi, can you be at Bob's session at 4 P.M. I said no because I had to have a meeting with my band, but I'll be there at six, where is it? She says Studio A. I said there's only about 1400 Studio As in New York but by then it dawned on me it was Columbia's studio so I asked her what did Bob want me to bring. She said what do you play. Well, I play about eight or nine instruments, but she said she didn't know what he wanted. So I told her to get in touch with Bob and call me back.

"After an hour, I called her and she said Bob left for the studio and was unreachable. So I asked who else was on the date but she didn't know. So I packed two or three guitars in my car and drove down. I finally reached Ramone on the phone and asked him who he got. He said he tried everyone but it was too short notice and it looked like no one was coming. So I said I got a band and just then Bobby walked into the studio and Phil asked Bob and he said sure bring the whole band over."

Dylan had been recording alone for a few hours. He played back those songs but then wanted to do some new ones, and Deliverance was forced to pick up the tunes cold.

"He seemed to be having a good time," said Charlie Brown, the electric guitarist. "His whole concept of making an album seemed to be to go ahead and play it and whichever way it comes out, well that's the way it is. It's what happens at the moment. He didn't want to do a lot of takes, and I don't blame him 'cause some of the songs are so long. We'd just watch his hands and pray we had the right changes."

Hammond said, "Bob said to me, 'I want to lay down a whole bunch of tracks. I don't want to overdub. I want it easy and natural.' And that's what the whole album's about. Bobby went right back the way he was in the early days and it works."

Weissberg was a bit more sardonic: "It was weird. You couldn't really watch his fingers 'cause he was playing in a tuning arrangement I had never seen before. If it was anybody else I would have walked out. He put us at a real disadvantage. If it hadn't been that we liked the songs and it was Bob, it would have been a drag. His talent overcomes a lot of stuff."

Once he got under way, Dylan seemed deadly serious. Security was extremely tight and visitors were few. However, Mick Jagger dropped by a few nights, unwinding from work in a nearby studio where he was editing Stones tapes. He danced and drank champagne straight from the bottle, and occasionally huddled with Dylan between takes, offering a production suggestion or two. There was no producer.

Dylan used Deliverance on a few tracks and brought bassist Tony Brown back on succeeding nights for additional work. New Rider Buddy Cage was then flown in to sweeten some of the more countryish tracks.

"Ellen Bernstein from Columbia played this tape of us doing 'You Angel You' for Bob and he told her to call me for his sessions," said Cage. "I felt knocked out and real nervous especially because he didn't use many people. Bob played the tapes for me and said listen to them and play on whatever tracks you want. Frankly, there wasn't that much room on many of them for me. Anyway, I started working on the first song and after four takes I was disgusted, it just wasn't right and Bob came over and said, 'Well shit, this is so difficult,' which was exactly what I was thinking. I think we were both kinda shy with each other.

"But Jagger, he was there, like, I'd rub elbows with him any time, it's so easy. It was like I had gone to high school with him. He was asked to do background vocals but he didn't. The second night we were all drunk and Jagger was going to play drums, but he never did. I finally asked him if he had Charlie's number and he said, 'Charlie who?' I wound up cutting three tunes, two of which Bob kept. The album's a beauty. All those songs, they're all hits."

It may seem strange that Dylan would record an album so soon after the back-to-back summer release of *Planet Waves* and *Before the Flood*, especially in light of his past habit of releasing an album a year. The immediacy of *Blood on the Tracks* may be due to the relative lack of impact, especially critical impact, of the last two albums. It is more likely that *Blood on the Tracks* is the beginning of a new cycle implicitly promised with *Planet Waves*. Pete Hamill, columnist and novelist, who Dylan asked to do the liner notes, viewed Dylan's current output in terms of Yeats's famous observation, "We make out of the quarrel with others rhetoric, but of the quarrel with ourselves poetry."

"Dylan has gotten the self and with the situation poets should deal with," Hammill said. "The whole notion that he should write 'Like a Rolling Stone Meets the Wolfman' or 'Gates of Eden Goes to Japan'— what the fuck does he want to do that for? What I love about Dylan is what he leaves out because then he gives us a chance to help create it. It's the most democratic form of art there is. Totalitarian art tells you every fucking thing. Dylan leaves the spaces. Listen, what I love about these love songs is that there's a terrific sophistication of feeling in them and a generosity of feeling. You know it's not just like 'You left me, you cunt,' or 'Come mother me, you bitch,' it's not at that level at all.

"Look, in my experience, when you've been with a good woman for a long time and it breaks up for whatever reason or other the generous human being remembers what was good about that and thanks himself and the woman and the world and fate for having had the privilege of having that long run, which is not like opening and closing a one-night stand with somebody. I can't really find the language to describe these songs. The album is just fucking wonderful."

And Dylan's art of late has been democratic, almost anarchistic, in its impressionistic quality. There is a thread that runs directly from the fragmented mysticism of *Planet Waves*'s "Never Say Goodbye" to the sketchy watercolors of *Blood on the Tracks*, a thread that suggests that Dylan is perfecting his craft, going back to, as Charlie Brown puts it, "being a poet again, which is exactly where he is, and a real great one." The criticism of late had to hurt, had to make Dylan more vunerable. He had to smart if he read comments like that of glitterrocker Todd Rundgren: "Dylan doesn't seem to be saying anything. He isn't doing anything sociologically, artistically, politically or spiritually important."

Planet Waves, an examination of the competing demands that complacent domesticity and mystical vision place on an artist, had less creative impact than was expected. *Before the Flood* was simply a live tour album. And to top it off, there are the gossipmongers, searching one more rumor blowing in that idiot wind. There's a line in that new song that says, "Those people in the press are saying terrible things about me, I wish they'd stop." But maybe it's understandable. When the times are hollow, you can easily lose perspective.

With Joan Baez and the Rolling Thunder Revue, Houston, Texas, 1976. *Photo copyright © David Gahr.*

Part Four

ROLLING THUNDER
1974–1984

JIM JEROME

BOB DYLAN: A MYTH MATERIALIZES WITH A NEW PROTEST RECORD AND A NEW TOUR (1975)

People Magazine, November 10, 1975

This article appeared in the mass-market magazine People *and shows Dylan reaching out to regain his audience on the eve of his famed Rolling Thunder Revue tour. It shows that Dylan had lost none of his ability to be both surly and communicative with an interviewer—often in the same response.—CB*

Bob Dylan at 34: "We each have our own vision and a voice inside that talks only to us. We have to be able to hear it."

It was a windowless recording studio, six floors above a deserted Manhattan side street. The artists were sealed off, as if under a siege that would not end until the tape was finally right. Meal breaks were out—instead, carrots, crunchy cauliflower, curry sauce, Camembert, French bread, beer, wine and tequila were brought in. The mood otherwise, though, was of a warm, conspiratorial intimacy. The harsh overhead lights were replaced by soothing red and green spots. A homey floor lamp illuminated the music stand of the lead singer. The producer was supportive: "Just hold that tempo, Bobby," he encouraged from the control room. "That last take was startin' to smoke." The star leaned into his mike and responded: "We're gonna get it, man, I know we are. Let's get this thing in the can and out on the streets." Bobby was Dylan and, after his latest 18-month retreat, he was returning to the streets again.

The recording is "Hurricane," a protest song with the gritty urgency and outrage that had once enflamed a whole American generation. It pleads against the controversial eight-year incarceration for murder of ex-boxer Rubin ("Hurricane") Carter. Simultaneously, Dylan was readying his first road show since his tumultous comeback tour of '74. The itinerary would detour the megabuck impresarios, the multiseat superdomes, the computerized ticket networks and re-create the modest small-club mini-tours that characterized the years when he first left Hibbing, Minnesota. But his entourage includes friends like his ex-lady Joan Baez, plus Ronee Blakley, the discovery of the movie *Nashville*. Undeniably, Dylan creates in a genre in which minimal art is almost impossible, and so his latest comeback may live up to its ironic title—the Rolling Thunder Review.

Dylan is himself, after all, the most infuential figure in American pop music (and thus pop culture) since 1960. His garbage was analyzed years before Henry Kissinger's. Every syllable or solecism of his life is subject to fearful scrutiny. Dylan, now 34 and as scruffy, wiry and taut as ever, looks back and sees it all as only a colossal accident. "It was never my intention to become a big star. It happened, and there was nothing I could do about it. I tried to get rid of that burden for a long time. I eat and sleep and, you know, have the same problems anybody else does, and yet people look at me funny."

If Dylan had his way, he would not be looked at—at all. He has granted very few major interviews in eight years, and this was his first in some 18 months. "I was playing music in the '50s," he begins, "and, man, it was all I did. It saved my life. I'm not a hermit. Exclusive, maybe, but not reclusive.

"I didn't consciously pursue the Bob Dylan myth," he continues. "It was given to me—by God. Inspiration is what we're looking for. You just have to be receptive to it." While reports of Dylan's ardent Zionism are almost certainly exaggerated, he has unquestionably returned to his Jewish roots, or at least to a generalized spiritualism.

"I was locked into a certain generation," he says. "I still am. A certain area, a certain place in the universe at a certain time." The middle '60s, a period of drug-boosted frenzy, were reflected in Dylan's electric, clamorous rock 'n' roll and in his manic jet-stream imagery—and they culminated on the edge of death on a shattered motorcycle in the summer of 1966. Then followed a two-year withdrawal which only intensified the myth. "I just wanted to be alone," he now says. He surfaced in 1968–69 with the subdued self-examination of *John Wesley Harding* and, later his watershed country LP, *Nashville Skyline*. Asked if he had it to do all over again, Dylan summons his samurai-quick sardonicism: "Maybe I would have chosen not to have been born at all—bypass the whole thing"

Dylan regards himself as an artist rather than a musician ("Put my guitar playing next to Segovia's and I'm sure you could tell who was the musician"), whose role is to create, not preach. "I can move, and fake. I know some of the tricks and it all applies artistically, not politically or philosophically."

He has a way of leaving reviewers as well as disciples in the dust. "I don't care what people expect of me," Dylan says defiantly. "Doesn't concern me. I'm doin' God's work. That's all I know." His classics like "Blowin' in the Wind" and "The Times, They Are A-Changin'" became anthems of the opposition, and the terrorist Weathermen took their name from his lyrics. But pressed about his influence, Dylan says only, "You'll have to ask them, those people who are involved in that state of panic where my works seem to take them. It's not for me. I wouldn't have time for that. I'm not an activist. I am not politically inclined. I'm for people, people who are suffering. I don't have any pull in the government."

The accusation that he copped out from the antiwar and other protest movements which his music catalyzed leaves him livid—especially criticism of his refusal to participate in Woodstock. "I didn't want to be part of that thing," he says. "I liked the town. I felt they exploited the shit out of that, goin' up there and gettin' 15 million people all in the same spot. That don't excite me. The flower generation—is that what it was? I wasn't into that at all. I just thought it was a lot of kids out and around wearing flowers in their hair takin' a lot of acid. I mean what can you think about that?

"Today the youth are living in a certain amount of fantasy," he adds. "But in a lot of ways they become more disillusioned with life a lot earlier. It's a result of the overload, the mass overload which we are all gonna have to face. Don't forget when I started singin', marijuana was known only in certain circles—actors, musicians, dancers, poets, architects, people who were aware of what it could do for you. You never went down to make a phone call at a phone booth and had some cop hand you a joint. But now it's almost legal. The consciousness of the whole country has changed in a very short time."

He is impatient with fans who expected his own expression to stay the same. "Those people were stupid," he snaps. "They want to see you in the same suit. Upheaval distorts their lives. They refuse to be loose and make themselves flexible to situations. They forget they might have a different girl friend every night, that *their* lives change too." Certainly there were formative changes in Dylan's life: marriage in 1965 to fashion model Sarah Lowndes; the accident; the growth of his own family to five (including one child from Sarah's previous marriage).

Yet, professionally, Dylan points out, "A songwriter tries to grasp a certain moment, write it down, sing it for that moment and then keep that experience within himself, so he can be able to sing the song years later. He'll change, and he won't want to do that song. He'll go on." But Dylan is not speaking of himself. Of his own massive anthology of poems, he says, "I can communicate *all* of my songs. I might not remember all the lyrics," he laughs, "but there aren't any in there I can't identify with on some level.

"I write fast," he continues. "The inspiration doesn't last. Writing a song, it can drive you crazy. My head is so crammed full of things I tend to lose a lot of what I think are my best songs, and I don't carry around a tape recorder.

"Music," Dylan says, "is an outgrowth of family—and my family comes first." He moved them to the beach at Malibu from Woodstock several years ago, and has been intermittently rumored to be splitting from Sarah. He concedes, "I haven't been able to spend as much time with my wife as I would like to," but pinning Dylan down on personal matters is like collecting quicksilver. A sample colloquy:

Q: Are you living with your wife?

A: When I have to, when I need to. I'm living with my wife in the same world.

Q: Do you . . . ?

A: Do I know where she is most of the time? She doesn't have to answer to me.

Q: So you don't live . . .

A: She has to answer to herself.

Q: Do you live under one roof?

A: Right now things are changing in all our lives. We will always be together.

Q: Where are you living now?

A: I live in more that one place.

Q: Can you be more specific?

A: I don't want to give out my address.

With Robbie Robertson during the Planet Waves tour, Chicago, 1975. *Photo courtesy of Neal Preston/Corbis.*

Q: Region?

A: I live where I have to live, where my priorities are.

Q: Right now, is that in New York City?

A: Right now it is, and off and on since last spring.

"Traveling is in my blood," said Dylan, as he rehearsed for his latest tour. "There is a lot of gypsy in me. What I'm trying to do is set my standards, get that organized now. There is a voice inside us all that talks only to us. We have to be able to hear that voice. I'm through listening to other people tell me how to live my life." Did Bob Dylan, of all Americans, feel himself mortgaged to others? "I'm just doing now what I feel is right for me," he concludes. "For my own self."

NAT HENTOFF

IS IT ROLLING ZEUS? (1976)

Rolling Stone, January 15, 1976

Nat Hentoff, long-time Village Voice *jazz critic, was also a long-time friend of Bob Dylan, having concocted with Dylan the famous* Playboy *interview of the mid-'60s. Invited to document Dylan's Rolling Thunder Revue tour, Hentoff wrote this wonderful warts-and-all glimpse of the tour and its participants.—CB*

Backstage at the Rolling Thunder Revue, Allen Ginsberg (who has just dedicated his book of First Blues to "Minstrel Guruji Bob Dylan") asks the convener of these revels, these winds of the old days, "Are you getting any pleasure out of this, Bob?"

The convener, who can use words as if they were fun-house mirrors when he's pressed, fingers his gray cowboy hat and looks at the poet. The first he had ever heard of Allen Ginsberg and the kind of people he hung out with was in *Time* around 1958 while he was still a kid in Minnesota. ("I'm Allen Ginsberg and I'm crazy." "My name is Peter Orlovsky and I'm crazy as a daisy." "My name is Gregory Corso and I'm not crazy at all." That had broken up the kid in Minnesota.)

Now, here on the road with this hooting, rocking carnival of time present and time past, both perhaps present in time future, is Allen, who has survived serene and curious, in a business suit.

"Pleasure?" Dylan finds the word without taste, without succulence. "Pleasure? I never seek pleasure. There was a time years ago when I sought a lot of pleasure because I'd had a lot of pain. But I found there was a subtle relationship between pleasure and pain. I mean, they were on the same plane. So now I do what I have to do without looking for pleasure from it."

"He is putting you on," said a friend to whom Ginsberg, later in the tour, had described Dylan's exorcism of the pursuit of pleasure.

"No," Ginsberg said firmly. "Bob's attitude is very similar to the Buddhist view of nonattachment. The belief that seeking pleasure, clinging to pleasure, evokes pain. It stunned me when Bob said that. It meant that he's reached a philosophical level very few come close to. And it's a long-range, practical, workable philosophical level. Bob has grown up an awful lot. He's alchemized a lot of the hangups of his past. Like his insecurity, which has now become," Ginsberg laughs, "an acceptance of and an ability to work with continuous change."

On the other hand, a musician in Minstrel Guruji's band tells of an epiphany early in the tour:

"Joan and Bob are doing a duet. I forget the name of it, it's one of his old tunes. She's really moving. I mean dancing. She starts doing the Charleston and the audience is digging it and we're digging it. Dylan though, he's plunking his guitar, moving his eyes around quick, like he does, looking at Joanie, looking at us, looking at the audience. Like, 'What the hell is she doing that's going over so damn big?' It's over, and Joan walks offstage, grinning, sees a friend in the wings, and says to him, 'You won't be hearing that number again from this old duo on this tour.' And laughs because neither the friend nor the others standing there can figure out what she's talking about. But she's right. Bob's never called for that tune since. He couldn't stand the competition. Big as he is, in some ways he's still a kid scrabbling for his turf."

"Not true," says Joan Baez of the kid characterization. "Or, not as true as it used to be." She had once described Dylan as "a huge ego bubble, frantic and lost, so wrapped in ego he couldn't have seen more than four feet in front of him." But now, "Bob has learned how to share," Joan told me one night after a three-and-a-half-hour show in Waterbury, Connecticut, at an old rococo movie theater that reminded me of Depression nights as a boy when we would go to just such a place to feel good anyhow and come home with some dishes besides. No dishes this time, but the most mellow feelings I've had from a concert since the Duke Ellington band on an exceptionally good night. The kicks were from the genuine mutual grooving of the music makers; but it was Dylan, as shaper of the thunder, who was responsible for lifting the audience and keeping it gliding.

A bounteous dispenser of thunder was Dylan this time around. At least three and a half hours every night, sometimes longer. (The first concert in Toronto, one of the tour's most exalted evenings, ran close to five hours.) And yet always, or nearly always, the pacing, though relaxed, didn't go slack.

The right mix of a backup band, driving strong but sinuously so it never sounded like an assault. If you could keep T-Bone Burnett, Steve Soles, Howie Wyeth, Mick Ronson, Luther Rix and David Mansfield together—I was thinking as a once and former A&R man—you could have one hell of a house insurance band. Especially with Mansfield, 19 and the kind of natural whom conservatory students prone to neurasthenia should never be allowed to hear or see. Mandolin, pedal steel, dobro, violin—Mansfield makes them all sing, for God's sake, as if he were the sorcerer, not the apprentice he looks like.

Up front Rob Stoner, who doesn't get in the way, and the authentically raffish Bob Neuwirth, who may, he says, be in the movies soon. Finally a Rhett Butler for our time. Put another way, I think you have to see Neuwirth to remember his singing.

Then the substars, Ronee Blakley, who earnestly needs direction, as her albums and her musical aimlessness on this tour rather painfully indicate. Roger McGuinn, who has become a large, jolly, historic rocker, almost right for a Christmas mime show. And surprisingly, most impressive of all in the second line some nights, Jack Elliott. With his rambling white cowboy hat and folk collector's glasses, Jack is real serious, however idiosyncratic, and on this tour quite moving in his seriousness. Watching and feeling what "Pretty Boy Floyd," let's say, still means to him, I started thinking of Cisco Houston. Not that they sang alike, Cisco being more of an original, but they trained a lot of memories. And Jack is still spreading seeds.

All the way up front, Joan Baez and, as she calls him, the Kid. Her voice has lowered and so the bodiless sound of medieval caroling in a cathedral is also gone. But now there is more warmth and flesh and survivor's humor ("Love is a pain in the ass"); and still that surging vibrato which is so strong that when Joan sings acapella, the vibrato becomes her rolling rhythm section.

In her duets with Dylan, Joan, most of the time, is a secondary strand. She could overpower him because her timbre penetrates deeper and because she is more resourceful with her voice than he is, but Joan is content to orchestrate Dylan. And Dylan—less coiled, even dancing from time to time—cannot ever be called relaxed but now is so in charge that even he believes he's in charge. His singing, therefore, is more authoritative than ever before. That is, the anxiety in his delivery has to do with the story he's telling rather than the way he's telling it.

It feels good to him, this tour. The itch was there last summer. One liquid night, if you believe Bob Neuwirth: "Me and Bob and Ramblin' Jack decided we were going to go out and tour in a station wagon, go out and play Poughkeepsie. That didn't turn out to be possible. So we did this instead. And this ain't no Elton John show, you know. This ain't no fucking one-fourth of the Beatles show or nothing like that. This show, we got it all, man. Between us we got it all. And it just gets better and better and better."

"The feeling is good," Joan handed me her glass of wine, "because everybody has some room onstage. Bob made sure of that. He didn't have to and I argued against it. I thought it would slow things up. But Bob insisted. He said the guys in the band have to work day and night, and so each of them ought to get some attention. Not that, as you saw, Bob has sworn off attention for himself."

He no longer seeks pleasure, he says. But what of the pleasure of attention? Why, that comes, it just comes.

Blood on the Tracks has been released and Allen Ginsberg, listening close, is moved to write the poet about a rhyme in "Idiot Wind": "idiot wind blowing like a circle around my skull from the Grand Coulee Dam to the Capitol."

It's an amazing rhyme, Ginsberg writes, an amazing image, a national image, like in Hart Crane's unfinished epic of America, *The Bridge*.

The other poet is delighted to get the letter. No one else, Dylan writes Ginsberg, had noticed that rhyme, a rhyme which is very dear to Dylan.

Ginsberg's tribute to that rhyme is one of the reasons he is here with Bob and Joan and the rest of the merry motley. It was, says Allen, "one of the little sparks of intelligence that passed between Bob and me and that led him to invite me on the tour."

Joan, in faded jeans and multicolored, boldly striped cotton shirt, is talking with amused affection about Dylan, about the tour, about herself. The Ghost of Johanna still marvels at the sparks that never cease coming from this "savage gift on a wayward bus." Throughout the tour, although Lord knows she knew his numbers well, Joan would slip into the audience to hear Dylan's sets or, if she were weary, she'd sit down backstage to listen.

"Bob has so powerful an effect on so many lives," Joan says. She has been saying this for some 13 years; and at the beginning, before his pop beatification, she pushed mightily to press that savage gift on those who had come to pay homage only to her. Dylan was the "mystery guest" unveiled at her concerts, lurching onstage to break the spell of high-born doom across the seas in someone else's history as he rasped about freak shows right outside.

"I'm still deeply affected by his songs," Joan says. And by him? "Well, of course, there's that presence of his. I've seen nothing like it except in Muhammad Ali, Marlon Brando and Stevie Wonder. Bob walks into a room and every eye in the place is on him. There are eyes on Bob even when he's hiding. All that has probably not been easy for him." She says this entirely without her usual irony.

"Sometimes," Dylan says to me on the phone in 1966, "I have the feeling that other people want my soul. If I say to them, 'I don't have a soul,' they say, 'I know that. You don't have to tell me that. Not me. How dumb do you think I am? I'm your friend.' What can I say except that I'm sorry and feel bad? I guess maybe feeling bad and paranoia are the same thing."

Onstage, all during the Rolling Thunder Revue, Joan had put her arm around Dylan's shoulders, wiped the sweat off his forehead, kissed his cheek, and looked into his eyes, giving rise to a frisson of voyeurism among those in the audience who yearn for "Diamonds and Rust" to have a sequel, several sequels, for where else these days can you find that old-time mysterious rhapsody in the romances of the famous? "It's on again," a woman behind me whispers eagerly as Dylan and Baez intertwine in close harmony onstage. "It's on again."

Later I ask the question and Joan laughs. "This is a musical tour for me. Actually, I don't see much of Bob at all. He spends most of his time on that movie he's making. The movie needs a director. The sense I get of it so far is that that movie is a giant mess of a home movie."

Joan, sitting back on the couch, as spontaneously straightforward as Dylan is cabalistically convoluted. And as he figures in who knows how many sexual fantasies of how many genders, so she is erotic, still freshly erotic, but probably stars in somewhat straighter fantasies. But who knows?

And she is funny, especially in self-defense. As on the day she showed up for her first rehearsal for the Rolling Thunder Revue.

"I'd like to hear that song off your new album," Dylan asks the once and former girl on the half-shell. "You know, 'Diamonds and Rust.'"

"You want me to do that on the show?" Joanie looks at him in solemn question.

"Yeah." There is a distinct collector's gleam in Dylan's eyes. "Yeah, I do."

"You mean," the ex-madonna grabs Dylan by the chin and looks him in the eye, "that song I wrote about my ex-husband."

Dylan has been aced. "I have to keep him spinning," Joan says of the rout, "in order to keep my balance."

"Those duets," Joan says of what she's sometimes been thinking while also wiping Dylan's brow and looking into his eyes, "are a hazard. It's hard singing with him because he's so devilish. There are times when I don't know what song he's plucking on that guitar until he starts singing. And he can be tricky. On one song, we'd been doing two choruses all along the tour but one night, just as I'm about to belt the second chorus, the song was all over. Done! Thanks a lot. Bob had worked out the new short ending with the band and hadn't told me. Oh, he's a lot of fun onstage."

Curtain! The second half of the nonpareil Rolling Thunder What-Might-Have-Been-and-What-Has-Been-Point-to-One-End-Which-Is-Always-Present Revue is about to start!

Under the cowboy hat, the klezmer, the Jewish hobo musician with roots—roots by the centuries—turns to the sad-eyed lady from Chavez country. That lady who, he used to say, "proved t' me that boys still grow." Dylan looks up to Baez and says, "Don't upstage me."

She smiles her luminous smile and says, "I'm going to use everything I have to do just that."

"I'm back from goose hunting in Maryland," [said President Ford]. He was disappointed at only bagging one goose in six hours. Shifting to the subject of country music, "Joan Baez really grabs me," Ford admitted. Party host Senator William Brock (R-Tenn.) agreed. "I wish I could get her to campaign for me . . . at least in some areas," said the senator.

The campaigner is still very fond of the klezmer. "I used to be too hard on him. I used to be too hard on a lot of people." Baez grins, sipping wine. "Well, I'm not as stiff as I used to be. I've lightened up on people. I don't expect Bob to champion my causes anymore. I've learned he's not an activist, which does not mean he doesn't care about people. If that were so, he wouldn't have written 'Hurricane.'"

Having shrived Dylan of her moral burden ("Singer or savior it was his to choose / Which of us know what was his to lose"), what does she want from him now?

"I'd like to see him keep making music, keep creating. Why, I would like him to be happy."

It all depends, of course. Or, as Jane Ace once said to Goodman Ace, "If it makes him happy to be happy, then let him be happy."

And what does she want for herself?

Joan Baez speaks to the wall. "There must be something I can do with my life that will be worthwhile."

You talk, I say, as if you've been a sybarite or a government official up to now.

"Oh, I've already done a fair amount of things; but in terms of what has to be done, how do you measure what you still ought to be doing? And maybe what I did wasn't done as efficiently as it could have been. Screaming at people may not be the most efficient way. I'm going to stay back a little from now on. I'm learning how to listen to people instead of preaching at them so much. And learning to listen to myself again. I'm 30,000 words into a book, an extension of *Daybreak*. And the songs. I'm going to write more personal songs. If they come. I go through some very long dry periods. But it's fun when it happens."

One part of Baez, interlaced with all the others, remains stubbornly intact. "I am," she says, "your basic camp counselor, I really am."

All campers are to be treated equally, with justic and fairness for all. Or else.

By the 12th stop on the Rolling Thunder Revue celebration of musical egalitarianism, the camp counselor is furious. She is preparing a pronunciamento and a graphic drawing for the tour's internal newspaper. She is protesting rank injustice in the heart of all this here cultural freedom.

"They make the security people, the bus drivers and the crew," the burning bush speaks, "eat at separate places and at separate hours from the rest of us. That is segregation."

Who is "they"—Lou Kemp?

"I don't know who it is. But this is going to stop. The drawing I'm putting in shows a pool of blood, and it's going to say that without these guys who are being segregated, one of us principals might be stranded, to say the least, in the wake of the Rolling Thunder Revue."

What if your protest is ignored?

"Then a lot of us," says Joan, "will go eat with the security people, the bus drivers and the crew. There are a lot of possible approaches to this kind of problem."

Is Bob aware of this segregation?

Joan, customarily spontaneous, customarily candid, weighs her answer. "I don't know," she says.

Allen Ginsberg also speaks of protest, but as in a vision. Where once was a time to howl, now is the time to begin the harvest and to give thanks to the harbingers, then and now.

In Springfield, Massachusetts, Arlo Guthrie moves onstage to play and sing with his father's other son, the hard-wishing, hard-traveling, earnestly self-adopted Jack Elliott. Backstage, the midwestern klezmer (to whom Woody was his "last idol") watches and listens.

"That's a strong lineage, Woody's," says Allen Ginsberg, "and Woody, of course, was part of an older lineage, that old good-time Wobbly idealism. That's all still going strong right in this show. Joan sings 'Joe Hill.' And 'Hurricane' is part of that too, an old classic social protest song."

Sound the news of injustice and the people will awake. How else can we begin?

"And look how we end," says Walt Whitman's friend.

The end, a reasonably jubilant "This Land Is Your Land," everybody onstage, even Ginsberg-the-keeper-of-the-vision making silvery his finger cymbals, as Joan soars and swoops from the mountains to the prairies and Dylan, smiling, stands his ground, and all the rest move to the hearty beat of the American Upanishad.

"There was a kind of vision of community in the Sixties," Ginsberg says after the show, "and many people thought that once they'd had the vision, everything was solved. But as Jack Kerouac once said, 'Walking on water wasn't built in a day.' Another thing going on in the Sixties was just people digging each other, digging each other's texture and character, hanging out. You can't do that fast either. You know, there was a lot of hanging out in the Fifties too, in Kerouac."

Dylan had been braced and shaped, in part, way back when, by Kerouac. *Doctor Sax*, *On the Road*, *Mexico City Blues*. The day after the Rolling Thunder Revue came to Lowell, Dylan, Ginsberg and Peter Orlovsky visited Kerouac's grave. Ginsberg had brought a copy of *Mexico City Blues* and Dylan read a poem from it. The three then sat on the grave, Dylan picking up Ginsberg's harmonium and making up a tune. When Dylan pulled out his guitar, Ginsberg began to improvise a long, slow 12-bar blues about Kerouac sitting up in the clouds looking down on these kindly wanderers putting music to his grave. Dylan is much moved, much involved, a state of introspection closely captured by the camera crew that has also come along.

Before Lowell, before Boston, before Plymouth, the day the Dharma Carnival was to leave New York, Allen Ginsberg meets Muriel Rukeyser on the street. This soft-voiced, slow-speaking, hugely honest poet, who of late has been in South Korea trying to stop the terminal silencing of an antideath poet there, is glad to see Ginsberg. She admires people with visions. She asks where he's going.

"I'm going on the bus," Ginsberg says cheerily. "It's a minstrel show!"

"But it's more than a minstrel show, isn't it?" she asks me the next day.

"It is a signal to the country," Ginsberg tells me on the road. "What happened in the San Francisco renaissance in the mid-Fifties was one of those signals that characterize the rise of a generation's poetic consciousness and its sense of social rebellion. And that happened in the very midst of McCarthyism. Then, in the mid-Sixties, the peace marches and the rise of rock—the Beatles and things like that—were among the signals for a further rising of consciousness, a wider sense of community. Now, the Rolling Thunder Revue will be one of the signal gestures characterizing the working cultural community that will make the Seventies."

I would truly like to believe, I tell the poet, but where, except in wish, is the basis for such joyous tidings in a time of torpor?

"Have you read Dave Dellinger's book, *More Power Than We Knew*?" The poet must resort to prose. "Dellinger shows that many of the demands that the youth generation or the left or the movement made in the Sixties have actually been met. Congress did cut off funds for the Vietnam war and who would have thought that possible in the mid-Sixties? Then there were all the protests about the police state, and a police state paranoia to go with them. Now a great deal of that has been confirmed and exposed in public investigations. Not that everything has been all cleaned up but the work of the Sixties did bear some fruit. It never was in vain.

"So now, it's time for America to get its shit together," the poet says idiomatically. "It's time to get back to work or keep on working, depending on who you are, because the work that went before has been good, even though people got discouraged. It's been as good as you can expect, considering what it takes to walk on water or reverse the machine age or deal with overpopulation or capitalism. Rolling Thunder, with its sense of community, is saying we should all get our act together. And do it properly and well." The poet, bouncing his vision, laughs. "Once you have a view of the right path, then you have to travel that path."

That means Dylan's getting his act together too?

"Having gone through his changes in the Sixties and Seventies, just like everybody else," Ginsberg says, "Bob now has his powers together. On the show, he has all the different kinds of art he has practiced—protest, improvisation, surreal invention, electric rock and roll, solitary acoustic guitars strumming, duet work with Joan and with other people. All these different practices have now ripened and are usable in one single show, just as there is also room for Mick Ronson and his very English kind of space-music rock, Joan and her sort of refined balladry and Roger McGuinn with his West Coast–style rock. All of these different styles turn out to be usable now."

"Do you know what Dylan is talking about doing?" a principal of the tour says to me. "Don't use my name, but he might start a newspaper! That blows my mind. It'll be like a community newspaper, but for a community all over the country."

I wonder who's going to be the music critic and, in particular, who is going to write about Dylan's records. Blind Boy Grunt?

"I am not able to tell you any details," says Allen Ginsberg, "but this tour may not end as all the other tours have. There is some desire among us to have a kind of permanent community and Dylan is stepping very, very slowly to find out if that can work. Recordings would be one way and there may be other ways. One must proceed slowly and soberly—unlike the Beatles when they tried to expand their sense of community. Remember John Lennon trying to put together that whole Apple enterprise as a sort of umbrella organization for all kinds of collective work? But he didn't have the right personnel and so it wasn't done soberly and practically enough. This would be. Keep watching. The thing is to keep the Rolling Thunder spirit alive."

Joan Baez's denunciation of class segregation aboard the Rolling Thunder Revue has appeared in the troupe's internal newspaper. Her sketch of some nameless star, lying on the ground with blood pouring out of his head, was not printed and has disappeared. But the accusatory text reads:

"We strongly suggest that the security people, the bus drivers and the crew be treated more like human beings and less like bastard children because without them one of the principals might be left dead in the wake of the Rolling Thunder Revue.

"[Signed], Joan Baez and a large supporting cast."

Did it work? I ask.

"Well," says the ceaseless strategist of nonviolent direct action, "things kind of came together a bit after that. A lot of people, each in his or her own way, began committing small acts of civil disobedience—like taking the bus driver to their table. So the tone has changed and the segregation has lessened." Some people, I am buoyed to see, are still overcoming.

The tour is old enough for retrospection.

Traveling with his then wife, Sara, at the London Airport, September 2, 1969. *Photo courtesy of UPI/Corbis-Bettmann.*

"When you got that call from Bob," an old acquaintance visiting Joan backstage says, "I suppose you got on the plane without even knowing what you were going to get paid."

Joan looks at the questioner as if the latter has just asked if the tooth fairy has gotten over its cold. "When I got that call," Joan says, "I had already planned my fall tour. So I told the people dealing with the money that although it seemed like fun, they'd have to make it worth my while to change my plans. Well, after my lawyers got involved and we worked out a contract, they made it worth my while. Sure I'm glad I came. This tour had integrity. And that's because of Bob."

"Tell me," the acquaintance asks, "what are his children like?"

Joan hoots. "I've never seen any of them. They're like mythology. It does gather around him, mythology. And he certainly helps it gather. Mythology and confusion. Like some of the songs. I know who 'Sad-Eyed Lady of the Lowlands' is, no matter who he says it is."

"But at least we know who 'Sara' is," the visitor observes.

"Dylan says," Ginsberg has overheard, "that song is about Sarah in the Bible." And Ginsberg laughs.

Mythology has become palpable. Sara Lowndes Dylan has joined the Rolling Thunder Revue, and with her are several Dylan children and a nanny. Allen Ginsberg is impressed. "Sara is very intelligent, very funny and I would say queenly. She's sort of aristocratic looking, like an old-time New York young Jewish lady who's been around a lot in the theater, which she has been. Sara and Joan," Ginsberg chuckles, "have had time to compare notes on Dylan."

"No, I had never known her before," Joan says of Sara, "and yes, we have been comparing notes, and that is all I'm going to tell you about that. But I will say that for me, Sara is the most interesting female on this tour. Why? Because she's not a bore. That's the best thing I can say about anybody."

Sara Lowndes Dylan has become part of the Rolling Thunder Revue Acting Company, adding her skills and fantasies to what Allen Ginsberg estimates to be more than 100 hours of film already in the can for the giant kaleidoscope being shot by Lombard Street Films, which is being financed—I am told for nonattribution by those close to Zeus—by Dylan himself. At least five or so complete concerts have been preserved and some special numbers, such as "Isis," have been filmed more times than that. And there have been scores of scenes enacted by diversely mixed members of the troupe. Sara Dylan, for instance, has now portrayed a madam in a bordello in which one of the nubile employees is enacted by Joan Baez in a brazen French accent.

Joan, at first rather standoffish about what she had earlier regarded as a huge mess of a home movie, has now become more involved. In another scene, for instance, she and Dylan are in a bar and the bartender is Arlo Guthrie. "My God, she has a lot of energy," says cineaste Allen Ginsberg. "And what a marvellous mime."

Also intermittently involved are members of the band, virtuosic David Mansfield among them. As an educational insert in the bordello sequence, Allen Ginsberg is seen in his business suit, making Mansfield (playing a chaste 14-year-old) lose his cherry, as Ginsberg puts it in the old-time vernacular. This being, in part, a musical, Mansfield of course has his violin along.

Like many of the scenes in this gargantuan movie—which will purportedly be cut and edited in the spring by Dylan and Howard Alk, who worked with Dylan on *Eat the Document*—the bordello section started as quite something else. Ginsberg had suggested a scene involving a number of women in the troupe, in part because he is much taken with the notion that the dominant theme in the Rolling Thunder Revue is respect for the "mother goddess, eternal woman, earth woman principle." He points to the songs in the show, such as "Isis" and "Sara," and notes as well that Sara Dylan has diligently researched this theme in such works as Robert Graves's *The White Goddess*.

The women having assembled, there was much discussion as to the roles they would play—perhaps the graces or the goddesses or the nine muses. Somehow, however, as Sara Lowndes Dylan said, "After all that talk about goddesses, we wound up being whores."

"Nonetheless," says Allen, "Sara, as the madam, did talk about Flaubert."

Dylan is consumed by this film. He conceives a good many of the situations, advises on the transmutation of others, does some of the directing, peers into the camera and works, picking up technique, with the film crew.

One day after much shooting, Ginsberg, wondering how Dylan keeps track of the direction of all this footage, asks him. Dylan wishes he hadn't.

"I've lost the thread," Dylan, with some bewilderment, admits to Ginsberg.

A couple of days later, Ginsberg asks Dylan if the thread has been relocated. The singing filmmaker nods affirmatively.

"So what is the thread of the film?" the poet asks.

"Truth and beauty," says his ever-precise friend.

Along with the Dylan children and their nanny, Joan Baez's six-year-old son, Gabriel, is now on hand, together with Joan's mother and a nursemaid for Gabriel. What would Kerouac have made of this way of doing the road?

Also suddenly, triumphantly materialized—a climactic reaffirmation of the eternal-woman principle—is Bob Dylan's mother, Beatty Zimmerman.

"A regular chicken soup Jewish mother," Allen Ginsberg says approvingly. "With a lot of spirit."

Toronto. A cornucopian concert with Gordon Lightfoot and Joni Mitchell added to the Astartean cast. And also added in the fertile finale, "This Land Is Your Land"—Bob Dylan's mother.

Seated at the back of the stage, Beatty Zimmerman is pulled up and onto stage center and begins to dance and wave to the audience, none of whom, she is sure, knows who she is.

It is getting near the start of the second chorus and Joan Baez, chronically gracious, pulls Mrs. Zimmerman toward the lead mike, the principals' mike. "All of a sudden," Joan says, "Dylan kicks me in the ass. Gently. It was his way of saying, 'I think I'd rather sing this chorus than have my mother do it.' So I had to gracefully Charleston Mrs. Zimmerman back a few steps and then leap to the mike and sing with Bob."

And there, back a few steps, is Mrs. Zimmerman, arms flailing, dancing to Woody's song and the music of Woody's children and the music of her own child, of all things. The first time she's ever been onstage with that child.

"Sara, Joan, his children, his mother," Allen Ginsberg meditates, "he's getting all his mysteries unraveled."

Not quite. Not yet. Earlier in the tour, listening to him as he chants what I took—wrongly, it turns out—to be kaddish for "Sara," there is that mysterious, demonic force, in and beyond the words, that will last a long while beyond the tour. That cracking, shaking energy which reminds me of another klezmer on the roof, another Tateh in ragtime, Lenny Bruce. But Lenny, who certainly had his act together, never learned how to get his defenses together. Dylan, on the other hand, has developed a vocation for self-protection. If he has a mania, it is for survival. ("I'm still gonna be around when everybody gets their heads straight.") And part of the way of survival is keeping some of his mysteries damn well raveled.

One morning, as the caravan is about to break camp, a rock musician says, "You know what makes him different. He sees the end of things. The rest of us, we're into something, it's as if it's going to last forever. Dylan, he's in just as deep, but he knows it's not going to last."

I am mumbling about a stiff singer who phrases, however authoritatively, like a seal and plays nothing guitar on the side. Why, then, do I once again (unlike the '74 tour) find him powerful? "It doesn't matter whether he's musical at all," I am instructed by Margot Hentoff, a writer on these matters. "He has in his voice that sense of the fragility of all things, that sense of mortality which everybody tries to avoid acknowledging but is drawn toward when they hear it. He's got it and nobody else has."

It was my wife (quoted in a *New York Times* epitaph I had written of the '74 tour) who had greatly annoyed Dylan, a friend of his told me. "He's not 'The Kid' anymore," she said in print, "so what can he be now?"

A year later, having come upon the Rolling Thunder Revue, she has an answer: "a grown-up. Maybe a suspicious, secretive, irritating grown-up. But no longer a kid. He's lost that. And now, as he grows older, he'll get still more powerful because he'll reach the further knowledge that there is no way out of loss, and so he'll have a new truth to talk about."

Late one night, at the Other End, before the trail boss was quite ready to get the wagon train going, Dylan and Bob Neuwirth and the rest of the gang are elevating their discourse.

"Hey, poet, sing me a poem!" one of them yells to Dylan.

"Okay, poet," says the Minstrel Guruji.

Delighted, Allen Ginsberg is saying, "It's like in a Dostoevsky novel, the way they've taken to calling each other 'poet.' It's no more 'Okay, cowboy.' It's 'Okay, poet.' They're using 'poet' as an honorific, practical thing, and that means they've grown old enough to see that poetry is tough, that it's a lasting practice bearing fruit after decades.

"Dylan has become much more conscious of himself as a poet," Ginsberg adds. "I've watched him grow in that direction. Back in 1968, he was talking poetics with me, telling me how he was writing shorter lines, with every line meaning something. He wasn't just making up a line to go with a rhyme anymore; each line had to advance the story, bring the song forward. And from that time came some of the stuff he did with the Band—like 'I Shall Be Released,' and some of his strong laconic ballads like 'The Ballad of Frankie Lee and Judas Priest.' There was to be no wasted language, no wasted breath. All the imagery was to be functional rather than ornamental. And he's kept growing from there.

"Like he's been reading Joseph Conrad recently. *Victory* in particular. I found out when we were talking about the narrative quality of some of the newer songs—'Hurricane' and 'Joey' and 'Isis.' Bob related the way those songs developed to what he'd been learning about narrative and about characterization from Conrad. The way characterization and mood shape narrative. Now he's asking about H. P. Lovecraft. I wonder what that's going to lead to?"

It is near the end. In Toronto, Joan Baez is backstage. Onstage, Dylan is beginning his acoustic set. A member of Gordon Lightfoot's band begins to move some equipment. Baez glares at him, and he stops.

"The jerk didn't know any better," she says later, "but I didn't want to miss a note. I didn't want to miss a word. Even after all these shows, the genius of the Kid was still holding it all together. I'd heard it all, every night, and here I'm sitting again as close to him as I can get. And not only me. You look around and you see every member of the band and the guys in the crew listening too."

What is it? What is it he has? I ask.

"It's the power," Joan says. "It's the power."

"Oh, I'm hurtin'." It is the next morning. Bob Neuwirth groans and coughs in a most alarming manner. "This is a rolling writers' show," Neuwirth manages to say. "Nobody on this tour who isn't a writer. Oh, I'm really hurtin'. Even the equipment guys, the bus drivers, they're all jotting things down. It's a goddamn rolling writers' convention. Oh my God, I can't even cough. It's going to be such a drag when this tour is over."

Joan Baez, mildly sympathetic when she's not laughing, says to the audibly aching Neuwirth, "Do let me describe what happened to you last night. Everybody has his own way of dealing with anxieties," she explains to me, "and his way was to get himself black and blue. He got very, very drunk and ornery and for an hour and a half four very large security guards were wrestling him in the hall because they didn't want him to leave the hotel and go wreck Gordon Lightfoot's house where we were having a party. Well, he got there anyhow and he did wreck the house just a little. But everybody had a grand time and now Neuwirth feels fine too, except he can't walk very well.

"You see, it's going to be rough for all of us when this is over. And Neuwirth's way of handling that was to have an early blowout. God, it's depressing at the end."

At the beginning, in Plymouth, Massachusetts, Elliott Adnopoz (long since transubstantiated into his vision, Ramblin' Jack Elliott) sees an old friend, the replica of the *Mayflower*, on whose rigging he, an expert sailor, had actually worked years before. Climbing to the top of the mizzenmast, Elliott explodes with a long, joyous, "Ahoy!" and waves to the Minnesota poet in the cowboy hat below as Allen Ginsberg proclaims, "We have, once again, embarked on a voyage to reclaim America."

At least it is steady work, especially for a minstrel.

NEIL HICKEY

BOB DYLAN (1976)

TV Guide, September 11, 1976

This interview/profile appeared on the eve of his first network tele-vision special, a filmed Rolling Thunder Revue performance. Dylan is reasonably helpful in this interview, and his comments about religion and faith are interesting in light of his conversion to Christianity a few years later.—CB

"My being a Gemini explains a lot, I think," Bob Dylan is saying. "It forces me to extremes. I'm never really balanced in the middle. I go from one side to the other without staying in either place very long. I'm happy, sad, up, down, in, out, up in the sky and down in the depths of the earth. I can't tell you how Bob Dylan has lived his life. And it's far from over." Outside the auto's air-conditioned shell, the Malibu coastline of California, baking in 95-degree heat, is slipping past. Dylan observes the bathers idly. "I'm not really very articulate. I save what I have to say for what I do." What Bob Dylan does is write songs and perform them. Over the last 15 years, since he was 20, he has created a body of work unique among American artists: songs of such power and pertinence that they stand as a definition of the country and the man in those years: songs of rage over inhumanity; songs of inexpressible love, bitter vindictiveness and ribald joy; songs of spiritual longing, confusion and affirmation; songs in such extraordinary numbers that it often seemed miraculous that a largely self-educated youth—son of a Jewish furniture dealer from the Mesabi iron range of northern Minnesota—could have created them all: "Blowin' in the Wind" (an anthem of the 1960s civil-rights movement), "Like a Rollin' Stone" (one of the greatest rock songs ever written), "Masters of War," "With God on Our Side," "A Hard Rain's A-Gonna Fall," "Don't Think Twice, It's All Right." He has been, in sum, the sin-gle biggest cultural influence on millions in his own generation. He has taken American music by the hand into uncharted regions. Dylan turns from consideration of the bathers, smothers a grin, and says: "Somebody called me the Ed Sullivan of rock and roll." He laughs loudly at the thought. "I don't know what that means," he says, "but it sounds right." Indeed, Dylan is both master and star of his own troupe, the so-called Rolling Thunder Revue, a company of strolling players who recently completed a 50-concert tour—one performance of which was taped at Colorado State University and will be visible on NBC Tuesday night (Sept. 14): Bob Dylan's first TV special, "Hard Rain."

Rarely interviewed (the last full-fledged one was seven years ago) and rarely seen publicly or privately over long periods, Dylan has chosen to be one of the least accessible figures in the entertainment world. Born in Duluth, Minnesota, he grew up in nearby Hibbing and migrated early to New York's Greenwich Village, where he acquired a recording contract and became a major concert star. After a motorcycle accident in Woodstock, New York, in July 1966, in which he almost died (indeed, rumors of his death were persistent), he remained in virtual seclusion for several years. In late 1969 he appeared at the Isle of Wight Festival of Music—his first paid concert in four years—and 200,000 people from Great Britain, the European continent, Canada and the U.S. showed up to hear him. Since then, he has toured the U.S. several times and issued a series of highly successful albums.

"I don't really talk about what I do," Bob Dylan is saying. "I just try to be poetically and musically straight. I think of myself as more than a musician, more than a poet. The real self is something other than that. Writing and performing is what I do in this life and in this country. But I could be happy being a blacksmith. I would still write and sing. I can't imagine not doing that. You do what you're geared for." This year, along the Presidential campaign trail, Jimmy Carter has been quoting Dylan in many of his stump speeches, and even in his acceptance speech at the Democratic convention. "I don't know what to think about that. People have told me there was a man running for President and quoting me. I don't know if that's good or bad." He laughs broadly. "But he's just another guy running for President. I sometimes dream of running the country and putting all my friends in office." He grins at the thought. "That's the way it works now, anyway. I'd like to see Thomas Jefferson, Benjamin Franklin and a few of those other guys come back. If they did, I'd go out and vote. They knew what was happening."

Sports cars bearing upturned surfboards stream along Pacific Coast Highway in the noon sun. "Over there," says Dylan, pointing to a roadside cafe rimmed with tables and benches. "There's a place to stop." Striding toward the cafe in a bent-kneed lope, Dylan—wearing jeans, sandals, a thin, frayed, black leather jacket and white burnoose swathing longish brown curls—resembles a hip shepherd from some Biblical Brigadoon. Settled with a beer, he fixes pale blue eyes on his companion and reflects on the press and its treatment of him. "The press has always misrepresented me. They refuse to accept what I am and what I do. They always sensationalize and blow things up. I let them write whatever they want as long as I don't have to talk to them. They can see me any time—doing what I do. It's best to keep your mouth shut and do your work. It makes me feel better to write one song than talk to a thousand journalists." He rarely watches television, he says, including news. "I'm not influenced by it. I don't feel that to live in this country you have to watch TV news." How does he absorb the world's information before processing it into the topical songs that are so substantial a part of his work?

"You learn from talking to other people. You have to know how people feel, and you don't get that from television news." (In 1963, when Dylan was a skyrocketing young folk balladeer, Ed Sullivan invited him to appear on his show and Dylan accepted. He'd sing a new composition of his own called "Talkin' John Birch Society Blues," Dylan told Sullivan—a satire on the right-wing political group. Sullivan liked the song and scheduled it, but CBS censors refused to let Dylan perform it. Dylan refused to alter his choice of material and angrily chose not to appear on the show. Since then, he has consistently declined offers of network television, except for two brief appearances: one on ABC's old *Johnny Cash Show*—out of friendship for Cash; another on a recent PBS tribute to Columbia Records executive John Hammond, who gave him his first recording contract.)

What does he read? He laughs. "You don't want to know that. It would sound stupid." Still, the on-screen credits for this week's TV special carry "thanks" to (among others) Arthur Rimbaud, the French symbolist, mystical poet; and to American novelist Herman Melville. "Yes. Rimbaud has been a big influence on me. When I'm on the road and want to read something that makes sense to me, I go to a bookstore and read his words. Melville is somebody I can identify with because of how he looked at life. I also like Joseph Conrad a lot, and I've loved what I've read of James Joyce. Allen Ginsberg is always a great inspiration." Dylan visited Israel in 1971, an event that triggered talk among Dylan experts that Judaic tradition was about to become an overt aspect of his art. "There was no great signficance to that visit," he insists. But, he says: "I'm interested in the fact that Jews are Semites, like Babylonians, Hittites, Arabs, Syrians, Ethiopians. But a Jew is different because a lot of people hate Jews. There's something going on here that's hard to explain." Many of Dylan's songs abound in religious mystical images: the album *John Wesley*

Harding for example ("the first biblical rock album," he calls it, and the first to be released after his motorcycle accident), contains songs based almost entirely on stories and symbols from the Bible.

"There's a mystic in all of us," he says. "It's part of our nature. Some of us are shown more than others. Or maybe we're all shown the same things, but some make more use of it." How does Bob Dylan imagine God? He laughts abruptly, and then says, "How come nobody ever asks Kris Kristofferson questions like that?" After a pause, he says, "I can see God in a daisy. I can see God at night in the wind and rain. I see creation just about everywhere. The highest form of song is prayer. King David's, Solomon's, the wailing of a coyote, the rumble of the earth. It must be wonderful to be God. There's so much going on out there that you can't get to it all. It would take longer than forever.

"You're talking to somebody who doesn't comprehend the values most people operate under. Greed and lust I can understand, but I can't understand the values of definition and confinement. Definition destroys. Besides, there's nothing definite in this world." He sips at his beer and asks solicitously, "Want to go and sit on the beach for a while?"

We return to the car and, Dylan driving, roll slowly northward. Dylan reminisces about Greenwich Village in the early 1960s and its role as the spawning ground for the great "folk boom" that swept the nation in those years. One reason he had traveled there was to track down Woody Guthrie, the folk poet and balladeer who was Dylan's idol. The village's cafes and coffeehouses were home to scores of guitar-playing folkniks whose music was filtering out to the marketplace. The enormously popular Newport Folk Festivals, ABC's overslick TV series *Hootenanny* and hundreds of record albums by folk-style performers all fed the public's new appetite for simple, homemade music. (The folk boom ended, effectively, when the Beatles took the U.S. by storm in 1964, and when Dylan himself turned to the use of electrified instruments at about the same time.) "There was a lot of space to be born in then," Dylan is saying. "The media were onto other things. You could develop whatever creative interests you had without having to deal with categories and definitions. It lasted about three years. There's just as much going on now, but it's not centrally located like it was then." A few skeptics have suggested that Dylan wrote his so-called protest songs in the 1960s because his finely attuned commercial antennae told him there was a market for them. He denies it. "I wrote them because that's what I was in the middle of. It swept me up. I felt 'Blowin' in the Wind.' When Joan [Baez] and I sing it [as they do on the TV special], it's like an old folk song to me. It never occurs to me that I'm the person who wrote that.

"The bunch of us who came through that time probably have a better sense about today's music. A lot of people in the '70s don't know how all this music got here. They think Elton John appeared overnight. But the '50s and '60s were a high-energy period."

And how did the Beatles fit into all this? Dylan wags his head earnestly. "America should put up statues to the Beatles. They helped give this country's pride back to it. They used all the music we'd been listening to—everything from Little Richard to the Everly Brothers. A lot of barriers broke down, but we didn't see it at the time because it happened too fast." Dylan draws up at the curb, exits the car and walks to a 20-foot-high bluff over a near-vertical incline leading down to the beach. He scrambles down agilely and turns to catch cans of beer thrown after him. Settled in the sun, burnoose in place, peering out at the ocean, he resumes: "I consider myself in the same spirit with the Beatles and the Rolling Stones. That music has meaning for me. And Joan Baez means more to me than 100 of these singers around today. She's more powerful. That's what we're looking for. That's what we respond to. She always had it and always will—power for the species, not just for a select group."

What records does he play for his own amusement? "Personally, I like sound-effects records," he says, laughing. "Sometimes late at night, I get a mint julep and just sit there and listen to sound effects. I'm surprised more of them aren't on the charts." He is still laughing. "If I had my own label, that's what I'd record." A teen-age girl approaches Dylan, Frisbee in hand, and asks if it belongs to him. "No," says Bob Dylan politely, and the girl nods and ambles off down the beach, obviously unaware that she has addressed (in the view of many) the generation's greatest rock-and-roll singer-writer. "I pass on crowded streets without being recognized. I don't want to be one of those big stars who can't go nowhere. Change that to anywhere. My mother might read this."

How is it, he is asked, that the Bob Dylan one encounters today, recumbent on this Malibu beach, seems so much more serene than the turbulent, often self-destructive, angry young man one recalls from the 1960s. (He's now the father of five, married to the former Sara Lowndes, living in the languor of Southern California rather than New York's bustle.) He squints toward the horizon. "Anger is often directed at oneself. It all depends on where you are in place and time. A person's body chemistry changes every seven years. No one on earth is the same now as he was seven years ago, or will be seven years from today. It doesn't take a whole lot of brains to know that if you don't grow you die. You have to burst out; you have to find the sunlight." Where is he, musically, these days? "I play rag rock. It's a special brand of music that I play. I'll be writing some new songs soon, and then, look out! The music will be up to a whole new level." Does he write every day, and does it come easily? "Are you kidding? Almost anything else is easy except writing songs. The hardest part is when the inspiration dies along the way. Then you spend all your time trying to recapture it. I don't write every day. I'd like to but I can't. You're talking to a total misfit. Gershwin, Bacharach—those people—they've got song-writing down. I don't really care if I write." Pause. "I can say that now, but as soon as the light changes, it'll be the thing I care about most. When I'm through performing, I'll still be writing, probably for other people." Any regrets? "The past doesn't exist. For me there's the next song, the next poem, the next performance." Any messages to the world? "I've been thinking about that. I'd like to extend my gratitude to my mother. I'd like to say hello to her if she's reading this."

Ever see her? Pause. "Not as much as when I was a kid." He plucks

At Madison Square Garden, 1978. *Photo copyright © David Gahr.*

his beer can from the sand. "I hope there's not a snake in my beer," he says, apropos of not very much. Then he reclines languorously and watches the sun descend slowly to the Pacific horizon.

CHARLES SHAAR MURRAY

WITH GOD ON HIS SIDE . . . (1979)

New Musical Express, August 25, 1979

A review of Dylan's first born-again album, Slow Train Coming, *which raises issues about the relationship between God and rock.*—CB

The relationship between rock and religion has always been fraught and filled with tension: back at its Southern rural roots, there was always a serious metaphysical choice involved. Not for nothing did Jerry Lee Lewis fear for the safety of his immortal soul when he debated the morality of his music with Sam Phillips during a Sun Records session back in the '50s; not for nothing did Little Richard veer crazily between his sinful boppin' and the call he felt snaking out to him from gospel music; not for nothing did Georgia Tom, bawdy bluesman supreme, kick it all in the head and become the Reverend Thomas A. Dorsey, composer and publisher of sacred songs.

Elvis Presley was assailed as an agent of the devil even when he recorded spirituals and hymns and even when he recorded a whole album in that vein—the young Presley duded himself up in a suit and tie and sat at a white piano for the cover of "His Hand in Mine," but his greasy hoodlum sneer indicated that he was just about to steal the damn piano and some of the Southern stations refused to play the tracks on grounds of sacrilege.

Meanwhile B. B. King cut gospel albums, Hank Williams recorded religious soliloquies under the name of Luke the Drifter, George Harrison became the biggest bore on heaven or earth, Jeremy Spencer and Peter Green were dragged around like men whose feet are caught in the stirrup of a runaway stallion, a million Rastas in a million echo chambers warn us of a million days of reckoning and Bob Dylan . . .

Like Sherlock Holmes after he took a flier off the Reichenback Falls, Bob Dylan may have recovered from his black night crash back in '66, but he was never the same afterwards. Already preoccupied with biblical imagery (consult "When the Ship Comes In," off *The Times They Are A-Changin'*, if you're interested) and fascinated with death and retribution as early on as his very first album, he became an avid student of Holy Writ while convalescing from his collision with the Reaper and soon the substance as well as the language of the King James Bible became part and parcel of his work. From Zen and Judaism, he ended up a few months ago undergoing rites of baptism with the California-based Vineyard Fellowship and emerges now with a prophet motive, a scourge of the unrighteous, preaching Doomsday and resurrection, breathing fire.

Slow Train Coming is the fruit of this fervor, and it's going to make a lot of people feel extremely uncomfortable (I know whereof I speak). As is common with Jews who have converted to Christianity, Dylan takes a severe, sulphurous Old Testament line on the New Testament, communicating little of the joy, warmth and salvation often found in Black American gospel music or in the Rasta testaments of Bob Marley or Burning Spear. The message, spread over nine songs of greater or lesser spiritual import, is: if you are not for Jesus, you are against him. Get it together. Repent or burn.

In other words, this album is not exactly a barrel of laughs (though Dylan's wit has certainly not deserted him). Bob has found God, and neither of them are pissing about. We're here to talk about your soul, brother. Have you been saved?

What certainly has been saved is the essence and core of Dylan's art.

After the ultimate decadence of *Bob Dylan at Budokan*—wherein he gave the lie to his magnificent Earls Court shows by singing like a greasy old hack—he returns to the finest vocal form he's ever had. He's never sung more like Dylan than he does here: Superdylan is more like it. Every note, every phrase is either caressed or cuffed, spat out or thrown away, twisted and shaped for emphasis and irony.

Every singer who has ever copped an inflection from Bob Dylan is hereby politely escorted to the back door and ceremonially thrown down the stairs. "Precious Angel" is a finer Graham Parker–style interpretation of Dylan's phrasing and tone than Geep himself has ever accomplished. Lou Reed is similarly seen off. Ian Hunter doesn't even come into it. No one sings Dylan like Dylan: the verse of "Precious Angel" beginning "Let me tell you, sister, about a vision that I saw / You were drawing water for your husband and suffering under the law" is some sort of peak in the history of vocal rock and roll.

Moreover, Dylan is still the chairman of the board of rock composers:

just as a judicious combination of Christian fervor and the guidance of producer Jerry Wexler (who's been recording great singers from Joe Turner and Ray Charles on up for 30 years now and ain't about to start taking bullshit off singers at this stage of the game) has worked wonders for his singing, the occasion has sharpened up his songwriting chops to the highest point they've attained since *Blood on the Tracks*. Almost every song (we'll reach the single, deliberate exception later) bristles with quotable stabs and pithy maxims. Far from having his wits addled by religion, Dylan would seem to have sharpened up his act all round.

Like any other dedicated evangelist, Dylan has concerned himself with packaging and marketing. Working with seasoned sessioneers (David Hood and coproducer Barry Beckett), members of a currently hot band (Mark Knopfler and Pick Withers from Dire Straits) and the first real producer that he's had since his days with Bob Johnston, Dylan has framed himself with smooth, streamlined music.

With a basic small band of Knopfler (lead guitar), Beckett (keyboards), Hood (bass) and Withers (drums) embellished only by discreet horns and choir here and there, the sound is strong and simple. Some of the backing tracks could've been directly filched from a late '60s or early '70s Albert King album, and Knopfler even attempts a few guitar solos (marred mainly by timidity, weedy tone and a silly, exaggerated finger vibrato) in the tradition of the big A.

An unadulterated ten out of ten for form, therefore, but let us press onwards into the realm of content. We open with a relaxed, but menacing soul-blues lope through "Gotta Serve Somebody" with Dylan telling us—with seemingly endless variation—that whatever your personal circumstances: "You gotta serve somebody sometime / It may be the devil and it may be the Lord / But you gotta serve somebody sometime." A rigid definition of good and evil and a black-and-white choice with a sole note of self-mocking levity when he informs us: "You can call me Terry, you can call me Jimmy / You can call me Bobby / You can call me Zimmy / You can call me, Archie, you can call me Ray / You can call me anything but no matter what you say . . ." I'd love to call you "Zimmy," Bob—in fact I will just to keep things from getting too serious—but what if I don't want to serve either God or the Devil?

The silky stomp of "Gotta Serve Somebody" gives way to the perky but muted strum of "Precious Angel" which—in the context of This Year's Britrock—resembles a collision/collusion between Dire Straits and the last Graham Parker album. Knopfler sounds as if he has a switch on his gui-

tar marked "Limpidly Beautiful" and his solo is as glibly, flawlessly sentimental as Dylan's vocal is gnarled and simultaneously polished. Again,
Zimmy tells us that "you either have faith or unbelief, there ain't no neu-
tral ground." This is the central polarity around which all religion—
indeed, the entire concept of religion—revolves, and throughout the album
Dylan presents it to us, time and time again.

In "I Believe in You," Zimmy puts new strings on his Martin, borrows
the opening lines of "Smoke Gets in Your Eyes" and presents the tale (told
in the first person) of a man persecuted for his faith, rejected and repulsed.
In the light of Dylan's identification with his Jewish heritage and the centuries of persecution and pogrom thereby involved, the song is lent both
resonance and irony: just who is the underdog here?

The sound rounds off with the title track as illustrated on the cover.
A train is seen with workers scurrying in its path laying down the rails
upon which the inexorable advance will roll; the figure nearest the fore-
ground (Dylan himself?) raises a pickaxe-cum-crucifix and the whole thing
is rendered in Old West woodcut. On the track itself, Knopfler reappears
as Albert King and the Muscles Shoals gang hit a "Born under a Bad Sign"
groove, over which Dylan appears, grim and spectral, to intone a series of
damning indictments against civilization (including a mini-tirade against
foreigners—specifically oil sheiks—controlling America's economic destiny and damaging her reputation overseas, causing Thomas Jefferson to
turn in his grave) culminating each time in a chorus which warns "There's
a slow train coming up around the bend." Retribution, it would seem, is
inevitable. You've been listening to your Marley records again, Bob.

The blues groove hardens up another pair of notches on "Changed
My Way of Thinking" over on side two. Loosely based on Taj Mahal's
"Done Changed My Way of Living," the writing draws on a rich vein of
blues aphorisms to rail ever more furiously against immorality: pornogra-
phy in schools, the lot. Again, Knopfler lets the side down by playing all
the right notes but with far too little attack although Dylan is at his most
caustic and commanding: "I got a good fine woman, one I can easily
afford . . . she can walk in the spirit of the Lord / Jesus said 'Be ready for
you know not the hour in which I come.' He said, 'He who is not for me
is against me' just so you know where he's coming from!" caws Dylan with
as much authority as he's ever sung anything.

He makes something of a turnabout on "Do Unto Me, Baby." Having
judged everything in sight, he then turns around coyly and announces:
"Don't wanna judge nobody, don't wanna be judged / Don't wanna touch

nobody / Don't wanna be touched." The song is intensely amusing (despite the line, "Don't wanna amuse nobody / Don't wanna be amused") and carries eerie echoes of "All I Really Wanna Do," but this time the message is a strictly transactional view of human relationships buffered with the cosy admonition, "If you do right to me, baby, I'll do right to you too / you gotta do unto others as you'd have them do unto you."

However, "When You Gonna Wake Up" finds him judging all over the place again, machine-gunning aphorisms like there was no tomorrow: "You got some big dreams, baby, but to dream you got to still be asleep! They tell you time is money as if your life is worth its weight in gold! You get men who can't hold their peace, women who can't control their tongue / The rich seduce the poor and the old are seduced by the young." Beckett's soulful, gospelly keyboards are the stuff of sheerest delight under Dylan's grim enquiry: "Have you ever wondered just what God requires? You think he's just an errand boy to satisfy your wandering desires?"

"Man Gave Names to All the Animals" is a children's song with the kind of mock-reggae groove that American session players think symbolizes innocent levity. Dylan implies that it was very presumptuous of man to name the animals when he can only perceive them in ridiculously naive ways. After all, only God knows their real names. It ends with a portentous reference to the Garden of Eden and the loss of innocence. It sounds like Jonathan Richman gone gospel, the bass line is silly/logical and it's very cute and catchy.

The Big Finale is Dylan alone with Barry Beckett's piano—who does he think he is? Ian Hunter? Bob Geldof?—testifying on "When He Returns." "Don't you burn," he warns, and achieves his final transformation. Now he is John the Baptist.

As a demonstration of Dylan's powers as a singer, composer and philosopher, *Slow Train Coming* verges on the awesome. To reemphasize: he has never sung better in his life, his verbal aim has never been more accurate, the fire of his critical ammunition has never been more withering, his records have never been more perfectly produced (though his sidemen have certainly shed more blood for his music in the past). He has much of present-day society totally sussed and numbered.

But . . . Dylan has divided the world into Good and Evil according to the precepts of a narrow and fundamentalist creed. Unlike the Rastas, he tells us damn little—there's another 2p for the swearbox. Shit!—of love and joy.

Religion can't all be a matter of vengeance and damnation; religion has to love as well as threaten or else the whole thing descends to a bunch of people rubbing their hands and muttering, "Boy, are you gonna catch it when teacher gets back!"

What Dylan is preaching talks not of liberation but of punishment, and in sour and elitist terms. If we aren't talking about a God of love then FORGET IT. The world is already too full of so-called Christians dealing in nothing but repression, and we don't need Bob Dylan opening a munitions factory to give them greater fire-power than they already possess.

Bob Dylan has never seemed more perfect and more impressive than on this album. He has also never seemed more unpleasant and hate-filled. Take your choice. It's your fiver—and your soul.

ROBERT HILBURN

"I LEARNED THAT JESUS IS REAL AND I WANTED THAT" (1980)

Los Angeles Times, November 23, 1980

Old friend Robert Hilburn, long-time music critic for the Los Angeles Times, *got the scoop that Dylan was "born-again." In this interview, conducted before a November 19 concert at the Warfield Theater in San Francisco, Dylan describes his conversion and what it meant to him. Clealry Hilburn is one of the few journalists with whom Dylan was prepared to discuss this subject.*—CB

Bob Dylan has finally confirmed in an interview what he's been saying in his music for 18 months: He's a born-again Christian.

Dylan said he accepted Jesus Christ in his heart in 1978 after a "vision and feeling" during which the room moved: "There was a presence in the room that couldn't have been anybody but Jesus."

He was initially reluctant to tell his friends or put his feelings into songs but he was so committed to his gospel music by late 1979 that he didn't perform any of his old songs during a tour. He said he feared that they might be "anti-God."

Believing now that the old and new songs are compatible, Dylan sings such stinging rockers as "Like a Rolling Stone" alongside such born-again treatises as "Gotta Serve Somebody" on a tour that includes a stop Wednesday at San Diego's Golden Hall.

Sitting in a hotel room here before a concert, Dylan, whose family is Jewish, sat on a couch and smoked a cigarette as he discussed his religious experience for the first time in an interview.

"The funny thing is a lot of people think that Jesus comes into a person's life only when they are either down and out or are miserable or just old and withering away. That's not the way it was for me.

"I was doing fine. I had come a long way in just the year we were on the road [in 1978]. I was relatively content, but a very close friend of mine mentioned a couple of things to me and one of them was Jesus.

"Well, the whole idea of Jesus was foreign to me. I said to myself, 'I can't deal with that. Maybe later.' But later it occurred to me that I trusted this person and I had nothing to do for the next couple of days so I called the person back and said I was willing to listen about Jesus."

Through a friend, Dylan met two young pastors.

"I was kind of skeptical, but I was also open. I certainly wasn't cynical. I asked lots of questions, questions like, 'What's the son of God, what's all that mean?' and 'What does it mean—dying for my sins?'"

Slowly, Dylan began to accept that "Jesus is real and I wanted that. . . . I knew that He wasn't going to come into my life and make it miserable, so one thing led to another . . . until I had this feeling, this vision and feeling."

Dylan, the most acclaimed songwriter of the rock era, had been unwilling to grant interviews since the release last year of the gospel-dominated *Slow Train Coming* album, suggesting that anyone who wanted to know what he felt could simply listen to that work.

Though the album became one of Dylan's biggest sellers, many of his own fans felt confused, even betrayed. The man who once urged his audience to question was suddenly embracing what some felt was the most simplistic of religious sentiments. Furthermore, some critics argued, Dylan's attitudes were smug. Surely, many insisted, this was just another peculiar turn in Dylan's ever-shifting persona.

Even when he returned last spring with another gospel album, the less commercially successful *Saved*, rumors abounded that he had abandoned his born-again beliefs. But his shows in San Francisco on this tour refuted that speculation. Ten of his seventeen songs on opening night were from the last two albums.

In the interview, too, Dylan stressed that his beliefs are deeply rooted: "It's in my system."

At the same time, Dylan showed that he hasn't lost his questioning spirit.

Asked about the political activism of fundamentalist Christian groups like the Moral Majority, he replied, "I think people have to be careful about all that. . . . It's real dangerous. You can find anything you want in the Bible. You can twist it around any way you want and a lot of people do that. I just don't think you can legislate morality. . . . The basic thing, I feel, is to get in touch with Christ yourself. He will lead you. Any preacher who is a real preacher will tell you that: 'Don't follow me, follow Christ.'"

Dylan still seemed uncertain about discussing his religious views when he began the current tour at the Warfield on November 9th, sidestepping questions on the topic at a mini-press conference backstage after the opening show. But once he touched on the subject in the hotel interview, he spoke freely.

The interview centers on his new direction in music because that was the topic I wanted to pursue in the time he had before the show, but it'd be wrong to infer that Dylan has become a "Jesus freak" stereotype, interested in only discussing that subject. During the interview and during other, more informal chats, he spoke with equal zest about various matters, including the decision to do his old material again.

Hilburn: *Some people would love you to go on stage and just sing the old songs, like a living "Beatlemania." Isn't there a danger in doing that? That's what Elvis Presley ended up doing.*

Dylan: Elvis changed. The show that people always talk about Elvis was that 1969 TV show, but it's not quite the same as when he did those songs in the beginning. When he did "That's Alright Mama" in 1955, it was sensitivity and power. In 1969, it was just full-out power. There was nothing other than just force behind that. I've fallen into that trap, too. Take the 1974 tour.

It's a very fine line you have to walk to stay in touch with something once you've created it. . . . Either it holds up for you or it doesn't. A lot of artists say, "I can't sing those old songs anymore," and I can understand it because you're no longer the same person who wrote those songs.

However, you really are still that person some place deep down. You don't really get that out of your system. So, you can still sing them if you can get in touch with the person you were when you wrote the songs. I don't think I could sit down now and write "It's All Right Ma" again. I wouldn't even know where to begin, but I can still sing it and I'm glad I've written it.

Hilburn: Why didn't you do any of the old songs on the 1979 tour?

Dylan: I truly had a born-again experience. If you want to call it that. It's an over-used term, but it's something that people can relate to. It happened in 1978. I always knew there was a God or a creator of the universe and a creator of the mountains and the sea and all that kind of thing, but I wasn't conscious of Jesus and what that had to do with the supreme creator.

Hilburn: After you had the vision, I understand you attended a three-month Bible course at a church in Reseda.

Dylan: At first, I said, "There's no way I can devote three months to this. I've got to be back on the road soon." But I was sleeping one day and I just sat up in bed at seven in the morning and I was compelled to get dressed and drive over to the Bible school. I couldn't believe I was there.

Hilburn: But you had already accepted Jesus in your heart?

Dylan: Yeah, but I hadn't told anybody about it because I felt they would say, "Aw, come on." Most of the people I know don't believe that Jesus was resurrected, that He is alive. It's like He was just another prophet or something, one of many good people. That's not the way it was any longer for me. I had always read the Bible, but I only looked at it as literature. I was never really instructed in it in a way that was meaningful to me.

Hilburn: I had assumed that these feelings came to you at a crisis point in your life, a time when you were desperately needing something else to believe in.

Dylan: No. I had gone so far that I didn't even think there was anything left. I thought, "Well, everybody has got their own truth." What works for one man is fine as long as it works for him. I had given up looking and searching for it.

Hilburn: But didn't you go to Israel? You seemed to be searching for some religious . . .

Dylan: Not really. If I was searching, it was just to . . . get down to the root reality of the way things really are, to pull the mask off. My thing was always to pull the mask off of whatever was going on. It's like war. People don't look at war as a business. They look at it as an emotional thing.

When you get right down to it, however, war—unless one people need another people's land—is a business. If you look at it that way, you can come to terms with it. There are certain people who make a lot of money off of war the same way people make money off blue jeans. To say it was something else always irritated me.

Hilburn: Did you start telling friends about it when you went to the Bible classes?

Dylan: No, I didn't want to set myself up. I didn't want to reflect on the Lord at all because if I told people and then I didn't keep going, they'd say, "Oh well, I guess it was just another one of those things that didn't work out." I didn't know myself if I could go for three months. But I did begin telling a few people after a couple of months and a lot of them got angry at me.

Hilburn: Did you have any second thoughts when that happened?

Dylan: No. By that time, I was into it. When I believe in something, I don't care what anybody else thinks.

Hilburn: Do you have any fear that what you're saying now may come back to haunt you in five years—that you aren't really committed?

Dylan: I don't think so. If I would have felt anything like that, I think I would have come up to the surface by now.

Hilburn: But we've seen so many rock stars get involved with gurus and maharishis and then move on.

Dylan: Well, this is no maharishi trip with me. Jesus is definitely not that to me.

Hilburn: When did you start writing the songs for Slow Train Coming?

Dylan: After about two months. I didn't even want to sing them. I was going to give them to Carolyn Dennis [a singer on the current tour] and have her sing them. I thought maybe I could produce her record.

Hilburn: Why didn't you want to sing them?

Dylan: I didn't want to step out there yet.

Hilburn: What did you think about some of the hostile reviews to Slow Train Coming?

Dylan: You can't look at reviews.

Hilburn: Do you see how people could think some of the messages in the album were heavy-handed?

Dylan: I didn't mean to deliver a hammer blow. It might come out that way, but I'm not trying to kill anybody. You can't put down people who don't believe. Anybody can have the answer I have. I mean, it's free.

Hilburn: What about the decision in 1979 to do only new songs?

Dylan: I wasn't in touch with those old songs then.

Hilburn: But you're singing them again now.

Dylan: It's like I said, this show evolved out of that last tour. It's like the songs aren't . . . how can I put it? Those songs weren't anti-God at all. I wasn't sure about that for a while.

Hilburn: Are the early songs still meaningful to you or do you just do them because people want to hear them?

Dylan: I love those songs, they're still part of me.

Hilburn: Is there any way you can talk about the changes in your life, how the religious experiences makes you feel or act differently?

Dylan: It's in my system. I don't really have enough time to talk about it. If someone really wants to know, I can explain it to them, but there are other people who can do it just as well. I don't feel compelled to do it. I was doing a bit of that last year on the stage. I was saying stuff I figured people needed to know. I thought I was giving people an idea of what was behind the songs. I don't think it's necessary anymore.

When I walk around some of the towns we go to, however, I'm totally convinced people need Jesus. Look at the junkies and the winos and the troubled people. It's all a sickness which can be healed in an instant. The powers that be won't let that happen. The powers that be say it has to be healed politically.

Hilburn: What about some of the new songs? Some seem only remotely religious.

Dylan: They've evolved. I've made my statement and I don't think I could make it any better than in some of those songs. Once I've said what I need to say in a song, that's it. I don't want to repeat myself.

Hilburn: So you can work from a larger canvas again?

Dylan: Yeah, but that doesn't mean that I won't keep singing these songs.

Hilburn: Is music still important to you?

Dylan: Music has given me a purpose. As a kid, there was rock. Later on, there was folk-blues music. It's not something that I just listen to as a passive person. It has always been in my blood and it has never failed me.

Because of that, I'm disconnected from a lot of the pressures of life. It disconnects you from what people think about you. Attitudes don't really make too much difference when you can get on stage and play the guitar and sing songs. It's natural for me. I don't know why I was chosen to do it. I'm almost 40 now and I'm not tired of it yet.

ERNIE SANTOSUOSSO

BOB DYLAN IN CONCERT (1980)

Boston Globe, May 5, 1980

This is a typical unsympathetic review of the born-again Bob in performance.—CB

Worcester—Bob Dylan has found Jesus and substituted prayer for protest. However, he could have used a miracle to fill several hundred empty seats Friday night in Worcester Memorial Auditorium (capacity 3000).

Recently recruited into the ranks of the born-again, Dylan demonstrated he has more guts than show-business savvy as he continually sermonized in song in this folk-rock tent show. This time Mr. Tambourine Man went into the trunk. No longer Blowin' in the Wind or bemoaning the fact that The Times They Are A-Changin', the "new" Dylan gave a performance long on yawns.

He sang of goodness, of how you "Gotta Serve Somebody," and asked "What Can I Do For You?" Since the show's concept was totally religious, it was difficult to comprehend the $15 and $12.50 ticket prices charged for the service.

In mostly the externals, Dylan appeared unchanged: Same black leather jacket, same black vest and slacks over white boots and scruffy facial hair. He wore the bored look of a worker who had just punched the time-clock on a job he couldn't escape. In the old days of the folk boom, they euphemistically called his aloofness charisma.

Dylan made it through the concert without smiling once and his stage announcements and sermonette-type introductions were almost completely garbled by abominable overamplification. Several of the songs, most containing creditable music, were extracted from his *Slow Train Coming* album memorializing the celebrated rebirth. Also included were songs whose titles he didn't bother to announce and would have been unintelligible delivered over the PA system, anyway.

Dylan was assisted by Spooner Oldham on keyboards, Fred Tackett on lead guitar, Tim Drummond on bass and Jim Keltner on drums. Opening the show in alternating lead vocal roles and later serving as backup vocalists was a generally excellent gospel group consisting of Regina Havis, Mona Lisa, Clydie King, Mary Bridges and Gwen Evans.

They managed to keep the exuberant crowd relatively attentive until Dylan appeared.

Strangely, most in the audience could hardly have been old enough to have been witness to the "folk boom" of the '60s, yet reacted with almost messianic fervor to each of Dylan's selections. Leaving the auditorium, this reporter overheard several young people hymning happily on the stone wall ringing the facility, an indication they had come to seriously celebrate Dylan's heavily publicized "reunion."

He took a swipe at the press, albeit with a velvet glove ("A lot of times," he said, "newspaper reporters come to my concerts and they're not too encouraging and don't think Dylan has any morality.") This reporter questions only his wisdom in choosing such a restrictive concept when others have been able to carry it off much more effectively and at much smaller cost to the public. Rather cryptically, he added: "God by Christ has reached out the word to me . . . don't be worried about your country now."

Hammering out his theme of spiritual love, the folk-rock superstar uninterruptedly posited his thesis with songs of similar sentiment, differing only in tempi: "I Believe in You," "When You Gonna Wake Up," "I Ain't Gonna Go to Hell for Anybody," "Shine Your Light," "Man Gave Names to All the Animals" (no improvement over the pallid album version), "Won't Let Go," "Slow Train," with scintillating guitar solo, "Saving Grace," embellished by Dylan's simulated mandolin effects, and, quite possibly, the concert's climactic moment featuring Dylan's mouth harp theatrics on "What Can I Do for You?"

Sustained standing ovations brought the performers back for two encores—"Are You Ready?" a tune built upon a blues riff and, with the star at the piano, "Pressin' On." And so went this churchy visit, to be repeated Saturday night, by Bob Dylan who formerly polemicized on "The Times They Are A-Changin'." Who could have foreseen that the singer himself would be included in the major alterations?

The issue of morality bore no relation to the empty seats in Worcester last Friday night. It was just that the word had gone out across the land that Bob Dylan had been born again—and that was conceivably good. However, this very personal mystical experience didn't relieve him of the responsibility to continue to entertain a paying audience.

LARRY YUDELSON

DYLAN: TANGLED UP IN JEWS (1991)

Washington Jewish Week, 1991

Here is a thoughtful look into Dylan's life as a prophet, both in relation to Judiasm and Christianity, and his many conversions and counterconversions from religion.—CB

Greenwich Village, 1961: Bob Dylan takes the stage at Gerde's Folk City. The 20-year-old Dylan hasn't yet written the soundtrack to the sixties, been anointed prophet of his generation, converted to Christianity or dabbled with Lubavitch Hasidism. But already he's going after an establishment—a Jewish establishment, for that matter.

"Here's a foreign song I learned out in Utah," he twangs into the microphone. He strums his guitar, and continues tunelessly: "Ha! Va! Hava! Ha-va-na! Hava Nagila. Yodeleihoo!"

With the yodel and a finishing harmonica flourish, Dylan had outlined an epitaph for the Hebrew folk songs sung by folksingers like Theodore Bikel and the Weavers as part of a vaguely leftist, working-man's ethnic repertoire. The mockery was prescient: The left would not be strumming love songs about Israeli soldiers much longer. Dylan, with his inspired instinct for the authentic, was first to smell the phoniness.

"Talkin' Hava Negeilah Blues" appears for the first time on the new *Bootleg Series* compilation of "rare and unreleased recordings," an album that fills in many gaps in Dylan's musical career—particularly this past decade, when the trail-blazing rock star seemed to weave between fundamentalist Christianity and Hasidic Judaism. This most recent period is well documented in Clinton Heylin's new biography, *Dylan: Behind the Shades*. Both the book and the record were released in time to salute Dylan's 50th birthday in May 1991—a suitable occasion to reexamine his Jewish life since the days when he mocked the quintessential American Jewish tune.

Dylan has, if only from the ironic sideline, taken part in—and sung at—the deepest spiritual crises of his generation of American Jews: the drama of the civil rights struggle, the comforts and exoticism of the Jewish homeland, and the spiritual excitements of Lubavitch.

He also became a Christian—the one leader he followed—and never really looked back and renounced it—because, like many a hasid, he found God through the music. And in America, the roots of the music is Christian.

Abe Zimmerman's Son

The young Dylan's desire for a story more real, exciting, romantic, and gritty than true initially led him to deny, or at least hide, his Jewishness. He affected an Okie accent when he first came to New York, recounted a tall-tale autobiography about running off to join the circus and told nobody that his name was really Robert Zimmerman.

Was this apparent self-hatred Dylan's attempt to efface his middle-class Jewish childhood in order to become "a real American"?

Some chroniclers have seen it that way. But biographer Clinton Heylin says no: The disguises were built up not against his religion but against the insularity of his life in the small Minnesota town of Hibbing. If anything, the son of store-owner Abraham Zimmerman was fortunate to have wide family ties which insulated against the town's cool anti-Semitic undercurrent. Dylan's Jewish education included summers at Camp Herzl and bar mitzvah training.

Much later, he would tell this tale:

> The town didn't have a rabbi, and it was time for me to be bar mitzvahed. Suddenly a rabbi showed up under strange circumstances for only a year. He and his wife got off the bus in the middle of winter. He showed up just in time for me to learn this stuff. He was an old man from Brooklyn who had a white beard and wore a black hat and black clothes. They put him upstairs above the cafe, which was the local hangout. It was a rock and roll cafe where I used to hang out, too. I used to go up there every day to learn the stuff, either after school or after dinner. After studying with him an hour or so, I'd come down and boogie.

The potent combination of religion and rock 'n' roll was written deep in Dylan's soul. The music he loved, from the blues to Hank Williams's country ballads, mixed faith with its funk and had its roots in African religion and Negro spirituals. But the new rock 'n' roll went only halfway, tacking shallow popular song lyrics onto denatured rhythm and blues, Dylan, perhaps inspired by his rabbi, pressed on to a higher calling. His musical path from the North Country via Highway 61 to the Mississippi Delta continued "all the way from New Orleans unto Jerusalem," as he sang in "Blind Willie McTell," the 1983 song that is a high point of the *Bootleg Series*.

Acidic Rebbe

When Dylan first came to New York in 1961, he was a hungry kid trying to make a name for himself as a new Woody Guthrie. Other hootenanny singers were combing newspapers to write topical songs on poverty, war and injustice, but Dylan, like Maggie's Ma, was already "telling all the servants about man and God and law." Those first months of his apprenticeship produced forgettable topical songs like "Who Killed Davy Moore."

The classic Dylan protest songs all have a shot of something more, be it God and Jesus in "The Masters of War" and "God on Our Side," or the more indirect sense of apocalypse and mystery of "A Hard Rain's Gonna Fall" and "Blowin' in the Wind."

A motorcycle accident in 1966 forced Dylan to slow down and drop out of the gypsy life of concert tours. While living in the upstate New York country town of Woodstock, he wrote music with the Band that was quieter, the lyrics more elemental. The songs show a new- found faith and hope, best captured by the most famous song of that period: "I see the light come shining / From the West down to the East / Any day now / Any way now / I shall be released."

Sixty-one biblical references have been counted on the next Dylan album, *John Wesley Harding*. "All Along the Watchtower" transformed Isaiah's images into a rock hit. But what was a nice Jewish boy doing singing that "I Dreamed I Saw St. Augustine"?

Over the next few years, the domestic life Dylan led with his wife and five children seemed to overpower his creativity. He recorded shallow love songs and duetted with whitebread country star Johnny Cash.

But now, far from the whirlwind of stardom, he began to explore his Jewish roots. The search may have been prompted by his father's death. Returning to Hibbing for the funeral, Bob surprised his brother by reciting the Kaddish prayer. On his 30th birthday he was in Israel and visited the Western Wall. He told one confidante of plans to buy an apartment in Israel; he investigated moving to a kibbutz.

This did not please the activist Left, who still hadn't forgiven the Voice of Their Generation for abandoning politics, and which since the 1967 war had increasingly supported Arafat's Fatah. The story was told that when Dylan met Black Panther leader Huey Newton, the singer chided the revolutionary for opposing Israel. ("Go ask Huey," Dylan told writer Anthony Scaduto when asked about the rumor; Newton was in exile at the time.)

Similar rumors pegged his 1974 comeback tour as a fundraiser for the Israel Emergency Fund. Folk Singer Mimi Farina even picketed his San Francisco concerts.

According to Stephen Pickering's book *Bob Dylan Approximately*, a bizarre blend of concert reportage and Jewish mystical musings which what can only be described as the teachings of an Acidic Rebbe, Dylan visited Georgia governor Jimmy Carter after an Atlanta concert. Carter praised Dylan's support for Israel; Dylan changed the subject. Two years later, accepting the Democratic presidential nomination, Carter quoted Dylan's phrase, "He not busy being born is busy dying."

Busy Being Born Again

In late 1978 Dylan himself was busy being born again. His widely publicized conversion to Christianity made him perhaps the most famous Jewish apostate in American history. Suffering from a painful divorce, a tiring world tour and too much alcohol, Dylan began looking for answers. He found one: "There was a presence in the room that couldn't have been anybody but Jesus. I truly had a born-again experience, if you want to call it that. . . . It was a physical thing. I felt it all over me. I felt my whole body tremble."

Pressed into vinyl as the slick *Slow Train Coming* album, Dylan's new beliefs won him his first Grammy Award. But on tour, he disregarded the savy advice of his spiritual mentors at the Vineyard Fellowship and obstinately refused to play any of his songs from before he found the light. Biographer Heylin downplays the catcalls from the audience, but the transcripts he includes show that Dylan felt obligated to save the souls of an audience he never liked all that much.

"I told you the times they are a-changin' and they did. I said the answer was blowin' in the wind and it was. I'm telling you now Jesus is coming back, and He is! And there is no other way of salvation."

The followup album, *Saved*, was as self-righteous as its title. (His record company refused to release a live album of this religious music Dylan had recorded at his own expense.)

But Dylan's evangelical phase didn't last long. His third "Christian" album included such departures from fundamentalism as "Lenny Bruce," a paean to the Jewish comedian.

More importantly, he had begun to synthesize his old vision with the new light. The results ranged from the soaring religious poem "Every Grain of Sand" to a trio of surrealistic songs left off the album but included on the *Bootleg Series* and the 1985 *Biograph* collection. "Angelina," "Caribbean Wind" and "Groom Still Waiting at the Altar" update the surrealistic landscape of "Desolation Row" for a darker apocalypse. The show is no longer "Shakespeare in the alley" but "The theatre of the Divine Comedy."

Prophet Motive

Soon after, the rumors went round that Dylan had returned to Judaism and was studying with the Lubavitch Hasidim in Brooklyn. The summer of 1982 he went to Israel for the bar mitzvah of his son, already 15, and was photographed at the Western Wall. Had he returned?

The inner sleeve of this 1983 album, *Infidels*, showed him crouching on the Mount of Olives above Jerusalem. Jesus had vanished from his lyric vocabulary (though New Testament allusions remained), replaced by "The Books of Leviticus and Deuteronomy." "Neighborhood Bully," his first political song since 1976, discomfited the rock press with a hard-rocking defense of Israel's attack on Iraq's nuclear reactor and invasion of Lebanon. In "Man of Peace," to this listener at least, Dylan seemed to turn on the Christian missionaries who had saved him.

And in what could be interpreted as a Jewish justification of his Christian phase, Dylan sang in "I and I": "Took a stranger to teach me, to look into justice's beautiful face / And to see an eye for an eye and a tooth for a tooth."

He told an interviewer about his born-again period, "That was all part of my experience. It had to happen. When I get involved in something, I get totally involved. I don't just play around the fringes."

The problem was, at least for one Washington-area rabbi who had painfully excommunicated Dylan from his record collection when the singer converted, was that Dylan's return to Judaism, if it was that, was taking place without the publicity of his departure. Dylan would not leave his Christian stepping stones behind. Even as he recorded *Infidels*, he still professed belief in the Book of Revelations.

"Whether you want to believe Jesus Christ is the Messiah is irrelevant, but whether you're aware of the messianic complex, that's all that's important . . . people who believe in the coming of the Messiah live their lives right now as if He was here. That's my idea of it anyway," he said in 1985.

Earlier he had acknowledged his heritage, while separating himself from the Jewish community: "Roots, man—we're talking about Jewish roots, you want to know more? Check on Elijah the prophet. He could make rain. Isaiah the prophet, even Jeremiah, see if their brethren didn't want to bust their brains for telling it right like it is, yeah—these are my roots, I suppose. Am I looking for them? . . . I ain't looking for them in synagogues with six-pointed Egyptian stars shining down from every window, I can tell you that much," he said in 1983.

Evidence of his Jewish involvement continues to mount. One friend of mine saw him at a Minneapolis bris (circumcision ceremony). Another heard he davens at the UCLA Hillel. One writer tells the story of how Dylan attended synagogue in jeans, scruffy beard and a battered hat and was recognized by the rabbi and invited to open the ark. The congregation was abuzz: Why was this apparent bum being honored?

Most recently, Dylan wrote a cover blurb for Rabbi Manis Friedman's *Why Doesn't Anyone Blush Anymore*, in which the influential Minneapolis Lubavitch rabbi defends traditional Jewish rules of sexual modesty.

In a musical contribution to Lubavitch—one well short of the album of Hasidic songs he was rumored to have recorded in 1983—Dylan appeared on a 1988 Lubavitch telethon playing harmonica while his Sabbath observing musician son-in-law played guitar and sang. The tune: "Hava Nagila."

An ironic choice, certainly, because whatever Dylan has gotten from Lubavitch, it does not seem to be the philosophy of singing and rejoicing extolled in "Hava Nagila." "Arise, brothers, with a happy heart!" is not the message of Dylan's recent music. His 1989 album *Oh Mercy*, which was hailed as his best of the decade, reveals instead an intensely lonely man of faith, closer to the spiritual uncertainty of the Kotzker rebbe than the gregarious Lubavitch.

The first side of the album focuses on a "Political World" where, as in the Kabbalistic myth, "Everything is Broken." His only solution: is to "Ring Them Bells" (so the world "will know that God is one"). The side ends with "The Man in the Long Black Coat," who comes to town quoting the Bible and takes the narrator's woman away. A Hasid, perhaps?

The flip side is soul-searching and introspection, summed up by one title: "What Good am I?"

The same religious tension suffuses the more recent *Under the Red Sky*, despite a light-hearted boogie-woogie tone: "God knows there's a purpose / God knows there's a chance / God knows you can rise above the darkest hour of any circumstance."

The album concludes with "Cat's in the Well," which, like much of the songs on this album, sounds at first like a nursery rhyme, a reminder that "Ring Around the Rosie" was about the plague. In Dylan's last words so far, the leaves fall like ashes, like the hard rain. "The cat's in the well and the servant is at the door / The drinks are ready and the dogs are going to war / The cat's in the well, the leaves are starting to fall / Goodnight my love, may the Lord have mercy on us all."

The age of 50, taught the Sages of the Mishna, is the age of counsel. Other rock stars of his generation may still be singing silly love songs, but Dylan seems, in his elusive way, to be counseling, even during the Grammy Awards where he preached, in the name of his father: "Son, it's possible to become so defiled in this world that your own mother and father will abandon you. And if this happens, God will always believe in your own ability to mend you ways."

For most of his career, Dylan shrugged off efforts to crown him a prophet. From the beginning he knew the spiritual power and responsibility of the singer. He described it in a hymn to his first folksinger idol, "Last Thoughts on Woody Guthrie." Toward the end of this long poem, released on *The Bootleg Series*, he asks: "Where do you look for this hope that yer seekin'?" He concludes with his own answer:

> You can either go to the church of your choice
> Or you can go to the Brooklyn State Hospital
> You'll find God in the church of your choice
> You'll find Woody Guthrie in Brooklyn State Hospital
> And though it's only my opinion
> I may be right or wrong
> You'll find them both
> In the Grand Canyon

Part Five

KNOCKED OUT LOADED
1985–1990

During rehearsals for his comeback tour with his then band, Los Angeles, 1984. *Photo courtesy of Neal Preston/Corbis.*

MIKAL GILMORE

DYLAN AT A CROSSROADS ONCE AGAIN (1985)

Los Angeles Herald-Examiner, October 13, 1985

Gilmore wrote two profiles of Dylan in the mid-'80s; this one and a following article a year later for Rolling Stone. *Both show Dylan with his defenses down, giving unique insight into his creative work in the period, particularly his collaboration with Tom Petty.*—CB

The man who showed up at my front door one afternoon a few weeks back looked exactly like I hoped and feared he would: With his mazy brown hair, and his taut smile and with smoky sunglasses masking his inscrutable stare, he looked just like Bob Dylan. Almost too much so. Dressed in sleeveless, torn T-shirt, weather-worn black jeans and black motorcycle boots and, at 44, looking far more fit than I had seen him in any recent photos or video appearances, he seemed remarkably like the image of the younger Bob Dylan that is burned into our collective memory: the keen, fierce man who often tore apart known views of the world with his acerbic gestures and eloquent yowls.

What brought Dylan to my door was simply that we had an interview to do, and since he had to come to Hollywood anyway that day, this was the easiest place for him to do it. While this certainly made the meeting a lot more thrilling for me, it also made it a bit scarier. More than 20 years of image preceded him. This was a man who could be tense, capricious and baffling, and who was capable of wielding his image at a whim's notice in a way that could stupefy and intimidate not only interviewers, but sometimes friends as well.

What I found instead was a man who didn't seem too concerned with brandishing his image—even for a moment. He offered his hand, flashed a slightly bashful smile, then walked over to my stereo, kneeled down and started to flip through a stack of some unfiled records on the floor— mostly LPs by older jazz, pop and country singers. He commented on most of what he came across: "The Delmore Brothers—God, I really love them. I think they've influenced every harmony I've ever tried to sing. . . . This Hank Williams thing with just him and his guitar—man, that's something, isn't it? I used to sing these songs way back, a long time ago, even before

179

I played rock and roll as a teenager. . . . Sinatra, Peggy Lee, yeah. I love all these people, but I tell you who I've really been listening to a lot lately—in fact, I'm thinking about recording one of his earlier songs—is Bing Crosby. I don't think you can find better phrasing anywhere."

That's pretty much how he was that afternoon: good-humored and gracious, but also thoughtful and often elaborate in his answers. And sometimes—when talking about his Minnesota youth, or his early days in the folk scene under the enthrallment of Woody Guthrie—his voice grew softer and more deliberate, as if he were striving to pick just the right words to convey the exact detail of his memory. During these moments he sometimes lapsed into silence, but behind his sunglasses his eyes stayed active with thought, flickering back and forth as if reading a distant memory.

For the most part, though, sipping a Corona beer and smoking cigarettes, he seemed generous and relaxed, sometimes even surprisingly candid, as he ranged through a wide stretch of topics. He talked about his recent work in videos: "Making these things is like pulling teeth. For one thing, because of that movie *Renaldo and Clara*, I haven't been in a place where I could ask for my own control over these things—plus, because my records aren't exactly selling like Cyndi Lauper's or Bruce's, I didn't feel I had the credibility to demand that control.

"But the company wanted me to try one more [to help boost *Empire Burlesque*'s sales], and I said I would, as long as I got to name Dave Stewart as director. His stuff had a spontaneous look to it, and somehow I just figured he would understand what I was doing. And he did: He put together a great band for this lip-sync video and set us up with equipment on this little stage in a church somewhere in West L.A. So between all the time they took setting up camera shots and lights and all that stuff, we could just play live for this little crowd that had gathered there.

"I can't express how good that felt—in fact, I was trying to remember the last time I'd felt that kind of direct connection, and finally I realized it must have been back in the Fifties, when I was 14 or 15 years old playing with four-piece rock and roll bands back in Minnesota. Back in those days there weren't any sound systems or anything that you had to bother with. You'd set up your amplifiers and turn them up to where you wanted to turn them. That just doesn't happen anymore. Now there are just so many things that get in the way of that kind of feeling, that simple directness. For some reason, making this video just made me realize how far everything has come these last several years—and how far I'd come."

His reaction to pop's new social activism, and such efforts as Live Aid, USA for Africa and Farm Aid, is somewhat mixed. "While it's great that people are supporting USA for Africa or Farm Aid, what are they really doing to alleviate poverty? It's almost like guilt money: Some guy halfway around the world is starving so, OK, put 10 bucks in the barrel, then you can feel you don't have to have a guilty conscience about it. Obviously, on some level it does help, but as far as any sweeping movement to destroy hunger and poverty, I don't see that happening.

"Still, Live Aid and Farm Aid are fantastic things, but then musicians have always done things like that. When people want a benefit, you don't see them calling dancers or architects or lawyers or even politicians—the power of music is that it has always drawn people together.

"But at the same time, while they're asking musicians to raise money, they're also trying to blacklist our records, trying to take somebody like Prince and Madonna off the radio—the same people that they ask to help raise funds. And it isn't just them: When they're talking about blacklisting records and giving them ratings, they're talking about everybody."

Dylan is pleased by Bruce Springsteen's growing popularity, but he has a warning, too. "Bruce knows where he comes from—he has taken what everybody else has done and made his own thing out of it—and that's great. But somebody'll come along after Bruce, say 10 or 20 years from now, and maybe they'll be looking to Bruce as their primary model and somehow miss the fact [that his music comes from Elvis Presley and Woody Guthrie]. In other words, all they're going to get is Bruce; they're not going to get what Bruce got.

"If you copy somebody—and there's nothing wrong with that—the top rule should be to go back and copy the guy that was there first. It's like all the people who copied me over the years, too many of them just got me, they didn't get what I got."

Dylan was a bit less expansive when it came to discussing his own historical presence in rock and roll. He seemed more moved or involved when discussing the inspiration he felt during his early immersion in rock and roll and the folk, beat and poetry scenes than in deliberating over any questions about his own triumphs—such as the seismic impact he had on international pop culture once he fused folk tradition, rock revolt, political insight and poetic ability into a personalized, myth-making style.

"There are certain things you can say you've done along the way that count," he said, "but in the end it's not really how many records you sell [Dylan has sold more than 35 million], or how big a show you play or even how many people end up imitating you. I know I've done a lot of things, but if I'm proud of anything, it's maybe that I helped bring somebody like Woody Guthrie—who was not a household name—to a little more attention, the same way that the Rolling Stones helped bring Howlin' Wolf more recognition. It's because of Woody Guthrie and people like him that I originally set out to do what I've done. Stumbling onto Woody just blew my mind.

"Then again, I never really dwell on myself too much in terms of what I've done. For one thing, so much of it went by in such a flash, it's hard for me to focus on. I was once offered a great deal of money for an autobiography, and I thought about it for a minute, then I decided I wasn't ready. I have to be sat down and have this stuff drawn out of me, because on my own I wouldn't think about these things. You just go ahead and you live your life and you move on to the next thing, and when it's all said and done, the historians can figure it out. That's the way I look at it."

Despite his reluctance, Dylan did look back recently at some length at the behest of Columbia Records, which has been trying for three years to elicit his cooperation and enthusiasm over *Biograph*, a five-LP retrospective of his career from 1962 to 1981. The package (which is due for release in early November, but may yet be held up by Dylan), features 53 tracks, including 18 previously unreleased recordings and three scarce singles. Just as importantly, the set also includes a 36-page booklet by author-screenwriter Cameron Crowe that features extensive commentary and reflections by Dylan. His own critiques of his political anthems, love songs, religious declarations, narrative epics, poetic fancies, rock inventions and long-buried gems are fascinating.

Except for Crowe's booklet, Dylan hasn't much use for the *Biograph* project. "I've never really known what this thing is supposed to be," he said. "There's some stuff that hasn't been heard before, but most of my stuff has already been bootlegged, so to anybody in the know, there's nothing on it they haven't heard before. I probably would've put different things on it that haven't been heard before, but I didn't pick the material, I didn't put it together and I haven't been very excited about this thing. All it is, really, is repackaging, and it'll just cost a lot of money. About the only thing that makes it special is Cameron's book."

Perhaps Dylan's objections to *Biograph* derive from an aversion to being consigned to any kind of definitive history when so much of his history remains to be written. Perhaps they also stem from an understanding that no single collection could ever bind or explain a career as wide-ranging and restive as his, nor could it ever satisfy the critics, detractors, defenders and partisans who have scrutinized, acclaimed, assailed and debated his work with more fervor and attention than any other American postwar musician has received. Beginning with his ninth album, *John Wesley Harding* (1968), virtually every subsequent release has been greeted as either a "comeback," a stinging disappointment or an out-and-out betrayal of his early promise and beliefs. While this later work hasn't affected pop culture as much as his early songs did (but then, what could?), it's also true that much of it amounts to a resourceful body of music—often beautiful and daring, sometimes perturbing or confused, but always informed by an aspiring and uncompromising conscience.

Still, while *Empire Burlesque* sold respectably (around the half-million mark), it didn't attain the commercial prominence that was expected. Does that bother or disappoint Dylan?

"Yeah," he said without hesitation. "In fact, it concerns me to a point where I was thinking about regrouping my whole thought on making records. If the records I make are only going to sell a certain amount, then why do I have to spend a lot of time putting them together? You see, I haven't always been into recording all that much. It used to be that I would go in and try to get some kind of track which was magical, with a vocal on it, and just wait for those moments. I mean, talk about (Bruce Springsteen's) *Nebraska*. People say to me, "When you gonna make a *Nebraska* album? Well, I love that record, but I think I've made five or six *Nebraska* albums, y'know?"

Dylan stopped, shrugged and poured a little more beer into his glass. "You know," he said. "I can't release all the stuff that I want to release. I've got a lot of just melodic instrumentals laying around. I was thinking the other day that maybe I should put them out, but I can't. I've also got a record of just me and Clydie King singing together and it's great, but it doesn't fall into any category that the record company knows how to deal with. It's like . . . well, something like the Delmore Brothers: It's very simple and the harmonies are great. If it was up to me I'd put that kind of stuff out, or I would've put some of it on *Biograph*, but it's not up to me. Anyway, who's to know what people would make of it?"

I'd heard similar stories from various sources over the last few years—about whole projects that had been discouraged, if not altogether nixed by CBS. I'd even heard tapes of some of the unreleased works, and many of them are stunning. Such still-unreleased tracks as "Blind Willie McTell," "Death Is Not the End" and "Lord Protect My Child" are among the most stirring work he has done, providing sharp commentaries on physical and spiritual despair and hard-earned moral hope. Hearing these, as well as the better material on *Infidels* and *Empire Burlesque*, one realizes that Dylan still has a great deal to say—that he is once again at a creative crossroads. At the same time, one fears that he may withhold such uncompromising work out of deference to the expectations of the marketplace.

That was one matter I didn't get to explore because, as quickly as Dylan can enter a room, he can also leave one. "It's late. I should go," he said, standing up, offering his hand and heading for the door. Looking out and realizing that night had fallen, he finally took off his sunglasses. It was nice to look, even if for just a moment, into those clear blue eyes.

In a way, I was glad that the question had gone unasked. How was I going to put it: Are you going to redeem every promise we've ever inferred from your work and legend? It was fitting to remember something Sam Shepard once said to Dylan: "The repercussions of his art don't have to be answered by him at all. They fall on us as questions and that's where they belong." That his art still inspires such questions tells me everything I need to know about his remaining promise.

MIKAL GILMORE

POSITIVELY DYLAN (1986)

Rolling Stone, July 17, July 31, 1986

"Subterranean," declares Bob Dylan, smiling with delight. It is just past midnight, and Dylan is standing in the middle of a crowded, smoke-laden recording studio tucked deep into the remote reaches of Topanga Canyon. He is wearing brown-tinted sunglasses, a sleeveless white T-shirt, black vest, black jeans, frayed black motorcycle boots and fingerless black motorcycle gloves, and he puffs hard at a Kool while bobbing his head rhythmically to the colossal blues shuffle that is thundering from the speakers above his head. Sitting on a sofa a few feet away, also nodding their heads in rapt pleasure, are T-Bone Burnett and Al Kooper—old friends and occasional sidemen of Dylan. Several other musicians—including Los Lobos guitarist Cesar Rosas, r&b saxophonist Steve Douglas and bassist James Jamerson Jr., the son of the legendary Motown bass player—fill out the edges of the room. Like everyone else, they are smiling at this music: romping, bawdy, jolting rock and roll—the sort of indomitable music a man might conjure if he were about to lay claim to something big.

Performing at the Gershwin Tribute concert at the Brooklyn Academy of Music, 1987. *Photo courtesy of Ezio Peterson/ UPI/Corbis-Bettmann.*

The guitars crackle, the horns honk and wail, the drums and bass rumble and clamor wildly, and then the room returns to silence. T-Bone Burnett, turning to Kooper, seems to voice a collective sentiment. "Man," he says, "that gets it."

"Yeah," says Kooper. "So dirty."

Everyone watches Dylan expectantly. For a moment, he appears to be in some distant, private place. "Subterranean," is all he says, still smiling.

"Positively subterranean," he adds, running his hand through his mazy brown hair, chuckling. Then he walks into an adjoining room, straps on his weatherworn Fender guitar, tears off a quick, bristling blues lick and says, "Okay, who wants to play lead on this? I broke a string."

Dylan has been like this all week, turning out spur-of-the-moment, blues-infused rock and roll with a startling force and imagination, piling up instrumental tracks so fast that the dazed, bleary-eyed engineers who are monitoring the sessions are having trouble cataloging all the various takes—so far, well over twenty songs, including gritty r&b, Chicago-steeped blues, rambunctious gospel and raw-toned hillbilly forms. In part, Dylan is working fast merely as a practical matter: rehearsals for his American tour with Tom Petty and the Heartbreakers start in only a couple of weeks, and though it hardly seems possible in this overmeticulous, high-tech recording era, he figures he can write, record, mix and package a new studio LP in that allotted term. "You see, I spend too much time working out the sound of my records these days," he had told me earlier. "And if the records I'm making only sell a certain amount anyway, then why should I take so long putting them together? . . . I've got a lot of different records inside me, and it's time just to start getting them out."

Apparently, this is not idle talk. Dylan has started perusing songs for a possible collection of new and standard folk songs and has also begun work on a set of Tin Pan Alley covers—which, it seems safe to predict, will be something to hear. At the moment, though, as Dylan leads the assembled band through yet another roadhouse-style blues number, a different ambition seems to possess him. This is Bob Dylan, the rock and roller, and despite all the vagaries of his career, it is still an impressive thing to witness. He leans lustily into the song's momentum at the same time that he invents its structure, pumping his rhythm guitar with tough, unexpected accents, much like Chuck Berry or Keith Richards, and in the process, prodding his other guitarists, Kooper and Rosas, to tangle and burn, like good-natured rivals. It isn't until moments later, as everybody gathers back into the booth to listen to the playback, that it's clear that this music sounds surprisingly like the riotous, dense music of *Highway 61 Revisited*—music that seems as menacing as it does joyful, and that, in any event, seems to erupt from an ungovernable imagination. Subterranean, indeed.

It was with rock and roll remarkably like this that, more than twenty years ago, Bob Dylan permanently and sweepingly altered the possibilities of both folk music and the pop-song form. In that epoch, the reach of his influence seemed so pervasive, his stance so powerful and myserious, that he was virtually changing the language and aspirations of popular culture with his every word and gesture. But Dylan barely got started in rock and roll before he stopped. In the spring of 1966, he was recording *Blonde on Blonde* and playing fiery, controversial electric concerts with his backing band, the Hawks (later renamed the Band); a few months later, he was nearly killed in a motorcycle accident and withdrew from recording and performing for nearly a year and a half.

For many, his music never seemed quite the same after that, and although much of it proved bold and lovely, for about twenty years now Bob Dylan hasn't produced much music that transfigures either pop style or youth culture. To some former fans, that lapse has seemed almost unforgivable. Consequently, Dylan has found himself in a dilemma shared by no other rock figure of his era: he has been sidestepped by the pop world he helped to transform, at a time when contemporaries like the Rolling Stones attract a more enthusiastic audience than ever before. This must hurt an artist as scrupulous as Dylan, who, for whatever his lapses, has remained pretty true to both his moral and musical ideals.

In the last couple of years, though, there have been signs that some kind of reclamation might be in the offing. For one thing, there's been his participation in the pop world's recent spate of social and political activism, including his involvement in the USA for Africa and Artists United against Apartheid projects and his appearance at the Live Aid and Farm Aid programs (the latter, an event inspired by an off-the-cuff remark Dylan had made at Live Aid). More important, there were intriguing indications in 1983's *Infidels* and 1985's *Empire Burlesque* that the singer seems interested in working his way back into the concerns of the real-life modern world—in fact, that he may even be interested in fashioning music that once more engages a pop-wise audience. And, as demonstrated by the strong response to his recent tour of Australia and Japan, as well as to his summer tour of America, there is still an audience willing to be engaged.

Of course, Dylan has his own views about all this talk of decline and renewal. A little later in the evening, at the Topanga studio, while various musicians are working on overdubs, he sits in a quiet office, fiddling with one of his ever-present cigarettes and taking occasional sips from a plastic cup filled with white wine. We are discussing a column that appeared in the April issue of *Artforum*, by critic Greil Marcus. Marcus has covered Dylan frequently over the years (he penned the liner notes for the 1975 release of *The Basement Tapes*), but he has been less than compelled by the artist's recent output. Commenting on Dylan's career, and about the recent five-LP retrospective of Dylan's music, *Biograph*, Marcus wrote: "Dylan actually did something between 1963 and 1968, and . . . what he did then created a standard against which everything he has putatively done since can be measured. . . . The fact that the 1964 'It Ain't Me Babe' can be placed on an album next to the 1974 'You Angel You' is a denial of everyone's best hopes."

Dylan seems intrigued by Marcus's comments, but also amused. "Well, he's right and he's wrong," he says. "I did that accidentally. That was all accidental, as every age is. You're doing something, you don't know what it is, you're just doing it. And later on you'll look at it and . . ." His words trail off, then he begins again. "To me, I don't have a 'career.' . . . A career is something you can look back on, and I'm not ready to look back. Time doesn't really exist for me in those kinds of terms. I don't really remember in any monumental way 'what I have done.' This isn't my career; this is my life, and it's still vital to me."

He removes his sunglasses and rubs at his eyes. "I feel like I really don't want to prove any points," he continues. "I just want to do whatever it is I do. These lyrical things that come off in a unique or a desolate sort of way, I don't know, I don't feel I have to put that out anymore to please anybody. Besides, anything you want to do for posterity's sake, you can just sing into a tape recorder and give it to your mother, you know?"

Dylan laughs at his last remark. "See," he says, "somebody once told me—and I don't remember who it was or even where it was—but they said, 'Never give a hundred percent.' My thing has always been just getting by on whatever I've been getting by on. That applies to that time, too, that time in the Sixties. It never really occured to me that I had to do it for any kind of motive except that I just felt like I wanted to do it. As things worked, I mean, I could never have predicted it."

I tell him it's hard to believe he wasn't giving a hundred percent on *Highway 61 Revisited* or *Blonde on Blonde*.

He flashes a shy grin and shrugs, "Well, maybe I was. But there's something at the back of your mind that says, 'I'm not giving you a hundred percent. I'm not giving anybody a hundred percent. I'm gonna give you this much, and this much is gonna have to do. I'm good at what I do. I can afford to give you this much and still be as good as, if not better than, the guy over across the street.' I'm not gonna give it all—I'm not Judy Garland, who's gonna die onstage in front of a thousand clowns. If we've learned anything, we should have learned that."

A moment later an engineer is standing in the doorway, telling Dylan the overdubs are done. "This is all gonna pass," Dylan says before getting up to go back into the studio. "All these people who say whatever it is I'm supposed to be doing—that's all gonna pass, because, obviously, I'm not gonna be around forever. That day's gonna come when there aren't gonna be any more records and then people won't be able to say, 'Well this one's not as good as the last one.' They're gonna have to look at it all. And I don't know what the picture will be, what people's judgment will be at that time. I can't help you in that area."

"Everyone's always saying to me, 'What's Bob Dylan like?'" says Tom Petty a few nights later, seated in the tiny lounge area of a Van Nuys recording studio. Petty and his band, the Heartbreakers, have gathered here to work out material for a forthcoming album and also to help supervise the sound mix for *Bob Dylan in Concert*, the HBO special documenting their recent tour of Australia with Dylan. "It's funny," Petty continues, "but people still attach a lot of mystery to Bob. . . . I think they figure that, since we've spent time around him, we can explain him, as if he's somebody who needs to be explained."

Petty shakes his head. "I mean, Dylan's just a guy like anybody else—except he's a guy who has something to say. And he has a personality that makes it his own. There's not many people that can walk into a room of 20,000, stare at them and get their attention. That's not an easy trick."

Petty may be a little too modest to admit it, but Dylan also has something else going for him these days. A good part of the excitement over Dylan's current U.S. tour owes to the singer's alliance with a band as rousing as the Heartbreakers—a band more given to propulsive rock and roll than any group Dylan has worked with in over a decade. Judging from the HBO special, the Heartbreakers can render the *Highway 61* sound—that unmistakable mix of fiery keyboards and stray-cat guitars—with a convincing flair. Yet rather than simply replicate the sound, the group reinvigorates it and applies it evenly to a broad range of Dylan's music, helping bring a new coherence to his sprawling body of styles. As a result, many of Dylan's more recent songs—such as "When the Night Comes Falling from the Sky" and "Lenny Bruce"—come across in concert with an uncommon force and conviction, perhaps even a bit more force than some of the older songs.

But Dylan isn't the only one whose music has benefited from this association. Ever since the end of the Australian tour, Petty and the Heartbreakers seem to be on an inspired streak, cranking out blues-tempered rock and pop songs in the same impromptu fashion that Dylan so often employs. It isn't so much that the group's new music resembles Dylan's (actually, it suggests nothing so much as the reckless blues of *Exile on Main Street*), but rather that it seems born of the same freewheeling intensity and instinctive ferocity that has marked Dylan's most ambitious efforts.

But there is something more to it—something that belongs only to Petty and the Heartbreakers. I have seen this band on numerous occasions, both in the studio and onstage, and though they've always seemed adept and exciting, they've never struck me as particularly inspired improvisers, in the way, say, that the Rolling Stones or the E Street Band can seem. Now, here they are, jamming with unqualified verve, playing not only head to head but also heart to heart and, in the process, creating what is probably their most inspiring music to date.

"We've never done anything like this before," says Petty, fishing a pack of cigarettes from his shirt pocket. "It's not like we're even thinking we're making a record. . . . Yet here we are with enough for a double album."

Petty plants a cigarette between his lips, lights it and settles back into the sofa. "Tonight was a good night," he continues. "In fact, this has been a good time for us in general. I think we feel pretty glad to be together."

Though nobody likes to admit it, following the 1982 release of *Long after Dark*, the Heartbreakers more or less dissolved. Petty withdrew into his home, where he was building a state-of-the-art studio and anticipating a solo project; drummer Stan Lynch joined T-Bone Burnett's band for a brief tour; keyboardist Benmont Tench played onstage and in the studio with Lone Justice; guitarist Mike Campbell began experimenting with some new aural textures on a twenty-four-track machine in his basement, where he would eventually compose "The Boys of Summer" for Don Henley; and bassist Howie Epstein did some session work and began assembling material for a possible record of his own.

"It was reaching a point," says Campbell, "where everybody was getting a bit stale with each other, inspirationwise. We just weren't committed as a band." Adds Stan Lynch, "It's like we all faced this ultimate question: If I'm not doing what I do now, what would I do? That's a horrible thing, but we faced it and realized we wouldn't roll over and die if we lost this gig."

Then, in 1984, inspired by some conversations with Robbie Robertson, Petty came up with an idea that couldn't be realized without the band's contribution. He wanted to make an album about the modern American South—the common homeland that most of the group's members had emerged from but had never quite forgotten. "I'd seen these people I'd grown up around struggling with that experience," Petty had said in an earlier conversation, "with all the things about that legacy they couldn't shake free of, and I think that was tearing at me." The result was *Southern Accents*—a work that examined the conflict between old ways and new ideals and that also aimed to broaden and update the band's musical scope. Though some band members now feel that the record was a bit overworked, they all credit it as a reconciliatory experience. "They've been real supportive of me through this record," Petty says. "I think in the last album we were in a lot of different camps. . . . Now they laugh about *Southern Accents* and its sitars. They had to let me get this out of my system."

Then along came Bob Dylan. He had already employed Tench on *Shot of Love*, and Tench, Campbell and Epstein on *Empire Burlesque*, and was now looking for an electric band to support him at Farm Aid. When Neil Young, one of the event's organizers, mentioned that Petty and the Heartbreakers had also committed themselves to the show, Dylan decided to ask the group to accompany him. "He called me," says Petty, "and I said, 'Yeah, come over,' and shit, we had a great time. We rehearsed about a week, playing maybe a million different songs. That was one of the best times I ever had. We were blazing. So we went off to Farm Aid and had a great night: the Heartbreakers had a good set, and Bob had a good set. But it was over too quick."

Well, not quite. Dylan had been considering offers for a possible Australian tour, but was reluctant to assemble a makeshift band. Plus, the Heartbreakers had just finished their own tour and were firming up their schedules for February. "The next thing I knew," says Petty, "we were doing the Australian tour, and we wanted to do it."

According to some reviews, the tour got off to a shaky start in New Zealand, where the opening-night audiences responded more fervently to Petty's set than Dylan's. But within a few shows, Dylan was storming into such songs as "Clean Cut Kid," "Positively 4th Street," "Rainy Day Women" and "Like a Rolling Stone," often facing off with Campbell and Petty in fierce three-way guitar exchanges and launching suddenly into songs that nobody had rehearsed, and that some band members hardly knew. "One night," Tench recalls, "Dylan turns around and goes, 'Just Like Tom Thumb's Blues.' We'd never played it. . . . At times, that tour sounded like some bizarre mix of the Stooges and Van Morrison."

"There's nothing tentative about Dylan onstage," adds Lynch. "I've seen gigs where the songs have ended in all the wrong places, where it's fallen aprt, and it's almost as if, in some perverse way, he gets energy from that chaos."

Dylan can also seem daunting in other ways. "He has more presence than anyone I've ever met," says Mike Campbell. "But when you're working together, you sort of forget about that. Then all of a sudden it will hit you. I mean, I can remember when I was in junior high school: I was in a diner eating a hamburger and 'Like a Rolling Stone' came on. I got so excited by the song and the lyric. I thought, 'There's somebody singing and writing for me.' I went out and got a guitar. I'd forgotten about that until one night in Australia, and I realized, 'This is the first song I ever learned on guitar, and here I am playing it with the person who wrote it.'"

Dylan was also the object of much intense feeling in Australia. "I pretty much saw it all," says Lynch. "I saw the girl who slept in the elevator claiming to be his sister from Minnesota; I saw the one who claimed to be his masseuse, who flew in from Perth and was riding up and down the elevator trying to figure out what floor he was on. I also saw the people that were genuinely moved, who felt they had to make some connection with him, that this was an important thing in their life. They wanted to be near him and tell him they're all right, because they probably feel that Bob was telling them that it was going to be all right when they weren't all right, as if Bob knew they weren't doing so well at the time.

"They forget one important thing: Bob doesn't know them; they just know him. But that's all right. That's not shortsightedness on their part. That's just the essence of what people do when you talk to them at a vulnerable time in their lives. It doesn't matter that he was talking to them by way of a record; he was still talking to them."

Two weeks later, Bob Dylan sits on a dogeared sofa in the Van Nuys studio where Petty is working, sipping at a plastic cup full of whiskey and water. He blows a curt puff of smoke and broods over it. His weary air reminds me of something he'd said earlier: "Man, sometimes it seems I've spent half my life in a recording studio. . . . It's like living in a coal mine."

Dylan and Petty have been holed up in this room the better part of the night, working on a track called "Got My Mind Made Up," which they have cowritten for Dylan's album. By all appearances, it's been a productive session: the tune is a walloping, Bo Diddley–like rave-up with Delta blues–style slide guitar, and Dylan has been hurling himself into the vocal with a genuinely staggering force. Yet there's also a note of tension about the evening. The pressure of completing the album has reportedly been wearing on Dylan, and his mood is said to have been rather dour and unpredictable these last several days. In fact, somewhere along the line he has decided to put aside most of the rock and roll tracks he had been working on in Topanga, and is apparently now assembling the album from various sessions that have accrued over the last year. "It's all sorts of stuff," he says. "It doesn't really have a theme or a purpose."

While waiting for his backup singers to arrive, Dylan tries to warm up to the task of the evening's interview. But in contrast to his manner in our earlier conversation, he seems somewhat distracted, almost edgy, and many questions don't seem to engender much response. After a bit, I ask him if he can tell me something about the lyrical tenor of the songs. "Got My Mind Made Up," for example, includes a reference to Libya. Will this be a record that has something to say about our national mood?

He considers the subject. "The kinds of stuff I write now come out over all the years I've lived," he says, "so I can't say anything is really that current. There may be one line that's current. . . . But you have to go on. You can't keep doing the same old thing all the time."

I try a couple more questions about political matters—about whether he feels any kinship with the new activism in pop music—but he looks exhausted at the possibility of seriously discussing the topic. "I'm opposed to whatever oppresses people's intelligence," he says. "We all have to be against that sort of thing, or else we have nowhere to go. But that's not a fight for one man, that's everybody's fight."

Over the course of our interviews, I've learned you can't budge him on a subject if he's not in the mood, so I move on. We chat for a while, but nothing much seems to engage him until I ask if he's pleased by the way the American public is responding to the upcoming tour. Demand has been so intense that the itinerary has been increased from twenty-six to forty shows, with more dates likely. In the end, it's estimated, he'll play to a million people.

"People forget it," he says, "but since 1974, I've never stopped working. I've been out on tours where there hasn't been any publicity. So for me, I'm not getting caught up in all this excitement of a big tour. I've played big tours and I've played small tours. I mean, what's such a big deal about this one?"

Well, it is his first cross-country tour of America in eight years.

"Yeah, but to me, an audience is an audience, no matter where they are. I'm not particularly into this American thing, this Bruce Springsteen–John Cougar–'America first' thing. I feel just as strongly about the American principles as those guys do, but I personally feel that what's important is more eternal things. This American pride thing, that doesn't mean nothing to me. I'm more locked into what's real forever."

Quickly, Dylan seems animated. He douses one cigarette, lights another and begins speaking at a faster clip. "Listen," he says, "I'm not saying anything bad about these guys, because I think Bruce has done a tremendous amount for real gutbucket rock and roll—and folk music, in his own way. And John Cougar's great, though the best thing on his record, I thought, was his grandmother singing. That knocked me out. But that ain't what music's about. Subjects like 'How come we don't have our jobs?' Then you're getting political. And if you want to get political, you ought to go as far out as you can."

But certainly he understands that Springsteen and Mellencamp aren't exactly trying to fan the flames of American pride. Instead, they're trying to say that if the nation loses sight of certain principles, it also forfeits its claim to greatness.

"Yeah? What are those principles? Are they Biblical principles? The only principles you can find are the principles in the Bible. I mean, Proverbs has got them all."

They are such principles, I say, as justice and equality.

"Yeah, but . . ." Dylan pauses. As we've been talking, others—including Petty, Mike Campbell, the sound engineers and the backup singers—have entered the room. Dylan stands up and starts pacing back and forth, smiling. It's hard to tell whether he is truly irked or merely spouting provocatively for the fun of it. After a moment, he continues. "To me, America means the Indians. They were here and this is their country, and all the white men are just trespassing. We've devastated the natural resources of this country, for no particular reason except to make money and buy houses and send our kids to college and shit like that. To me, America is the Indians, period. I just don't go for nothing more. Unions, movies, Greta Garbo, Wall Street, Tin Pan Alley or Dodgers baseball games." He laughs. "It doesn't mean shit. What we did to the Indians is disgraceful. I think America, to get right, has got to start there first."

I reply that a more realistic way of getting right might be to follow the warning of one of his own songs, "Clean Cut Kid," and not send our young people off to fight another wasteful war.

"Who sends the young people out to war?" says Dylan. "Their parents do."

But it isn't the parents who suited them up and put them on the planes and sent them off to die in Vietnam.

"Look, the parents could have said, 'Hey, we'll talk about it.' But parents aren't into that. They don't know how to deal with what they should do or shouldn't do. So they leave it to the government."

Suddenly, loudly, music blares up in the room. Perhaps somebody—maybe Petty—figures the conversation is getting a little too tense. Dylan smiles and shrugs, then pats me on the shoulder. "We can talk a little more later," he says.

For the next couple of hours, Dylan and Petty attend to detail work on the track—getting the right accent on a ride cymbal and overdubbing the gospel-derived harmonies of the four female singers who have just arrived. As always, it is fascinating to observe how acutely musical Dylan is. In one particularly inspired offhand moment, he leads the four singers—Queen Esther Morrow, Elisecia Wright, Madelyn Quebec and Carol Dennis—through a lovely a capella version of "White Christmas," then moves into a haunting reading of an old gospel standard, "Evening Sun." Petty and the rest of us just stare, stunned. "Man," says Petty frantically, "we've got to get this on tape."

Afterward, Dylan leads me out into a lounge area to talk some more. He leans on top of a pinball machine, a cigarette nipped between his teeth. He seems calmer, happy with the night's work. He also seems willing to finish the conversation we were having earlier, so we pick up where we left off. What would he do, I ask, if his own sons were drafted?

Dylan looks almost sad as he considers the question. After several moments, he says: "They could do what their conscience tells them to do, and I would support them. But it also depends on what the government wants your children to do. I mean, if the government wants your children to go down and raid Central American countries, there would be no moral value in that. I also don't think we should have bombed those people in Libya." Then he flashes one of those utterly guileless, disarming smiles of his as our talk winds down. "But what I want to know," he says, "is what's all this got to do with folk music and rock and roll?"

Quite a bit, since he, more than any other artist, raised the possibility that folk music and rock and roll could have political impact. "Right," says Dylan, "and I'm proud of that."

And the reason questions like these keep coming up is because many of us aren't so sure where he stands these days—in fact, some critics have charged that, with songs like "Slow Train" and "Union Sundown," he's even moved a bit to the right.

Dylan muses over the remark in silence for a moment. "Well, for me," he begins, "there is no right and there is no left. There's truth and there's untruth, y'know? There's honesty and there's hypocrisy. Look in the Bible: you don't see nothing about right or left. Other people might have other ideas about things, but I don't, because I'm not that smart. I hate to keep beating people over the head with the Bible, but that's the only instrument I know, the only thing that stays true."

Does it disturb him that there seem to be so many preachers these days who claim that to be a good Christian one must also be a political conservative?

"Conservative? Well, don't forget, Jesus said that it's harder for a rich man to enter the kingdom of heaven than it is for a camel to enter the eye of a needle. I mean, is that conservative? I don't know, I've heard a lot of preachers say how God wants everybody to be wealthy and healthy. Well, it doesn't say that in the Bible. You can twist anybody's words, but that's only for fools and people who follow fools. If you're entangled in the snares of this world, which everybody is . . ."

Petty comes into the room and asks Dylan to come hear the final overdubs. Dylan likes what he hears, then decides to take one more pass at the lead vocal. This time, apparently, he nails it. "Don't ever try to change me / I been in this thing too long / There's nothing you can say or do / To make me think I'm wrong," he snarls at the song's outset, and while it is hardly the most inviting line one has ever heard him sing, tonight he seems to render it with a fitting passion.

It is midnight in Hollywood, and Bob Dylan, Tom Petty and the Heartbreakers are clustered in a cavernous room at the old Zoetrope Studios, working out a harmonica part to "License to Kill," when Dylan suddenly begins playing a different, oddly haunting piece of music. Gradually, the random tones he is blowing begin to take a familiar shape, and it becomes evident that he's playing a plaintive, bluesy variation of "I Dreamed I Saw St. Augustine." Benmont Tench is the first to recognize the melody, and quickly embellishes it with a graceful piano part; Petty catches the drift and underscores Dylan's harmonica with some strong, sharp chord strokes. Soon, the entire band, which tonight includes guitarist Al Kooper, is seizing Dylan's urge and transforming the song into a full and passionate performance. Dylan never sings the lyrics himself but instead signals a backup singer to take the lead, and immediately "I Dreamed I Saw St. Augustine" becomes a full-fledged, driving spiritual.

Five minutes later, the moment has passed. According to Petty and Tench, Dylan's rehearsals are often like this: inventive versions of wondrous songs come and go and are never heard again, except in those rare times when they may be conjured onstage. In a way, an instance like this leaves one wishing that every show in the current True Confessions Tour were simply another rehearsal: Dylan's impulses are so sure-handed and imaginative, they're practically matchless.

Trying to get Dylan to talk about where such moments come from—or trying to persuade him to take them to the stage—is, as one might expect, not that easy. "I'm not sure if people really want to hear that sort of thing from me," he says, smiling ingenuously. Then he perches himself on an equipment case and puts his hands into his pockets, looking momentarily uncomfortable. Quickly, his face brightens. "Hey," he says, pulling a tape from his pockets, "wanna hear the best album of the year?" He holds a cassette of *AKA Grafitti Man*, an album by poet John Trudell and guitarist Jesse Ed Davis. "Only people like Lou Reed and John Doe can dream about doing work like this. Most don't have enough talent."

Dylan has his sound engineer cue the tape to a song about Elvis Presley. It is a long, stirring track about the threat that so many originally perceived in Presley's manner and the promise so many others discovered in his music. "We heard Elvis's song for the first time / Then we made up our own mind," recites Trudell at one point, followed by a lovely, blue guitar solo from Davis that quotes "Love Me Tender." Dylan grins at the line, then shakes his head with delight. "Man," he says, "that's about all anybody ever needs to say about Elvis Presley."

I wonder if Dylan realizes that the line could also have been written about him—that millions of us heard his songs, and that those songs not only inspired our own but, in some deep-felt place, almost seemed to be our own. But before there is even time to raise the question, Dylan has put on his coat and is on his way across the room.

"I'm thinking about calling this album *Knocked Out Loaded*," Bob Dylan says. He repeats the phrase once, then chuckles over it. "Is that any good, you think, *Knocked Out Loaded*?"

Dylan and a recording engineer are seated at a mixing board at the Topanga recording studio, pouring over a list of song titles and talking about possible sequences. Dylan seems downright affable, more relaxed than earlier in the week. Apparently, the album has fallen into place with sudden ease. In the last few days, he has narrowed the record's selection down to a possible nine or ten songs, and tonight he is polishing two of those tracks and attempting a final mix on a couple of others.

So far, it all sounds pretty good—not exactly the back-snapping rock and roll I'd heard a few weeks earlier but, in a way, something no less bold. Then Dylan plays one more track, "Brownsville Girl," a piece he wrote last year with playwright Sam Shepard. A long, storylike song, it begins with a half-drawled, half-sung remembrance about a fateful scene from a western the singer had once seen, then opens up from there into two or three intersecting, dreamlike tales about pursued love and forsaken love, about fading heroes and forfeited ideals—about hope and death. It's hard to tell where Dylan ends and Shepard begins in the lyrics, but it is quite easy to hear whom the song really belongs to. In fact, I've only known of one man who could put across a performance as exhilirating as this one, and he is sitting there right in front of me, concentrating hard on the tale, as if he too were hearing its wondrous involutions for the first time. If this is the way Bob Dylan is going to age as a songwriter, I decide, I'm happy to age with him.

Twelve minutes later, the song closes with a glorious, explosive chorus. I don't know exactly what to say, so Dylan picks up the slack. He lights a cigarette, moves over to the sofa, takes off his glasses and smiles a shy smile. "You know," he says, "sometimes I think about people like T-Bone Walker, John Lee Hooker, Muddy Waters—these people who played into their sixties. If I'm here at eighty, I'll be doing the same thing. This is all I want to do—it's all I can do. I mean, you don't have to be a nineteen- or twenty-year-old to play this stuff. That's the vanity of that youth-culture ideal. To me that's never been the thing. I've never really aimed myself at any so-called youth culture. I directed it at people who I imagined, maybe falsely so, had the same experiences that I've had, who have kind of been through what I'd been through. But I guess a lot of people haven't."

He falls silent for a moment, taking a drag off his cigarette. "See," he says, "I've always been just about being an individual, with an individual point of view. If I've been about anything, it's probably that, and to let some people know that it's possible to do the impossible."

Dylan leans forward and snuffs out his cigarette. "And that's really all. If I've ever had anything to tell anybody, it's that: You can do the impossible. Anything is possible. And that's it. No more."

LYNN VAN MATRE

STILL COMPELLING: A LONG LOOK BACK AT TWO DECADES OF DYLAN (1985)

Chicago Tribune, November 10, 1985

This review of Dylan's Biograph *set gives a good career overview of his work to that point.—CB*

In the two decades since the surgingly surreal "Like a Rolling Stone" and the corrosively bitter "Positively 4th Street" catapulted Bob Dylan into pop Top 10 territory, the Minnesota-born singer-songwriter has, among other things, been hailed as "the voice of a generation," fallen from favor, made various comebacks, found religion and—in one way or another—revolutionized the world of pop music like few other performers.

Along the way, he has been the subject of countless books and articles, from glossy coffeetable tomes to earnest academic attempts to find the "true meaning" behind his frequently evocative imagery. Now comes *Biograph*, a handsomely boxed, five-album Dylan retrospective from Columbia Records which tells Dylan's story in the most important way: through his music.

Of the 53 songs included on the 5 albums, 35 have been previously released, either on one of Dylan's nearly 30 albums or as a single. Nine are alternate takes or live concert versions of songs already released on studio albums. The final nine songs never appeared on any of Dylan's albums (except, perhaps, on bootleg versions).

As is the case with any such project, the choice of songs included could be argued; had he put together this retrospective himself, Dylan might have done things differently. Nevertheless, the release of *Biograph* ranks as a happy event, a testimony to the talent of an artist whose idiosyncratic style and evocative visions have made him one of rock's most fascinating figures.

Plenty of people have outsold Dylan. The 35 million albums the singer has sold worldwide, while a respectable enough total, is hardly extraordinary (Barry Manilow, for instance, has sold 50 million); only two of his albums (1976's *Desire* and 1979's *Slow Train Coming*) have sold more than a million copies, and at least eight of his albums sold less than half that. But few performers can match the impact that Dylan had on contemporary music in the 1960s. Though his self-created "mystique" became tiresome—just as the smugly self-righteous, overly preachy stance that accompanied his move into Christian music in the late 1970s would become tiresome—and his secular "comebacks" often have been largely routine (though the most recent one, *Empire Burlesque*, frequently showed sparks of the "old" Dylan), his past accomplishments have ensured that Dylan's reputation as one of pop's most compelling artists will remain intact.

While the alternative versions of various songs are often entertaining, and many of the previously released songs are among Dylan's finest, the previously unheard songs, obviously, are of the greatest interest to Dylan fans. Nearly all are worth hearing; many are gems.

The most interesting ones—with the exception of "Caribbean Wind," an enigmatic outtake from the 1981 *Shot of Love* album—date from the early to middle 1960s, the years in which Dylan (born Robert Allen Zimmerman of Jewish middle-class parents) went from an acoustic folk singer with a hard-travelin' drifter persona borrowed from Woody Guthrie and Ramblin' Jack Elliott to a trend-setting performer whose aggressive merger of topical folk and rock infuriated folk purists but electrified the much wider pop audience.

Just as he had borrowed bits and pieces from older folk legends to piece together his own image, the young Dylan's early melodies were often borrowed from traditional folk tunes. One of the previously unheard *Biograph* songs from this era, the poignant "Lay Down Your Weary Tune," is particularly typical of this period; in the extensive liner notes, Dylan says that the song's melody was taken from an old Scottish ballad he first heard on an old 78 r.p.m. record.

Another previously unheard song from the early 1960s, the raucous, bluesy "Baby I'm in the Mood for You," comes from the recording sessions for Dylan's second album, *The Freewheelin' Bob Dylan*, by which time he was doing mostly original material, though his early folk and blues influences were still strongly apparent.

A third unreleased song from this period, "Percy's Song," is a longtime early favorite that Dylan used to perform in concert but which never made it onto an album until now. Combining a melody line borrowed from folk singer Paul Clayton with lyrics about a young man who is sentenced to 99 years for manslaughter, the song is one of many that Dylan (sometimes naively and self-righteously) would go on to write about incidents that he viewed as miscarriages of justice.

Even more heartfelt is the moving "I'll Keep It with Mine," which has turned up on several bootleg albums over the years and features Dylan accompanying himself on piano. Two more "new" songs from the '60s are 1965's "Jet Pilot," which has nothing to do with airplanes (it's a humorous, throwaway bit about a transvestite that figured in an early version of the song "Tombstone Blues" during the recording sessions for *Highway 61 Revisited*) and "I Wanna Be Your Lover," a not particularly memorable folk-rock number recorded during an early recording session with the Hawks, later known as the Band.

In addition to the previously unissued songs, *Biograph* contains alternative/live versions of a number of songs from the '60s, including "Visions of Johanna," "I Don't Believe You," "It's All Over Now, Baby Blue" and "Quinn the Eskimo," plus such previously released Dylan classics as "Blowin' in the Wind," "Subterranean Homesick Blues," "The Times They Are A-Changin'," "The Lonesome Death of Hattie Carroll" and "Like a Rolling Stone," the song that catapulted Dylan into the Top 10 in 1965.

Earlier that year, after leaving the traditional folk format behind in favor of electric backing and forsaking more or less straightforward folk/political protest for a more rambling poetic approach, Dylan had cracked pop's Top 40 with the surreally humorous and biting "Subterranean Homesick Blues," which contained the classic advice, "Don't follow leaders, watch the parking meters." By the middle 1960s, however, fans were according the singer and his music a significance that frequently bordered on the absurd, laboriously dissecting and analyzing his enigmatic lyrics in search of some sort of ultimate meaning that very likely never was there to begin with.

(Those who suspected this all along—though the lack of literal meaning in Dylan's lyrics is irrelevant given that, like the best art, his finest songs do make sense on some elusive level—might be interested in what the singer has to say about "Caribbean Wind." The song dates from Dylan's early 1980s *Shot of Love* period but is being released for the first time on *Biograph*; it tells of a woman who "was the rose of Sharon, from paradise lost, from the city of seven hills near the place of the cross," who "told about Jesus, told about the rain . . . told me about the jungle where her brothers were slain by the man who invented iron and disappeared so mysteriously." Notes Dylan in the booklet that accompanies the albums, "That one I couldn't quite grasp what it was about after I finished it.")

By 1966, Dylan had sold 10 million records; his influence and impact were at their peak. But a motorcycle accident that summer took him off of the scene for more than a year. When he was heard from again, it was in 1968 with *John Wesley Harding*, a country-folk flavored effort that was recorded in Nashville and marked the beginning of a new, far more mellow approach for Dylan that would characterize much of his output over the next few years.

His early 1970s albums were largely forgettable, and it was not until 1974's *Blood on the Tracks* and 1975's *Desire* that Dylan regained some of his old magic. *Biograph* includes four unreleased tracks from this period—an alternate version of "Up to Me," live versions of "Romance in Durango" and "Isis" and the previously unissued "Abandoned Love"—in addition to a number of other songs from studio and live albums released from 1970 through 1975, including "If Not for You," "Most Likely You Go Your Way," "You Angel You," "Million Dollar Bash," "On a Night Like This" and an alternate version of "Forever Young" from 1973.

While Biblical imagery had figured off and on in Dylan's writing for years, in the late 1970s his new (or renewed) interest in Christianity triggered a switch to an unabashedly religious approach that surfaced in 1979's *Slow Train Coming*, 1980's *Saved* and 1981's *Shot of Love*. Though much of Dylan's output during this time was so self-righteous as to be virtually devoid of Christly compassion, a few of the songs were memorable—among them "Every Grain of Sand," which represents this era on *Biograph* along with "Groom's Still Waiting at the Altar" (released originally as the B-side of a single), "Caribbean Wind," "Solid Rock" and a previously unreleased live version of "Heart of Mine." The most recent material included is from 1981; there are no cuts from Dylan's last two studio albums, *Infidels* and *Empire Burlesque*.

A few months ago, Dylan stood on stage at Live Aid in Philadelphia and closed the show with several songs of social commentary he wrote in the early 1960s. The songs, for the most part, were largely unfamiliar to an audience that included pop fans who weren't even born when "Blowin' in the Wind" established Dylan as a musical force—and who might have been wondering why a hotter, flashier performer wasn't bringing the day's events to a grand finale. But the choice was particularly appropriate, given Dylan's musical history of commitment to the sort of social causes that have once again become causes celebres in pop music.

In the years between then and now, Dylan has made a lot of music—some of it great, some of it not so great, but most of it interesting. *Biograph* collects some of the best of it in one boxed set.

ROBERT HILBURN

BOB DYLAN: STILL A-CHANGIN' (1985)

Los Angeles Times, November 17, 1985

In this interview at the time of the release of both Empire Burlesque *and* Biograph, *Dylan looks both backward and forward. As always when he speaks with Hilburn, he tends to be more straightforward and more revealing than with other journalists.*—CB

Maybe it's because he didn't do interviews at all for years, or maybe it's just that he's the most important songwriter of the modern pop era, but I can't imagine passing up the chance to talk to Bob Dylan—even if strings are attached.

The interview invitation from Columbia Records suggested that Dylan only wanted to discuss his latest albums: *Empire Burlesque*, the studio collection from last summer, and *Biograph*, the ambitious retrospective set that just hit the stores.

Dylan himself, however, quickly cut the strings. He showed little interest in those subjects as he sat on a chair in the backyard of his Malibu home.

"The new releases . . . ?" Dylan asked, almost sheepishly.

"I hope you don't make this look like some carny trying to hawk his records. I don't know if you even want to hit on the records. When people think of me, they are not necessarily going to buy the latest record anyway. They may buy a record from years ago. Besides, I don't think interviews sell records."

So why did Dylan agree to a series of interviews, including his first formal network TV interview [for *20/20*]?

"I really haven't had that much connection or conversation (over the years) with the people at Columbia," he said, referring to his record label for most of two decades. "Usually, I turn in my records . . . and they release them. But they really liked this record [*Empire Burlesque*], so they asked me to do some more videos and a few interviews to draw attention to it.

"But that doesn't mean I want to sit around and talk about the record. I haven't even listened to [*Empire*] since it came out. I'd rather spend my time working on new songs or listen to other people's records. Have you heard that new Hank Williams album . . . the collection of old demo tapes? It's great."

Reviews for *Empire Burlesque* were mostly positive, but sales quickly leveled off. A recent live video of "Emotionally Yours" failed to revive it.

Biograph, however, is a long-awaited five-record set that includes 21 selections never before available on an album, plus 32 digitally remastered versions of previously released tracks. The project has been rumored for years, but the release was held up to avoid conflicting with other Dylan works.

About the project, Dylan said: "Columbia wanted to put out a [retrospective] album on me a few years ago. They had pulled out everything [from earlier albums] that could be classified as love songs and had it on one collection. I didn't care one way or another, but I had a new record coming out, so I asked them not to do it then.

"I guess it's OK for someone who has never heard of me and is looking for a crash course or something. But I've got a lot of stuff that is lying around all over the place in cassette recorders that I'd put out if I was putting the set together."

One thing about *Biograph* that does please Dylan is a 36-page booklet written by Cameron Crowe, who did numerous *Rolling Stone* magazine profiles and wrote the film *Fast Times at Ridgemont High*. The text is a brief, affectionate look at Dylan's life, with generous quotes from the songwriter.

The most interesting part of the liner notes is Dylan's reflections on the songs. Though he has tended to avoid discussing his work, he commented freely this time on both the development and themes of several of the songs in the LP.

About his celebrated "The Times They Are A-Changin'," for instance, he remarked in the liner notes: "This was definitely a song with a purpose. I knew exactly what I wanted to write and for whom. . . . I wanted to write a big song, some kind of theme song, ya know, with short concise verses that piled up on each other in a hypnotic way. . . ."

On "Forever Young," perhaps the most recorded of all Dylan's post-'60s songs: "I wrote [it] . . . thinking about one of my boys and not wanting to be too sentimental. The lines came to me, they were done in a minute . . . the song wrote itself."

Dylan, 44, isn't being open just to the press these days. For years, he has tended to be isolated even when doing a guest spot on a benefit concert—avoiding photographers and, often, other artists backstage by arriving just before showtime and leaving quickly after the last number.

At September's Farm Aid concert at the University of Illinois, however, he was almost leisurely—hanging out with Tom Petty, whose band backed him on the show, and chatting with other performers, including Randy Newman, Lou Reed and Emmylou Harris. Normally camera-shy, Dylan didn't even turn away when a TV crew and a few photographers pointed their lenses at him as he sat on the steps outside his dressing room trailer.

One reason for the naturalness, a backstage observer joked at Farm Aid, was that Dylan wanted to prove—after his disastrously spacey performance with the Stones' Keith Richards and Ron Wood at Live Aid—that he still had his faculties.

"Yeah," Dylan grumped about last summer's Live Aid concert in Philadelphia. "They screwed around with us. We didn't even have any [sound] monitors out there. When they threw in the grand finale at the last moment, they took all the settings off and set the stage up for the 30 people who were standing behind the curtain. We couldn't even hear our own voices [out front] and when you can't hear, you can't play . . . you don't have any timing. It's like proceeding on radar."

Dylan's Malibu house, on a bluff overlooking the ocean, is quite secluded, and a guard shack at the only entrance to the property keeps the curious away. The atmosphere is rural: A dirt driveway runs through the property, and lots of small animals, including chickens and a couple of large dogs, roam around.

On this cool afternoon, Dylan was wearing the same outfit that he's always seemed to be wearing in recent years: jeans that looked as if they were ready for the hamper, a wrinkled T-shirt and motorcycle boots. Except for Europe last year, he hasn't toured much in the '80s. Still, he is on the road so much—Minnesota, New York, London or some more isolated, exotic places—that he doesn't really call any place home.

"I'm just not the kind of person who seems to be able to settle down," he said as two dogs edged against his chair. "If I'm in L.A. for, say, two months, I'll be in the studio for maybe a month out of that time, putting down ideas for songs.

"On the other days, I'm usually recuperating from being in the studio. I usually stay in a long time . . . all night, part of the day. Then, I'll go off to New York or London and do the same thing. I'm going to London soon to work on some stuff with Dave Stewart."

Stewart, the co-leader of Eurythmics, joined Dylan on guitar on the "Emotionally Yours" video.

Dylan expects to concentrate on performance videos because he has not been pleased with the concept clips based upon his songs—either the arty "Jokerman" video or more conventional narrative of "Tight Connection."

He'd probably just as soon not do a video at all, but realizes their importance in the marketplace.

"It used to be that people would buy a record if they liked what they heard on the radio, but video has changed a lot of that," he said. "If someone comes along now with a new song, people talk about, 'Well, what does it look like?' It is like, 'I saw this new song.'"

He also suggested wryly that the controversial new system of putting stickers on records to warn parents about explicit material may also end up as a factor that teen-agers will consider in buying records.

"They [the stickers] will just mean more people are going to buy the records," he said. "The thing that would bother me is if they label [a record] subversive or un-American. Those things do matter. As a parent, I was more concerned with what [kids] saw on television than what they heard on a record. There's almost nothing you can see on TV that means a thing. It's for morons. It's just putting your brain to sleep. I may have been part of the last generation to grow up without any television. It was only on three hours a day where I lived when I was growing up."

Dylan, whose influence on Bruce Springsteen has been widely cited by critics, declined to discuss Springsteen at length, except to say he related to much of the *Nebraska* album, and seemed amused by Springsteen's image.

"It's funny how people refer to Bruce as the Boss," Dylan noted. "Ten years ago, the boss was a dreaded figure—the guy you punch your time clock for or that you inhale oil into your lungs for . . . someone you can never get out from under his thumb. So, all of a sudden Bruce is the Boss and it's a lovable figure. It's strange."

One continuing question involving Dylan is his much-publicized "born-again" Christian phase. He has said he doesn't like the term born again, and his music has moved away from the aggressive dogma of the *Slow Train Coming* album. But Dylan still refuses to define his exact religious stance.

Asked about the issue, his only reply was: "I feel like pretty soon I am going to write about that. I feel like I've got something to say . . . but more than you can say in a few paragraphs in a newspaper."

But he did smile at the mention of the hostile reactions generated during his "born-again" Christian tours of 1979 and 1980. "If you make peo-

Performing with George Harrison following his induction into the Rock and Roll Hall of Fame, 1988. *Photo courtesy of Ezio Peterson/ UPI/Corbis-Bettmann.*

ple jump on any level, I think it is worthwhile because people are so asleep."

Beyond music, Dylan's special interest these days is art. He maintains an artist's studio behind the main house and showed off his character sketches with the nervous excitement of a proud parent. He hopes to put them in a book and write something to go with each drawing. Dylan's also thinking about a book of short stories. "That may sound presumptuous," he said, "but there is a lot of things I'd like to say that I can't say in songs."

Regarding his continued energy, he said: "It's kinda funny. . . . When I see my name anywhere, it's [often] 'the '60s this or the '60s that.' I can't figure out sometimes if people think I'm dead or alive.

"But I'm not through. . . ."

This man, who has been hounded, dissected, idolized and ridiculed over the years, stepped outside the studio. The sun had set and the dogs raced over to him. He paused—as if searching for a summary statement.

"I've had some personal ups and downs, but usually things have been pretty good for me," he finally said. "I don't feel old, but I remember in my 20s [when] I'd think about people in their 30s as old. The thing I really notice now is time.

"Things used to go a lot slower. . . . The days [now] go by so very fast. But I've never felt numb [about life]. There is something about the chords, the sound of them that makes you feel alive. As long as you can play music, I believe, you'll feel alive."

Part Six

GOOD AS I BEEN TO YOU
1990–TODAY

ROBERT HILBURN

FOREVER DYLAN: ON THE NEVER-ENDING TOUR WITH ROCK'S GREATEST POET (1992)

Los Angeles Times, February 9, 1992

Long-time Dylan friend and music critic Hilburn spends some time on the road with Dylan and his cohorts in the midst of their Never-Ending Tour.—CB

Bob Dylan stares idly at the paperback book that someone has brought aboard his custom tour bus, which is speeding through the snowy Wisconsin countryside in the midnight hour. He has just finished a concert in Madison and is now on his way to South Bend, Indiana, where he'll play again in 20 hours.

The shiny, 278-page book, titled *Tangled up in Tapes Revisited*, is an exhaustive chronicle of the last half of Dylan's 32-year career and a testimony to the public's continuing obsession with the most influential songwriter of the rock era. The book lists every song Dylan has sung—and in what order—at most of his concerts from 1974 to 1989.

If the book's contents reveal every detail of his recent performing career, the color portrait on the cover—an expressionless Robert Allen Zimmerman, circa the late '80s, eyes concealed by dark glasses—is a teasing reminder of everything else Dylan has kept hidden these many years. Like the man himself, the drawing gives away almost nothing.

On the bus this night, the real Dylan, who has placed his own dark glasses on the table in front of him, flips quickly through the book. He's sitting in the dining nook and shows more interest in when the coffee will be ready than in the book.

Other performers might be curious enough to look back on, say, an earlier show they played in Wisconsin. (For example, from page 164: On November 1, 1978, at the Dane County Memorial Coliseum, Dylan sang 27 songs, opening with "She's Love Crazy" and "Mr. Tambourine Man," closing with "Forever Young" and "Changing of the Guards.") Or maybe a more recent one along the same highway, 11 years later. (Page 209: July 3, 1989, at the Marcus Amphitheater in Milwaukee; 17 songs, starting with "Early Morning Rain" and ending with "Maggie's Farm.")

Dylan finally just hands the book back to the man who brought it aboard the bus.

Told he is welcome to keep it as a souvenir, Dylan says, "Naw, I've already been all those places and done all those things."

Then he pauses slightly and adds, with a trace of a smile, "Now if you ever find a book out there that's going to tell me where I'm going, I might be interested."

Bob Dylan has always been a pop outsider, and there are few signs, as he enters his sixth decade, that he is surrendering his independence. When he first appeared in the folk clubs of New York's Greenwich Village in the early 1960s, there was an element of choirboy innocence—and mischief—in the smoothness of his cheeks and the gentleness of his smile. He not only taught rock and roll to think during that decade but he also showed a stubborn refusal to play by anyone else's rules.

Today, Dylan can still disarm you with a sudden smile, but there is wariness in the eyes. It's the instinctive suspicion of a survivor who knows, after years of public scrutiny, the dangers of letting down his guard.

On May 24, 1991, Dylan turned 50, and the media thought it would be the ideal time to try to put this cultural hero—and puzzle—into perspective. But he refused more than 300 requests for interviews, agreeing only to a brief telephone Q&A that ended up in *Spy* magazine, another in a journal published by the National Academy of Songwriters and a radio interview syndicated by Westwood One.

Instead, he hit the road, in year four of what Dylan-watchers now call the "Never-Ending Tour"—an ongoing road show that to date has racked up 450 performances and been seen by about 3 million fans in the United States, Europe and South America. By design, the tour has avoided the usual media glare. Dylan has concentrated on smaller venues and turned his back on the sort of superstar hoopla that would put him in a national spotlight. Madison was one of the final stops on a trek last year that took him from Burlington, Vermont, to Zurich, Switzerland.

A notable exception to his low-profile stance during his fiftieth-birthday year was the infamous Grammy Awards appearance in New York City last February. During the '60s, a conservative pop Establishment declined to honor the prolific Dylan with a Grammy. The ice broke a bit in 1979, when Dylan won the Best Male Rock Vocal award for his single "Gotta Serve Somebody." At the 1991 awards ceremony, a new generation of directors of the National Academy of Recording Arts & Sciences tried to make up for the years of slight with a Lifetime Achievement award.

Instead of a mellow Dylan, caught up in the sentimentality of the occasion, taking the stage, he remained the outsider.

Exhausted after a flight from Europe and suffering from the flu, he looked disheveled and distracted. And on a night when most of the country was caught up in the fervor and patriotism of the month-old Persian Gulf War, he and his band launched into a blistering if all but unintelligible version of "Masters of War":

> Come you masters of war,
> You that build all the guns,
> You that build the death planes,
> You that build the big bombs.
> You that hide behind walls,
> You that hide behind desks,
> I just want you to know
> I can see through your masks.

It was classic Dylan—enigmatic and provocative. Fans and reporters asked themselves what happened. There were whispers about drugs or drinking. But Dylan remained outside of the controversy: no apologies made, no answers offered.

For much of his career, Dylan's reluctance to explain himself or his actions seemed to be a strategy to heighten interest in his legend. Now, on the bus to South Bend, with a reporter allowed along for the ride, he sounds genuinely uninterested in his own notoriety. He wants no part of the confessional talk that fuels most celebrity interviews. Most of all, he has no patience with dissections of his famous past.

"Nostalgia," he says sharply, "is death."

As he gazes across the tour bus table, Dylan even smiles wickedly as the reporter suggests the hackneyed headlines that editors might have tacked on the birthday retrospectives that never appeared:

"Mr. Tambourine Man Turns 50!"

"Bringing It All Back Home."

Or—and this suggestion draws a full-scale laugh—"Knockin' on Heaven's Door."

There's no hostility in his manner, but he fences instinctively, warding off certain questions. He listens to—and ignores—one after another until one catches his interest. He dismisses old-day inquiries as "ancient history" and counters a query about his personal life with, "Do people ask

Paul Simon questions like that?" Like a lot of artists, he feels that his work expresses all that people need to know about him.

"It wasn't me who called myself a legend," he says sternly and suddenly in response to a question about his revered place in rock. "It was thrown at me by editors in the media who wanted to play around with me or have something new to tell their readers. But it stuck.

"It was important for me to come to the bottom of this legend thing, which has no reality at all. What's important isn't the legend, but the art, the work. A person has to do whatever they are called on to do. If you try to act a legend, it's nothing but hype."

But isn't it flattering that critics and artists have pointed to him as rock's most important songwriter? He just shakes his head.

"Not really," he continues, more softly. "Genius? There's a real fine line between genius and insanity. Anybody will tell you that."

Chicago's Ambassador East, on the historic and tony Gold Coast, is one of the city's grand old hotels, the home of the Pump Room restaurant, where everyone from gangsters (Al Capone) to Presidents (Nixon and Reagan) have dined. The hotel also has its share of show-biz ties. Alfred Hitchcock shot scenes with Cary Grant here in the late '50s for *North by North-West*, and Led Zeppelin caused a stir in 1977 by throwing a couch out of an 11th-floor window.

On the Never-Ending Tour, Dylan does a lot of sleeping on one of the two tour buses as they eat up the miles between concert cities. But today, Dylan has unobtrusively checked into the Ambassador, which is a short drive from the Evanston campus of Northwestern University, where he is scheduled to perform at 9 P.M.

It was in Chicago in 1974 that Dylan, with the Band in tow, returned to live performing after an eight-year hiatus prompted by a reported motorcycle accident in 1966 and his subsequent desire to spend more time with his family. The atmosphere then, however, was dramatically different.

About 6 million mail orders were received for tickets to the tour's 40 shows. The city was abuzz with reporters from around the world, all seeking an exclusive interview, and with scores of fans hoping for private audiences with the man frequently referred to as the "spokesman for his generation." Dylan's hotel at that time was on alert—security had been warned about Dylan-seekers—fans with a "glazed look" in their eyes.

Today, the midafternoon atmosphere at the Ambassador East is relaxed—just the usual flow of guests, most of them in town on business.

Dylan is upstairs in his room, relaxing until the bus picks him up around 7 P.M. for the ride to Northwestern's McGaw Hall, a basketball gym-cum-auditorium. Tonight he'll play for about 3,500 fans, a crowd a little more than a fifth the size of the one that gathered at Chicago Stadium in 1974. But these small halls are his choice; he prefers the intimacy and audience rapport they provide.

By the time he has driven over freezing streets to the concert site, a heavily bundled crowd is filing into the hall. As they unwrap their mufflers and take off their hats, another contrast between then and now is made clear. Until the mid-'80s, Dylan played chiefly to fans from his own generation. Now he performs to mostly college-age audiences, young people who weren't even alive when "Blowin' in the Wind," recorded by Peter, Paul and Mary, hit no. 2 in 1963, fans who see him less as a superstar or personal savior than as a gifted artist, an American icon.

Kevin Martell is 20 years old and seeing Dylan for the first time. He and two friends sit quietly in the hall waiting for the show to begin, displaying none of the raucous exuberance usually found at rock shows. When he talks about why he wanted to see the show, he sounds a bit like he's signed up to hear an honored novelist or historian deliver a lecture.

"There are a few bands today, like U2, that talk about real issues," he says. "But I think the '60s artists were the ones who were really into it, and Dylan is one of the few you can still see. I think songs like 'Masters of War' are as important today as when he wrote it. He's like a legend."

A few rows away, Robert Blackmon, 19, a chemical engineering student, can reel off a long list of his favorite new bands—including Jane's Addiction, Nirvana and Primus—that he feels speak directly to the frustrations and aspirations of his generation. But, like Martell, he sees Dylan from a broader perspective: "He has a timeless, universal quality," Blackmon says.

The band walks out on stage first, a three-man group made up of guitarist John Jackson, bassist Tony Garnier and drummer Ian Wallace—veterans whose collective resumes range from Asleep at the Wheel, the lighthearted Western swing band, to King Crimson, the arty veteran British rock group. They've been on the road with him now for more than a year.

There is a charge of electricity as the houselights dim. Without a word of greeting, Dylan, in a black shirt and striped black pants, steps to the microphone. With a quick glance back at the band, he starts to play. The lighting is so dim that it's hard to make out his features, but his familiar raspy voice is unmistakable.

Dylan seemed at times in the '70s and early '80s to be fighting his way through concerts—stiff and largely motionless as he faced challenging audiences that often complained about anything in his song selection or arrangements that didn't conform to their expectations. But now, in his introverted way, he enjoys the interaction with the audience. He's comfortable enough on stage to move a bit, and there's an occasional trace of playfulness in his eyes. And there's no rush to get it all over with—the instrumental interludes between verses get more of an airing-out than in the past.

Over the next 90 minutes, he runs through songs from the '60s, '70s and '80s—love songs and social commentaries, mostly his own songs and some by other writers. Dylan surprises the older fans early in the set by gliding into a tender, shields-down rendition of Nat King Cole's pop ballad "Answer Me, My Love." He stands stock-still, his head slightly tilted as if to recall the emotion that the song triggered the first time he heard it. Later, looking like a young rock upstart in a Memphis roadhouse, he bobs and weaves to kick off a spirited version of Johnny Cash's old "Folsom Prison Blues." The band supports Dylan with a frisky, rockabilly-and-blues-accented sound.

At first, the audience simply watches politely. It takes Dylan's old "All Along the Watchtower," a song that the younger listeners may best recognize from a recent recording by U2, to get them moving. By the end of the set, hundreds have raced to the edge of the stage, moving in time with the music.

Dylan looks down at them briefly, seems pleased and just keeps playing. As usual, he has said little during the entire concert beyond an occasional "thank you." No introductions, no eye contact, no chitchat. The show ends and there's a tremendous burst of applause when Dylan returns for a quick two-song encore. Then he bows slightly toward the audience, turns abruptly and heads offstage, directly into the chill of the night and onto the bus—no post-show handshaking or small talk. His only question to his aides: "How was the sound out there?"

When the bus arrives around midnight at the entrance of the Ambassador East, the band members file off, heading for their rooms. But Dylan stands on State Street, shifting his weight back and forth in the cold and staring into the distance. He wants to stop at a blues club in the neighborhood for a while and then get some dinner.

After an hour of blues, Dylan, his bodyguard and a tour aide end up in a nondescript diner a few blocks from the hotel. Sipping at a bowl of soup, Dylan says he likes the mandolin riff in R.E.M.'s "Losing My Religion," which is playing on the radio. He listens to a run-through of comments from the new generation that filled the seats at the Northwestern show.

"Older people—people my age—don't come out anymore," he says. "A lot of the shows over the years was people coming out of curiosity and their curiosity wasn't fulfilled. They weren't transported back to the '60s. Lightning didn't strike.

"The shows didn't make sense for them, and they didn't make sense for me. That had to stop, and it took a long time to stop it. A lot of people were coming out to see The Legend, and I was trying to just get on stage and play music."

He shifts restlessly in the chair. The brightly lit room is almost empty, and no one recognizes him at first. After a few minutes, however, the diner manager and a customer at the other end of the room start huddling and looking his way. Dylan doesn't notice. He's still thinking about the comments of the students and their interest in the '60s.

"A lot of people say the '60s generation didn't turn out well—that they didn't live up to their dreams or follow through or whatever—and they may be right. But there still was a lot that no one else has been able to do," he says firmly.

"People today are still living off the table scraps of the '60s. They are still being passed around—the music, the ideas.

"Look at what's going on today: There used to be a time when the idea of heroes was important. People grew up sharing those myths and legends and ideals. Now they grow up sharing McDonald's and Disneyland."

When Dylan and his party leave the diner half an hour later, the manager approaches the singer at the cash register and asks for a photo or an autograph. "Maybe tomorrow or something, OK," he says, not very convincingly. But he doesn't want to be rude. Just before he walks out, he shakes the manager's hand.

Back at the hotel, Dylan pauses at the entrance to the Pump Room and stares at some of the hundreds of celebrity photos on the wall. He moves slowly down the hallway as his aide and his bodyguard point to faces they recognize—Frank Sinatra, Cary Grant, Marilyn Monroe, even David Bowie and Mick Jagger. Dylan's picture is not on the wall.

He stares briefly at a photo of Humphrey Bogart and Lauren Bacall, but then loses interest. It's 2:30 by now, and the outsider heads toward the elevator.

The next night, Dylan paces impatiently backstage at the Dane County Memorial Coliseum in Madison. A snowstorm had snarled traffic, and it has taken Dylan's bus four hours instead of two to get here from Chicago. He seems anxious to get the whole evening over with. Finally, he goes back to the bus to wait out the opening act.

On stage, instead of the relaxed mood he brought to the concert at Northwestern, he struggles for inspiration. The audience cheers as much as the fans at Northwestern, but Dylan's vocals—on the very same songs—lack the emotional edge of the previous show. The exception is the ballad "I Believe in You":

> They ask me how I feel
> and if my love is real
> And how I know I'll make it through
> They look at me and frown
> They'd like to drive me from this town
> They don't want me around
> 'Cause I believe in you.

It's a nakedly personal song, a reflection on the isolation of an outsider's life, and the tension in Dylan's performance emphasizes its poignancy.

Despite a standing ovation at the end of the concert, Dylan can't seem to wait until he is on his way to the next town. He again walks directly from the stage to the bus. The heater is on but he sits bundled up in a rumpled sweat shirt and jacket at a small table in the front compartment. Across the aisle, in the TV-lounge area, the band members are laughing as they listen to a bootleg tape of Buddy Rich. On the tape, the great jazz drummer is delivering a tongue-lashing to his band. Dylan, who plans to produce a movie of the late drummer's life, has heard the tape before and his mind is elsewhere.

"That was a useless gig," he says flatly.

When someone mentions that the audience seemed to enjoy it, he waves his hand. "Naw, it just wasn't there. Nothin' wrong with the audience. Sometimes the energy level just doesn't happen the way it should. We didn't invite this weather to follow us around."

He lapses into silence.

The night before, after the Northwestern show, he had been more talkative, and more philosophical about the ups and downs of touring.

"You hear sometimes about the glamor of the road," he said then, "but you get over that real fast. There are a lot of times that it's no different from going to work in the morning. Still, you're either a player or you're not a player. It didn't really occur to me until we did those shows with the Grateful Dead [in 1987]. If you just go out every three years or so, like I was doing for a while, that's when you lose touch. If you are going to be a performer, you've got to give it your all."

At the blues club in Chicago, he had let his guard down—briefly—when an old friend, who had heard that Dylan was in town, tracked him down. The tour bodyguard braced as a middle-aged man in a business suit walked up to Dylan and put an arm around him. But the smile on Dylan's face said it was OK. The man's name was Arnie, and he had gone to high school with Dylan in Hibbing, Minnesota.

Dylan sat bemused while Arnie regaled the reporter with tales. "Back in English class," Arnie confided, "Bob wrote me a note: 'Arnie, I'm going to make it big. I know it for sure, and when I do, you bring this piece of paper and for two months, you can stay with me, no matter where I am at.' I still have it at home."

Dylan laughed easily.

"You know, I took off and joined the Navy and Bob went down to the University of Minnesota and the next thing I know, he's got this record out," Arnie continued. "I've got some of his albums at home and some picture books of his life story. The song I like the best is 'Slow Train'—that and 'Lay Lady Lay.'"

Dylan stepped in only when the reporter asked Arnie his last name. "Naw," he said protectively, "don't drag him into all this."

Tonight on the bus, just out of Madison, Dylan is much less at ease. He looks like a street person—as drained as he appeared on last year's Grammy telecast, as he waits for someone to bring him whiskey and coffee, trying to separate himself from the frustrations of the night.

When the band members retire to their bunks in the back of the bus, Dylan begins to loosen up a bit. Still, with no Arnie to make the revelations, Dylan keeps the veil tightly drawn around his personal life. Any talk about his former, 13-year marriage to Sara Lowndes, or their four now-grown children, is strictly off-limits. So is his longstanding relationship with Carole Childs, an Elektra Records artists and repertoire executive.

The music, however, is not off-limits. He is intrigued by a comparison between the message of "I Believe in You" and the speech he had delivered at the Grammy Awards. "It's possible to be so defiled in this world that your own mother and father will abandon you," he said that night. "And if this happens, God will always believe in your ability to mend your own ways."

When the reporter tells him that the song and speech both seemed to be about the need to be true to one's own beliefs, Dylan responds easily. "That song is just about overcoming hardship," he volunteers. "Songs are mostly personal—something happens in your life or flashes through and then it's gone, and sometimes it's a song and sometimes it's just lost. Sometimes things work, sometimes they don't.

"These days," he says, "they don't more often than they do." At one point in the conversation, he pulls a notebook from his jacket and starts scribbling. "It's a song I'm workin' on," he offers, and then adds: "Part of the secret of being a songwriter is to have an audacious attitude. There was a time when the songs would come three or four at the same time, but those days are long gone."

It's a delicate topic, but Dylan continues.

"Once in a while, the odd song will come to me like a bulldog at the garden gate and demand to be written. But most of them are rejected out of my mind right away. You get caught up in wondering if anyone really needs to hear it. Maybe a person gets to the point where they have written enough songs. Let someone else write them." Still, he writes enough for a new album every couple of years, and some—including 1989's *Oh Mercy*—are widely acclaimed.

He shrugs at the mention of all the "new Dylans" who have been touted over the years—displaying a rare flash of pride.

"That's never been a worry," he says. "There wasn't anybody doing my thing—though I'm not saying it was all that great. It was just mine and no one was going to cover that territory. No one frames language with that same sense of rhyme. It's my thing, just like no one writes a sad song like Hank Williams or no one writes a bitter song like Willie Nelson. My thing is the forming of the lines."

Dylan is loose now. He's not letting the questions go unanswered. He could easily say he was tired and call an end to the discussion. But he is leaning back on the seat, involved in the conversation rather than fencing. Like most songwriters, he doesn't like to dissect his material, but he agrees to give his opinion about some of the reporter's favorite Dylan songs.

He nods when "Every Grain of Sand" is mentioned.

"That's an excellent song, very painless song to write," he says without hesitation. "It took like 12 seconds—or that's how it felt."

He doesn't seem as enthusiastic at the mention of "Tangled Up in Blue," one of his most-performed post-'60s songs. "I always thought it was written too fast, too rushed. Sometimes that happens in a song—just too many lines, as if I were racing to get from here to there."

Dylan nods again at the mention of "Just Like a Woman."

"That's a hard song to pin down," he says. "It's another one of those that you can sing a thousand times and still ask what is it about, but you know there's a real feeling there."

Dylan pauses, as if suddenly self-conscious.

"I'm not trying to say any of these are great songs—that they'd be high up on a list of all the songs ever written."

His answers become increasingly short at the mention of other, older songs, but he does comment on the large number of love songs on the critic's list as opposed to the political songs that earned him his greatest fame in the '60s.

"They call a lot of my songs political songs, but they never really were about politicians," Dylan says, lighting a cigarette. "The politicians don't make a difference. It's the businessmen behind them."

Dylan smiles, then adds: "'Along the Watchtower' may be my [only] political song," apparently referring to the line in the song: "Business men, they drink my wine, plowmen dig my earth / None of them along the line know what any of it is worth."

It's well past 1 o'clock when the driver announces that the bus is approaching Chicago, about a third of the way to South Bend, and the conversation has switched to Hollywood's fascination with rock and roll. Given his role in the culture of the '60s, it seems probable that some filmmaker would want to use his story to explain America in the '60s.

Would he welcome such a film?

"Absolutely not," he says almost contemptuously. "No one knows too much about [my life], so it's going to have to all be speculation. Who was it that said it: Fame is a curse. There's a lot of truth in that."

Looking through the side window at the lights on the outskirts of Chicago, he adds: "Look at Elvis—he's bigger now then when he was living. He lives on in people's mind. But you wonder if people are remembering the right things about his music, rather than all the stuff that people wrote about him."

When the tour bus stops to let the reporter off at a motel near O'Hare International Airport, Dylan says he wants a cup of fresh coffee. One would assume that somebody would go and get it for him. Instead, Dylan walks into an all-night diner and sits at the counter with a tour aide. He's unnoticed amid a handful of truckers and motorists taking a break from the icy highway. It's a bleak scene, worthy of an Edward Hopper painting, and seeing Dylan as part of it suggests, at least momentarily, a clear image of faded glory.

Not everyone at 50 would want to spend all these months on the road, especially in the numbing cold of the winter.

If Dylan maintains the pace of the Never-Ending Tour, he'll do about 120 shows this year. "That may not sound like a lot," he says. "Willie [Nelson] and B. B. King do a lot more, but it's a comfortable number for me." He also says that he reserves the right to halt the tour at any time. "Whenever it does start feeling like work, that's when I want to stop," he says. "Get away from it for a while. You don't want to be a prisoner of this [touring] any more than you want to be a prisoner of anything in life if you can avoid it."

But for now, the road is his choice and he seems grateful for the chance, after all these years, to be able to move about the world at his own pace, freed somewhat from the prison of his '60s mantle.

In the last analysis, the reasons for Dylan's cultural impact are as much a puzzle to the enigmatic performer as they are to others.

"There's no one to my knowledge that isn't surprised by their longevity, including myself," Dylan said wearily, wiping the sleep from his eyes as the bus made its way from concert to concert. "But it's very dangerous to plan [far ahead], because you are just dealing with your vanity. Tomorrow is hard enough. It's God who gives you the freedom, and the days you should be most concerned with are today and tomorrow.

"It's one thing to say 'There's a new record out and people are responding to the new songs,' which is encouraging. But that's not the case. There's no new album, and it's hard for me to know just what that means, why people come out and what they are looking for or listening for. . . . Maybe the same things I was looking for when I wrote them."

EDNA GUNDERSEN

DYLAN ON DYLAN: "UNPLUGGED" AND THE BIRTH OF A SONG (1995)

USA Today, May 5–7, 1995

Here Dylan reflects on his Unplugged *experience and the demands of both the MTV age and his own attempts to remain "current."*—CB

On the eve of his *MTV Unplugged* album, the usually reclusive Bob Dylan agreed to an exclusive chat about his current activities. After a string of West Coast dates this month, he and his band resume touring in Europe in June, then return for a full U.S. tour this fall. He spent three weeks in January writing new songs but probably won't record them before 1996. What else? Read on.

Gundersen: How did you plan this Unplugged *project?*

Dylan: I wasn't quite sure how to do it and what material to use. I would have liked to do old folk songs with acoustic instruments, but there was a lot of input from other sources as to what would be right for the MTV audience. The record company said, "You can't do that, it's too obscure." At one time, I would have argued, but there's no point. OK, so what's not obscure? They said "Knockin' on Heaven's Door."

Gundersen: And "Like a Rolling Stone," your signature.

Dylan: I was hearing a lot about how Eric Clapton did "Layla" acoustically for *Unplugged*. That influenced me to do the same for "Like a Rolling Stone," but it would never get played that way normally.

Gundersen: Would you consider an Unplugged *sequel?*

Dylan: I'd consider doing *Unplugged* again in a relaxed setting where I didn't feel like I was on the spot. I felt like I had to deliver, and I delivered something that was preconceived for me. That wasn't a problem, but it wasn't necessarily what I wanted to do.

Gundersen: Do you prefer playing acoustic over electric?

Dylan: They're pretty much equal to me. I try not to deface the song with electricity or nonelectricity. I'd rather get something out of the song verbally and phonetically than depend on tonality of instruments.

Gundersen: Was performing before TV cameras difficult?

Dylan: It's hard to rise above some lukewarm attitude toward TV. I've never catered to that medium. It doesn't really pay off for me.

Gundersen: Was the studio audience a typical Dylan crowd?

Dylan: I'd never seen them before. [Laughs] As I recall, they were in the polite category.

Gundersen: Did you approve of the finished show?

Dylan: I can't say. I didn't see it.

Gundersen: You've been touring a lot in recent years. Obviously you enjoy playing live.

Dylan: There's a certain part of you that becomes addicted to a live audience. I wouldn't keep doing it if I was tired of it. I do about 125 shows a year. It may sound like a lot to people who don't work that much, but it isn't. B. B. King is working 350 nights a year.

Gundersen: Was playing at Woodstock a special moment?

Dylan: Nah, it was just another show, really. We just blew in and blew out of there. You do wonder if you're coming across, because you feel so small on a stage like that.

Gundersen: Do any of your songs feel dated or stale to you?

Dylan: I rarely listen to my old records. Songs to me are alive. They're not based on any con game or racket or humbug. They're real songs and they're right now. They're not songs people can listen to and say, "Oh gee, I remember where I was when I first heart that" or "That speaks for me." My songs aren't like that. They're not disposable. Folk and blues songs aren't either.

Gundersen: But you've discarded some songs along the way.

Dylan: Let's face it, some of my songs don't hold up live. I can't think of any right now, but I've tried them over the years and now I just don't do them.

Gundersen: Do current events, like the Oklahoma bombing, impact on your songwriting?

Dylan: Chaos is everywhere: lawlessness, disorganization, misrule. I don't know if it impacts my songwriting like it used to. In the past few years, events have affected me and I've addressed them. But unless a song flows out naturally and doesn't have to be chaperoned, it just dissipates.

Gundersen: Do you write with immortality in mind?

Dylan: No. It's a here-and-now thing. A lot of songs are just interrogation of yourself. I wouldn't classify myself as any type of songwriter. I try not to force myself anywhere.

Gundersen: Are there many unwritten songs inside your head?

Dylan: Probably more that have never come out than ones that have. I get thoughts during the day that I just can't get to. I'll write a verse down and never complete it. It's hard to be vigilant over the whole thing.

Gundersen: At 53, do you feel a greater urgency about writing?

Dylan: Yeah, it's either that or be completely mindless about it. I've written a whole bunch of songs, so I can't say I didn't get to what I wanted to. As you get older, you get smarter and that can hinder you because you try to gain control over the creative impulse. Creativity is not like a freight train going down the tracks. It's something that has to be caressed and treated with a great deal of respect. If your mind is intellectually in the way, it will stop you. You've got to program your brain not to think too much.

Gundersen: And how do you do that?

Dylan: Go out with the bird dogs.

JOHN DOLEN

A MIDNIGHT CHAT WITH BOB DYLAN (1995)

Fort Lauderdale Sun Sentinel, September 29, 1995

*Here Dylan comments on his recent touring band and reper-
toire.*—CB

When Bob Dylan calls, it's nearly midnight. When he speaks it is with a
clear, distinctive voice. Even though he's at the end of his day, having just
returned to a Fort Lauderdale hotel after a band rehearsal, he is contem-
plative, enigmatic, even poetic.

The Southern leg of his current tour cranks into high gear tonight
with the first of two concerts at the Sunrise Musical Theatre. The tour,
which has been in progress for more than a year, has earned rave reviews
from critics in New York, San Francisco, Dublin. In a nearly hour-long
interview with Arts & Features Editor John Dolen, the first in-depth interview he has given to a newspaper this year, Dylan talks about his songs,
the creative process and the free gig at the Edge in Fort Lauderdale last
Saturday.

*Q: Like many others, over the years I've spent thousands of hours listen-
ing to your albums. Even now, not a month goes by without me reaching
for* Blonde on Blonde, Highway 61 Revisited, Slow Train Coming, Street
Legal, Oh Mercy. *Do you sit back and look at all these albums and say,
hey, that's pretty good?*

A: You know, it's ironic, I never listen to those records. I really don't
notice them anymore except to pick songs off of them here and there to
play. Maybe I should listen to them. As a body of work, there could
always be more. But it depends. Robert Johnson only made one record.
His body of work was just one record. Yet there's no praise or esteem high
enough for the body of work he represents. He's influenced hundreds of
artists. There are people who put out 40 or 50 records and don't do what
he did.

Q: What was the record?

A: He made a record called *King of the Delta Blues Singers*. In '61 or '62. He was brilliant.

Q: *Your performance at the Rock and Roll Hall of Fame concert in Cleveland earlier this month drew a lot of great notices. Is that important to you? What's your feeling about that institution?*

A: I never visited the actual building, I was just over at the concert, which was pretty long. So I have no comment on the interior or any of the exhibits inside.

Q: *But how do you feel about the idea of a rock hall of fame itself?*

A: Nothing surprises me anymore. It's a perfect time for anything to happen.

Q: *At the Edge show Saturday, you did a lot of covers, including some old stuff, like "Confidential." Was that a Johnny Ray song?*

A: It's by Sonny Knight. You won't hear that again.

Q: *Oh, was that the reason for your "trying to turn bullshit into gold" comment at the show? Were these covers just something for folks at the Edge? Does that mean you aren't going to be doing more material like that on your tour, including the Sunrise shows?*

A: It will be the usual show we're used to doing on this tour now, songs most people will have heard already.

Q: *In the vein of non-Dylan music, what does Bob Dylan toss on the CD or cassette player these days?*

A: Ever heard of John Trudell? He talks his songs instead of singing them and has a real good band. There's a lot of tradition to what he is doing. I also like Kevin Lynch. And Steve Forbert.

Q: *Are there new bands you think are worth bringing to attention?*

A: I hear people here and there and I think they're all great. In most cases I never hear of them again. I saw some groups in London this summer. I don't know their names.

Q: At this stage of your career, when you've earned every kind of honor and accolade that a person can get, what motivates you?

A: I've had it both ways. I have had good and bad accolades. If you pay any attention to them at all, it makes you pathological. It makes us pathological, to read about ourselves. You try not to pay attention or you try to discard it as soon as possible.

Q: For some writers the motivation is that burden, that you have to get what's inside of you out and down on paper. How is it with you?

A: Like that, exactly. But if I can't make it happen when it comes, you know, when other things intrude, I usually don't make it happen. I don't go to a certain place at a certain time every day to build it. In my case, a lot of these songs, they lay around imperfectly. . . .

Q: As a songwriter, what's the creative process? How does a song like "All Along the Watchtower" come about?

A: There's three kinds of ways. You write lyrics and try to find a melody. Or, if you come up with a melody, then you have to stuff the lyrics in there some kinda way. And then the third kind of a way is when they both come at the same time. Where it all comes in a blur: The words are the melody and the melody is the words. And that's the ideal way for somebody like myself to get going with something. "All Along the Watchtower" was that way. It leaped out in a very short time. I don't like songs that make you feel feeble or indifferent. That lets a whole lot of things out of the picture for me.

Q: How did you feel when you first heard Jimi Hendrix's version of "All Along the Watchtower"?

A: It overwhelmed me, really. He had such talent, he could find things inside a song and vigorously develop them. He found things that other people wouldn't think of finding in there. He probably improved upon it by the spaces he was using. I took license with the song from his version, actually, and continue to do it to this day.

Q: "Angelina," off The Bootleg Series, is such a great song, but no matter how hard I try I can't figure out the words; any clues for me?

A: I never try to figure out what they're about. If you have to think about it, then it's not there.

Q: A song that always haunted me was "Senor," from Street Legal. *Have you played that at all in the last few years?*

A: We play that maybe once every third, fourth or fifth show.

Q: In the '70s, after years abroad, I remember the incredible elation I felt coming back to the States and hearing your Christian songs, a validation of experiences I had been through in Spain. I remember the lines,

You talk about Buddha
You talk about Muhammad
But you never said a word about
the one who came to die for us instead. . . .

Those were fearless words. How do you feel about those words and the songs your wrote during that period now?

A: Just writing a song like that probably emancipated me from other kinds of illusions. I've written so many songs and so many records that I can't address them all. I can't say that I would disagree with that line. On its own level it was some kind of turning point for me, writing that.

Q: With the great catalog you have and with the success this year with the MTV Unplugged *disc, why does this concert tour have such a heavy guitar and drums thing going?*

A: It's not the kind of music that will put anybody to sleep.

Q: The other night at the Edge you left the harmonicas on the stand without touching them, any reason for that?

A: They are such a dynamo unto themselves. I pick them up when I feel like it.

Q: You've made several passes through here in the past 10 years. Your thoughts on South Florida?

A: I like it a lot, who wouldn't. There's a lot to like.

Q: Now there is Bob Dylan on CD-ROM, Bob Dylan on the Internet and all that stuff. Are some people taking you too seriously?

A: It's not for me to say. People take everything seriously. You can get too altruistic on yourself because of the brain energy of other people.

Q: Across the Atlantic is a fellow named Elvis Costello, who, after you, takes a lot of shelf space in my stereo. Both of you are prolific, turn out distinctive albums each time, have great imagery, have a lot to say, and so on. Is there any reason that in all the years I've never seen your names or faces together?

A: It's funny you should mention that. He just played four or five shows with me in London and Paris. He was doing a lot of new songs, playing them by himself. He was doing his thing. You so had to be there.

Q: Is America better or worse than, say, in the days of "The Times They Are A-Changin'"?

A: I see pictures of the '50s, the '60s and the '70s and I see there was a difference. But I don't think the human mind can comprehend the past and the future. They are both just illusions that can manipulate you into thinking there's some kind of change. But after you've been around awhile, they both seem unnatural. It seems like we're going in a straight line, but then you start seeing things that you've seen before. Haven't you experienced that? It seems we're going around in circles.

Q: When you look ahead now, do you still see a Slow Train Coming?

A: When I look ahead now, it's picked up quite a bit of speed. In fact, it's going like a freight train now.

ERIC WEISBARD

THE FOLK SLINGERS (1998)

Village Voice, January 13, 1998

This appreciation of Bob Dylan as folksinger, takes him full circle in his career. The reissue of Harry Smith's mammoth Anthology of American Folk Music *in 1998 brought much commentary about the folk revival and Dylan's role in it. In this article, Weisbard compares the work of three revivalists: folklorist Alan Lomax, anthologist Harry Smith, and performer Bob Dylan.—CB*

1959: Ozarks traditionalist Almeda Riddle sings to folklorist Alan Lomax the ancient ballad "The House Carpenter"; about a woman who abandons her child to run off with a demon lover and is sent to hell for it. Heard on volume 6 of Rounder's 1997 Lomax reissue, *Southern Journey*, her impassive tone both demonstrates the subtle—some might say interminable—techniques of a cappella mountain singing and imparts a fatalistic morality.

1930: Medicine show veteran Clarence Ashley cuts the same song for a Columbia single, later compiled on Harry Smith's 1952 *Anthology of American Folk Music,* rereleased this year to sweeping acclaim. Ashley sings it faster, putting on a show, his banjo swirling out the modal patterns said to have preceded the blues. He leaves hell out—the recording device's three minutes were up.

1961: It's only two years after Riddle, but you could be hearing a different century. Bob Dylan is still recording his first album (this was an outtake, released 30 years later on *The Bootleg Series*). He hasn't yet desecrated the Newport Folk Festival—center of the "folk revival" sparked by Lomax's songbooks, Smith's LPs, and Freewheelin' Bob's charisma—with electricity. Dylan spits out the lines, singing "it's all for the lu-uv of thee" with a dip that's pure Elvis. He also made sure the hell part returned—found it sexy, I bet.

Here, in three renditions, are three kinds of folk. A field recording, the dullest to listen to, but with the fullest lyric (and the spookiest). A wheedling commercial record, sexier for it, from a minstrel following his own demon lover: money. And a revival, fascinating as much for the circumstances of its rebirth—which in this case include hearing a celebrity respond to it—as for the original ballad itself. We blur these distinctions all the time—in *Entertainment Weekly*, David Browne had Harry Smith, six when Ashley sang, field recording his *Anthology*—but without them folk music is lumpy nostalgia, like so much roots rock.

In 1997, a folk label announced that it would place in circulation the lifework, projected at over 100 CDs, of an arrogant, romanticizing folklorist without peer. A different folk label reissued the thrift-store-derived 78-rpm collection of a brilliant crackpot who never set foot in the field. And a former folksinger, the voice of a generation, a wasted rock star, released *Time Out of Mind*, quickly recognized as his best work in decades, possibly the best album of a year that had been consigned to electronica at its start. This music mattered in the here and now just as much, even though it sounded more like old blues ground up; this Jewish son of a Minnesota appliance salesman had turned into the sardonic voice of the hills.

Folk can be any notion of the genuine we project onto other people, or assume unto ourselves. But all folk music is a kissing cousin of what anthropologists call ethnography—an attempt to define a people's way of being (or our own). Anthropologists have learned to question the assumptions behind even accepted classics of ethnography. Recordings, seemingly transparent cultural reflections, deserve no less scrutiny. Especially now, as new landfills worth of past come on sale each year. The folk explosions of the '30s and '60s are the folk implosion of the '90s, sucking us into the vortex of mankind's first century of recorded sound. If we're going to rush back, or be pulled back, into folk, we might think about what exactly this thing is that we're all so quick to fawn over.

The Lomax story truly does span a century; it was about 90 years ago that Alan's dad John, a Texas farm child who'd raised himself up, at age 40, into a Harvard grad student on fellowship, suggested to a professor that he write a paper on folk songs. One can only imagine the will that turned that project into the 1910 landmark anthology *Cowboy Songs and Other Ballads*, a songbook compiled through advertisements in hundreds of Western newspapers and field recordings on Edison cylinders too weak to provide more than lyrics and a melody line. Suddenly, America had its own folk tradition.

Even in this first book, most of the hallmarks of the Lomax approach were visible. (1) Romanticization of the primitive—that Harvard prof, Barrett Wendell, gushed in the introduction: ". . . the wonderful, robust vividness of their artless yet supremely true utterance . . . expression straight from the heart of humanity . . . their very rudeness refreshes us with a new sense of brimming life." (2) Fear of modern contamination—a handwritten preface by Theodore Roosevelt, which legitimized the book, worries about "music hall" making the ballad disappear. (3) A modern taste for slick packaging—deviating from standard folk preservationism, Lomax published "composite ballads," taking the bits he liked best from multiple versions. "Frankly," he wrote in justification, "the volume is meant to be popular." And (4), an uneasy relationship to black culture—though the book's cowboy theme is, explicitly, the "Anglo Saxon ballad spirit," its pop coup was "Home on the Range," learned from an African American communicant who, Lomax reported in the revised edition, told him: "I's too drunk to sing today. Come back tomorrow."

Deepening the race question, *American Ballads and Folk Songs*, a 1934 book compiled with help from a teenage Alan, centered around African American lyrics, gathered from convicts with exotic names like Iron Head, Chin Shooter, and Ing Shing; the Lomaxes liked convicts on the spurious theory that they had "the least contact with jazz, the radio, and with the white man" (blacks, after all, were "naturally imitative"). Were they forced to sing, these convicts? Well, there were armed guards nearby, they were urged to cooperate, and they called John Lomax boss. One prisoner was more than eager: Lead Belly, who was soon brought North, where he became John Lomax's "companion" (chauffeur, house helper) and performed in convict's stripes, before breaking off on his own. Lead Belly's most popular song, "Goodnight Irene," was co-copyrighted by the Lomaxes: the profits would launch Alan on his European field trip of the 1950s.

Still, the Lomaxes discovered Lead Belly, one of a list of accomplishments far too long to merit prolonged scoffing. John Lomax recorded and compiled thousands of folk songs, and helped establish the Library of Congress's Archive of American Folk Song.

Alan Lomax directed the Archive, undertook full-length oral histories of Lead Belly (whom he remained friendly with), Woody Guthrie, and Jelly Roll Morton, promoted folk on CBS radio early and PBS TV later on, took countless song hunting trips of his own around the world, wrote books for scholars, fans, and children, staged concerts and "ballad operas," and inspired even more work by others than he generated himself. Balancing the racial scale, the *Blues in the Mississippi Night* LP (taped in 1946, released in 1959 with the participants' names obscured, then with full disclosure in 1990) was the first candid discussion of race by blues musicians ever recorded.

Alan Lomax was both more of an agitator and more of an academic than his father. Exemplifying the politics, which were straight Popular Front (that union of communism and American popular culture), is *Hard Hitting Songs for Hard-Hit People*, an agitprop songbook compiled by Lomax in the '30s (though only published in 1967), with musical transcriptions by Pete Seeger, sentimental liner notes by Woody Guthrie, a foreword by John Steinbeck, and sharecropper photos from the Farm Security Administration. Exemplifying the scholarship is Lomax's work on what he dubbed Cantometrics at Columbia University, an attempt at an "aesthetic anthropology" that translated varying ethnic musics into some 30-odd categories of song style.

The idea of Cantometrics was to facilitate more assured cross-comparisons between different cultures. Yet, like the Popular Front, which often reduced "the people" to a caricature, and like the multimedia "Global Jukebox" that's been Lomax's final obsession, Cantometrics ultimately makes human expression seem far too abstract, too categorical: the inspirational part of art leaks out. The same thing happens with his field recordings. (Thus far, the reissues in Rounder's *The Alan Lomax Collection* include eight diverse volumes of the 1959 *Southern Journey*; an earnest Fred McDowell single disc; two CDs of *Prison Songs* taped in 1947 Mississippi, the sound of captivity; innocuous 1962 Caribbean children's music; and a disorienting series sampler.) The range of what's been captured is amazing, the individual performances often skillful and stylistically illuminating, especially combined with the exemplary liner notes. But you wouldn't call it listenable. What's missing is human beings trying to win over other human beings, or at least get something out of themselves. These are performances recorded for a time capsule.

This is music chosen to illustrate language like the blurb Lomax attaches to the *Prison Songs* volumes: "They were born of the very rock and earth of this country, as black hands broke the soil, moved, reformed it, and rivers of stinging sweat poured upon the land. . . . They tell us the story of the slave gang, the sharecropper system, the lawless work camp, the chain gang, the pen." Lomax's 1993 memoir of his southern journeys, *The Land Where the Blues Began*, makes the problem even plainer. He's enormously knowledgeable about form, explaining exactly how a work song is structured to keep a convict's energy up. But his characters are as romantically drawn as his conclusions, he repeats discredited myths, and his longing to cross "over the border into unconventional America" is palpable: "There was a jug there that gurgled, and it was so hot that Son

House and his buddies stripped to the waist as they played. Of all my times with the blues this was the best one." Not all field recordings sound the same. *Angola Prison Blues*, recorded by ethnomusicologist Harry Oster around the time of Lomax's '59 set, includes a track of a female inmate singing a current radio hit in a laundry room, making her voice play off the machine—a slice of the modern life Lomax preferred to ignore. Mike Seeger's '97 fieldwork retrospective for Smithsonian Folkways, *Close to Home*, shows how such recordings can attain a family feel—these are musicians he plainly idolized and cultivated. And another '97 Rounder release outside the Lomax Collection, *A Treasury of Library of Congress Field Recordings*, lays the '30s and '40s work of John and Alan side by side. Lo and behold: the more conservative John got more relaxed performances.

Part of what enticed the Lomaxes into field recording was the supposed objectivity of the machinery. In 1941 they rhapsodized: "The needle writes on the disc with tireless accuracy the subtle inflections, the melodies, the pauses that comprise the emotional meaning of speech, spoken and sung. . . . The field recording, as contrasted with the field notebook, shows the folk song in its three-dimensional entirety." The Lomax recordings did tremendous service, helping to document concretely the distinctiveness of American folk traditions and African retentions in our culture. But they also prove how drastically the reasons for a recording, and the person conducting it, can affect what ends up on the grooves.

In 1933, the same Depression that had radically curtailed the music industry, particularly "specialty" folk recordings (which had sold well ever since Fiddlin' John Carson's first hit in 1923), cost John Lomax his bank job and sent him back into the field. As a result, history looped around: for Northerners and intellectuals, who'd never heard the earlier, regionally released commercial material, folk meant the Lomax songbooks and recordings, Lead Belly, Woody Guthrie, and Pete Seeger. By 1952, when Folkways put out Harry Smith's *Anthology of American Folk Music*, history looped back again. The Popular Front was in retreat: the Weavers blacklisted, Lomax off to Europe. The *Anthology* revived the original commercial folk artists, now symbols of authenticity; among the resurrected were Mississippi John Hurt, the Carter Family, Clarence Ashley, and Dock Boggs.

In a weird way, then, the music of the *Anthology*, recorded between 1926 and 1934, is both chronologically older and culturally younger than the Lomaxes' work. The effect is heightened by the fact that most of the performers Smith compiled were younger when they recorded than those

Alan Lomax taped: Buell Kazee, 28; Ashley, 35; Blind Lemon Jefferson, 31; John Hurt, 34; Maybelle Carter, 30; and Sara Carter, 19. And the older Smith artists, like Uncle Dave Macon, had remained working musicians, where most of Lomax's informants were retired from regular playing or had never been professionals. Further, Alan Lomax paid for his performances only in liquor; *Folk Song Style and Culture* made clear who his true friends were: "The principal debt of the Cantometrics Project is to a generation of field workers who have taken the pains to record song and dance after having cajoled the temperamental artists of the world to perform for them." In contrast, A&R man Ralph Peer, the hero of Smith's *Anthology*, was able to take down performances by the Carter Family, Jimmie Rodgers, and Blind Willie McTell in the same week because he could advertise in the newspapers that, in one year, the Stoneman Family had made $3600 working with him. Forget cajoling.

The *Anthology* showcases accomplished performers, at the height of their powers, working all out. Over half the recordings are by duos or groups, manifesting the kind of aggressive ensemble cohesion Lomax rarely captured (check out *Southern Journey* Vol. 8 for a rare exception, "You Got Dimples in Your Jaws"—recorded, atypically, in a juke joint). They aren't preserving a culture—they're developing one. They strain their voices silly when it'll help, milk the scary ballads, throw in goofy effects, and when they project a regal dignity, as many do, they're being cool on their own terms (or the terms of wherever they're from). That one rarely encounters such a complete package in a field recording isn't surprising, given who was performing for what reasons; another exception is the earliest John Lomax recordings of Leadbelly, from when he was still in prison but tasting freedom, and just afterward, tasting celebrity.

Of course, many commercial records are miserable failures; credit for the *Anthology* belongs to Harry Smith, not capitalism. Throughout the six discs and 84 songs you hear a mixture of mountain balladeers, early bluesmen, and off-kilter Cajuns, jug band groans and string band kick. Yet Smith also proceeds topically: Volume 1's ballads progress from ancient times up to McKinley's assassination and the boll weevil; Volume 2's *Social Music* takes in dance instrumentals and church testimonies; Volume 3's more varied *Songs* include male and female plaints, couplings, and deep blues. There aren't enough female voices (you're 17 songs in before the first appears), yet John Fahey's comment in the reissue booklet is on target: the key here is balance. Smith knew that "certain musicultural traditions are sympathetic to each other while others are not." Finding functional and personal connections in apparently disparate sources, Smith pulls off an anti-Lomax: his work leaves the folk seeming more mysterious, not less so.

Ironically, what seems to have launched Smith as a collector of old 78s, judging from an interview he gave in 1968, was a list Lomax published in 1940 of 350 folk songs on commercial recordings, a list which included many of the artists on the *Anthology* and about a dozen of its songs. It's an odd document: Lomax would never sound as sanguine about commercial culture again. "I have come away from this listening experience with the certainty that American folk music, while certain folklore specialists have been mourning its decline, has been growing in new directions to compete with 'thick' commercial music, and that it is today in its most 'distorted' form in a healthier condition, roving the radio stations and recording studios, than it has been or ever will be in the notebooks of collectors."

His more self-serving memoir reverses this judgment, saying the musicians were "simply 'going through the motions'" and "the material could not compare to the music we were then recording in the rural South." Lomax had it right the first time. As cultural sociologist Richard Peterson explains in his recent *Creating Country Music*, early record men pushed regional artists to record previously uncopyrighted folk songs, which provided easy publishing income for both the artists (most prominently the Carter Family and Jimmie Rodgers) and their handlers. Thus began an insane hunt for folk material; by the end of 1929, some 3500 old-time titles were recorded in the country field alone. Few old ballads or folk tunes were overlooked, and the records that resulted forever affected how later performers shaped their songs. (The Lomax Collection includes many such borrowings.) In other words, commercial recordings came first, and were often superior aesthetically. The Ralph Peers of the world, hating the music they recorded (asked for the names of those he'd recorded in 1947, Peer replied, "Oh, I tried so hard to forget them"), often did better by it than the loving ethnomusicologists who followed.

Partly because the rights and the master tapes to early commercial recordings have been difficult to obtain (the *Anthology* was essentially a bootleg), folk music Harry Smith–style remains difficult to come by, save for a very few artists and a series of haphazardly compiled, poorly annotated, but still fascinating sets on Yazoo. A parallel series on Shanachie, *The Secret Museum of Mankind*, documents similar early recordings worldwide. And John Fahey recently joined the fray with his Revenant label, releasing a compilation of *Raw Gospel from 1926–36* and slotting retrospectives on Dock Boggs and Buell Kazee. One can only hope that the commercial roots of American folk will soon be preserved in the best Rounder and Smithsonian/Folkways tradition.

It's hard to say whether Harry Smith would have approved. A film-maker, mystic, collector of Easter eggs and many other nonmusical objects, bebop fan (he'd paint jazz solos), and amateur anthropologist, his life resisted all attempts at ordering—later volumes of the *Anthology* went unreleased because Smith never got around to writing the notes and sold his records to the New York Public Library when he needed money. Like Lomax, Smith believed in field recordings, but his efforts were willfully haphazard. He documented Indian peyote rituals and accumulated "Materials for the Study of Religion and Culture in the Lower East Side." Debra DeSalvo, who played in the hardcore band False Prophets and knew Smith's longtime friend Allen Ginsberg, recalls Smith "showing up with his high-end Sony recording Walkman at our rehearsals, mumbling about how slam dancing was the latest outbreak of Dionysus among the young."

Yet without entailing a bit of fieldwork, the *Anthology* became the ultimate field recording, compiled without in any way altering the culture of those it surveyed. (Another viable approach, used later by Mike Seeger but very rare, involved taping live local radio shows.) Smith's unruly, paradigm-busting set fits perfectly revisionist anthropologist James Clifford's call, in *Writing Culture*, for noninterventionist ethnographies that replace overarching single interpretations—incorporating the idio-syncrasies of speech and gesture and making sure "many voices clamor for expression."

The leading lights of the 1960s folk revival came from a variety of backgrounds: longtime folklorists like Lomax and Pete Seeger, rediscover-ies like Fred McDowell and Maybelle Carter, borderline pop acts like the Kingston Trio and Peter, Paul, and Mary. Yet the biggest heroes, the sexi-est idols to the collegiate crowds at the Newport Folk Festival, were Bob Dylan and Joan Baez, young interpreters of the tradition far less knowl-edgeable, or skilled, than the oldtime musicians who surrounded them. And when Dylan went electric the rent he tore in the folk-revival audience brought Newport down.

Bob Dylan's family owned the first television set in Hibbing, Minnesota, back in 1952—that made-up last name of his was initially Dillon, after the sheriff in *Gunsmoke*. Bobby Zimmerman formed his first rock band in 1955, heard his first folksinger (Leadbelly) in 1959 as rock's allure subsided; far from a born nostalgic, he rode the waves of his moment. And as Dylan, the method actor and born pop provocateur, he insisted that the folk be as brash and hip as the contemporary world, rather than conserve the past. As a result, his transformations—in Ellen Willis's words, "from proletarian assertiveness to anarchist angst to pop detachment"—became the essence of those a-changin' times. In 1997, Newt Gingrich was as eager as Bill Clinton to hail Bob Dylan at the Kennedy Center honors. We all agree he changed something, but we don't know what it is.

There's a famous story of Alan Lomax fistfighting with Dylan's manager, Albert Grossman, at Newport in 1965, over insulting comments Lomax had made onstage about another of Grossman's acts, the Paul Butterfield Blues Band. What infuriated Lomax wasn't simply electric guitars; he'd already, in the discography to his 1960 *Folk Songs of North America*, hailed Bo Diddley, Ray Charles, and Fats Domino. It was the idea that some kids with a few stolen blues licks, a blatant copy, could be more popular than the real thing. The idea of pop culture, mass media, swooping in and distorting the true folk. That Alan Lomax had been, in folk historian Georgina Boyes's words, "a creator of the role of modern celebrity collector," probably never occurred to him.

Lomax had cause for gloom; one reason it's taken so long to reissue Smith's box is that, between Bob Dylan and all the other rock folkies, few made time to hear the old stuff. The rock artist, as Dylan established him, is the third stage in folk's cultural evolution: regional music disseminated through a pop system of larger-than-life representative individuals, from Carlos Santana to Lou Reed to Youssou N'Dour. The rock artist has roots—roots his national and international audience cares about mainly because they're his roots. His career twists and turns according to his whim, far more freely than the performers Lomax or Smith knew. And his audience follows along, trying to understand him. There may be an element of ethnography to his work, of trying to interpret the world. But it's hugely overshadowed by all the anthropology directed his way by admirers trying to comprehend his mysteries.

I couldn't possibly survey Dylan's obsessively documented live and studio oeuvre here; the amount of material, released and especially unreleased, has no precedent in earlier eras of pop. Over time, the bootlegs turn into genuine offerings—the true answer to the old "Dylan's best album since *Blood on the Tracks*" hype is *The Basement Tapes*, *Biograph*, and *The Bootleg Series*. And not all of the unearthed gems date to the '60s—if anything, Dylan's gotten more perverse since about which treasures he buries. Greil Marcus has just based an entire book around a bootleg five-CD set of basement tapes. Paul Williams's Dylan study places on the short list of masterpieces the solo version of "She's Your Lover Now," released in a band version (not good enough!) on *The Bootleg Series*; Clinton Heylin makes similar claims for 1983's electric "Blind Willie McTell." When Dylan actually did that song electric at Jones Beach this summer, I was swept up with excitement, and it's not even one of my favorites, maybe because it always makes me mad that I've never heard the real Blind Willie McTell.

Fans and critics endlessly construct their own straw Dylan. And he only adds to the speculation. He no more has a true singing voice than Madonna has a naked body. The speedfreak image-mongering that created *Bringing It All Back Home*, *Highway 61 Revisited*, and *Blonde on Blonde* within 15 months would have killed him. So his best work since (*Blood on the Tracks* excepted) substitutes smaller beauty, rude carnality, apocalyptic belches, private surrealism, pop readymades, and nods to his cultural idols. Sometimes he sounds emotionally committed (often on the rare tracks his devotees crave, thinking they're getting the "true" man); often he doesn't bother to conceal his boredom and contempt, rhyming moon-June-spoon with phlegm in his throat. In the early '90s he played vocal games live; in the later '90s he's shifted his attention to his guitar. Lines blaze out of dull songs, songs out of dull sets or albums.

If he's now a folk text, Dylan started out a folk interpreter—a "sponge," as his contemporaries put it. He didn't exactly merge folk and rock: more a vast heritage of popular song with pure popcult iconography. His first album, mostly covers, was as death-obsessed as *Time Out of Mind*: "See That My Grave Is Kept Clean" played with the sophomoric intensity of Elvis Costello's debut. By the cover versions on *The Basement Tapes* outtakes, he was learning to treat his sources like a cornucopia; his emotions, and musical accents, became broader and craggier than ever before as he developed much of the palette he's drawn from ever since.

Where Alan Lomax hoped his books and recordings would teach people to appreciate and perform "genuine" folk music, and many folk revivalists lost themselves trying to do the same, Dylan has soul and blues feeling because he sang his own culture: bringing in rock, the movies, whatever was out there. Yet he never fully broke with the folk revival, or stopped wanting to be Willie McTell, never sorted out his own feelings about the folk. And that mixedup confusion of categories is a major part of his enduring originality. Within Dylan, many voices clamor for expression.

When Dylan covers a song—or evokes one in his own compositions—cultural landscapes, sensual associations, and ethical lessons flood through him. Scan his liner notes to the 1993 folk set *World Gone Wrong* to see what I mean. A jumble once removed in kinship from Dylan's own "chains of flashing images" they're unlike any music writing I've ever read. A similar effect occurs in the music of *Time Out of Mind*. Languid, impersonally played, the album's filled with little references, little nods. Dylan, you feel certain, knows the roots of all of it. What you're hearing is something like the sediment that's accumulated at the bottom of his brain, after a lifetime locked up in the tower of song.

Cultural critic W. T. Lhamon Jr. wrote an essay in the 1970s about Bob Dylan as "poplore," his term for "a younger lore than folklore." Poplore, Lhamon argued, found imagery of substance within the jetstreams of mass media; it created the sense of folk, but in the present tense. By flaunting its power, teasing the limits of noise, poplore overcame the fatalism of traditional folk.

I would argue that *The Anthology of American Folk Music* is poplore too, unlike Alan Lomax's work, because the folk it included was recorded in the present tense and retains its riveting, noisy charge—even when, as is sometimes the case (less than you'd expect), the tone is fatalistic. At the beginning of recording history no less than today, a basic question dangled: should folk document a contemporary moment, or the unrecorded and disappearing past? My vote goes to the contemporary moment, which will always contain an echo of the past if you look hard enough. Because by focusing deliberately on a vanishing ideal, you all but eliminate art's vitality. Your sin, to paraphrase Dylan, will be your lifelessness.

The folk of the present tense isn't even vaguely representative. The colossal appeal of the bad man hangs over the whole story—Teddy Roosevelt wrote John Lomax that he particularly relished how Jesse James had replaced Robin Hood; Harry Smith and Dylan both licked their lips over the murder ballads that, through Nick Cave albums and Louvin Brothers reissues, are still an alternaworld growth portfolio—displacing female domestic dramas. White men have seized the lion's share of the space talented artists need to freely reveal themselves. Where corrective redress is needed, field recordings can make useful surrogates. Yet I'd also suggest folklorists learn to listen to the present better; aren't there echoes of back country *Highway 61* in the eerie Chicago house of Phuture, in the inner grooves of Norfolk, Virginia's, Timbaland?

After a century of recordings, the folk echoes everywhere; we're far from the homogenizing "cultural gray-out" Alan Lomax warned of. You can document the folk systematically; you can also just enjoy its occult webs and folds, as Harry Smith did. A few weeks back I went to an evening of tributes to WNEW DJ Vince Scelsa, whose *Idiot's Delight* show has kept the folk revival moving steadily forward through the rock era. The moment that knocked me over came when Ronnie Spector belted a tune by the late Johnny Thunders. Johnny Thunders, the New York Doll, the punk band formed out of the shadows of the girl groups, and Ronnie Spector has heard herself in there? And how perfectly in keeping with my own attitudes that the undeniable lyric was contradicted by her undeniable performance: "You can't put your arms around a memory / So don't try, don't try."

R. EMMETT TYRRELL, JR.

DYLAN RECEIVES KENNEDY CENTER HONORS (1998)

American Spectator, February 1998

Dylan's winning a Kennedy Center Honor sent shock waves through the conservative and liberal communities together. The conservatives, like R. Emmett Tyrrell, were less than happy that a symbol of drug-using hippiedom was so honored; the liberals were somewhat shocked to think that Dylan would take his place in the Establishment. These articles from two opposite ends of the political spectrum reflect typical reactions.—CB

Bob Dylan came to Washington in early December. He snuffled his way through the Kennedy Center Honors, wiped his nose on his sleeve, and went home—wherever that might be. He was here as an honoree, along with several older American performers. Age is a matter of grim consternation to Dylan and his peers. Suffice to say that he is one of the earliest members of what we call the baby boomer generation. Accordingly, he, as the hacks wrote it up, "upstaged" the older honorees, Lauren Bacall, Charlton Heston, Jessye Norman, and Edward Villella.

A medal was placed on Dylan's bony shoulders, and the august confines of the State Department dining room resounded with a raucous three-minute standing ovation. Improbable war whoops punctuated the din as paunchy suburbans emoted with nostalgia, delusions of their rockabilly days, and enough self-love to embarrass Narcissus. "Upstaged," indeed—here was another cloying spectacle of the boomers celebrating themselves.

Doubtless, Dylan was not disposed to see through their exploitation of his mediocre self. Nor did he snicker as the country's first boomer president and first boomer Speaker of the House spent the weekend in desperate competition to proclaim their love for him. Speaker Newt Gingrich won the competition with his "The idea of even meeting Lauren Bacall is unbelievable. The idea of having met God's associate [this being a threadbare joke about the career of Charlton Heston] is almost inconceivable." And then: "The sheer magic, for I think everyone in my generation, is to finally have our nation recognize Bob Dylan."

Well, Newt, as a member of your generation I should like to be left out of the revels. I have heard it all before. In artistic and intellectual terms our wildly overpraised generation is a gigantic bust. In terms of political achievement, neither you nor the Boy President are showing student government of the 1960's and 1970's to be a match for a Hollywood studio back at midcentury. Put the aging Ronald Reagan of 1980, who only became a politician in middle age, next to either of these career politicians—the Hot Springs goody-goody or Newt, whining here about some imagined national rebuff of Dylan—and you have a first-class statesman towering over student government machiavels at play.

Dylan, the impudent egotist who ransacked the lovely old repertoire of folk music, sneered at the bourgeoisie, and then took up the bourgeoisie's electric guitar to exploit its every mawkish emotion, was up to his old tricks while in Washington. He looked scroungy, smelled bad, and variously affected timidity and rage. He failed to join in singing the national anthem—"He has absolutely no political problem singing the national anthem," insisted his publicist Eliot Mintz. It is, of course, all an act, another edition of the down-and-out-in-Paris claptrap of the humbug intellectual. That is not to say that Dylan does not suffer occasional side-effects from his feigned bohemianism. Some time ago he became deathly ill from a contagion borne in bird feces. He still looks sick.

Just listening to the preposterous praise he evokes from his fellows would make a normal man uneasy. They called him the "poet of his generation." Given the mediocrity of his generation, the thing is possible. Yet when Gregory Peck compared him to Walt Whitman and Mark Twain things were clearly out of hand. All he has ever written are jingles freighted with ominous blah. Moreover the blah about war and peace was all wrong. The Pentagon and the State Department won the Cold War, not some teen-aged waif with a flower stuck between her teeth. As for Dylan's pish-posh about sex, drugs, and authenticity, all his so-called free spirits have shown themselves to be dreadful frauds, the drugs have led to insanity or enslavement, and the sex to Anita Hill. Frankly if Dylan is a prophet, the world he prophetized is all pratfalls and misery.

Actually he is just another boomer success story. Like his president he walks on both sides of the street and talks out of both sides of his mouth. Or should I say mumbles? There he was in Washington the other month accepting another award as a celebrated rebel. Once there was a time when the celebrated rebel refused these awards. They were recognized as being an insult to the whole idea of the independent artist. Sinclair Lewis, for instance, aided and abetted by Mencken and Nathan, rejected his Pulitzer. When Lewis was awarded his Nobel Prize he accepted it. He was drunk. Mencken and Nathan could not get past his drunken wife.

ELSA DIXLER

THE TIMES, THEY ARE A— (1997)

The Nation, December 29, 1997

"How does it feel," Bob Dylan's voice taunted from the speaker hidden behind the hanging ferns. It was 1979, and my former boyfriend and I were having a glass of chablis for old times' sake. My friend covered my hand with his. "Listen, dear," he murmured. "They're playing our song."

A joke, of course, but since the early sixties, Bob Dylan has been playing my generation's song, using, as Don McLean put it, "a voice that came from you and me." Odd as it was to see pictures of Dylan receiving his Kennedy Center award in a tux, and to read the outpouring of praise from the likes of Bill Clinton and Newt Gingrich—is it really a surprise that a man who invited Fleetwood Mac to play at his inauguration was responsible for welfare repeal?—there was delight in it too.

Everybody knows that Dylan, more than any other musician, led rock and roll's transformation into an art form. John Lennon claimed that Dylan was the first person to turn the Beatles on. That's culturally if not literally true; Dylan liberated the Beatles and the Stones and many others to take their own chances. And although the award was meant to honor the past, it turns out that the recently released *Time Out of Mind* is Dylan's best album in decades.

Headline writers amused themselves with Dylan lyrics, and reporters noted the irony of seeing the people who once sang Dylan songs on the Washington Mall in evening dress at the Kennedy Center. Irony, sure; it's what keeps you from crying. We live now in a very different world from the one we envisioned, but Bob Dylan's music continues to remind us of who we were and who, despite time's passing, we remain.

GREG KOT

BRILLIANCE STILL SHINES IN DYLAN'S ENDLESS NIGHT (1997)

Chicago Tribune, December 15, 1997

Here is a recent review of Dylan in concert.—CB

Don't Look Back, D. A. Pennebaker titled his famed 1967 documentary on Bob Dylan, providing a defiant slogan for budding rock revolutionaries. Back then, rock 'n' rollers were expected to trash the old order and make up the new rules.

Now those rebels are well into middle age, and in rock 'n' roll the second act is the toughest. What do rock stars do after they change pop culture with a song, a record, even a decade of accomplishment? The Rolling Stones, Pink Floyd, Fleetwood Mac, Rod Stewart—the list of the old favorites who keep on keeping on is endless. And the question is always the same: How to escape the comforting embrace of nostalgia?

Bob Dylan came to town over the weekend with no easy answers to that question. But he provided a few hints as to how a man once saddled with the ridiculously impossible burden of "spokesman for a generation" has not only been making do in the supposed twilight of his career, but flourishing.

What a year—what a decade—it has been for Dylan. At first quietly, and now emphatically, the 56-year-old singer-songwriter has been making some of the best music of his life. Since 1989, Dylan has squeezed off a series of mostly impressive albums, bookended by two masterful studio releases recorded with producer Daniel Lanois. The latest of these, *Time Out of Mind*, is being hailed as a masterpiece, and it has put Dylan back in the pop-culture glitter parade: Cover of *Newsweek*, lead review in *Rolling Stone*, an audience with the Pope. The album has already gone gold (500,000 sales), only weeks after its release, and it's been popping up on year-end top-10 lists; even *Spin* magazine, traditionally contemptuous of Baby Boomer–era acts, named *Time Out of Mind* the fifth-best record of '97, right alongside hipsters Sleater-Kinney, Radiohead and Bjork.

His secret? Do what he's always done: tour virtually year-round, play for anyone who will have him, and don't look back. Even a potentially fatal heart infection earlier this year barely slowed him down; his Metro dates over the weekend were his third and fourth appearances in the area since late August.

Dylan, impeccably outfitted in black suit and red tie with patent-leather shoes gleaming in the spotlights, eased his rail-thin frame across the stage as though gingerly parodying Chuck Berry's duck walk. He brought with him a killer band whose members looked as if they had rolled off a nineteenth-century riverboat with their felt hats, snappy suits and switchblade riffs. And together they spoke a language that allowed for, even encouraged, the possibility of failure rather than succumbing to rote professionalism.

Dylan compensates for his utterly ravaged voice by racing through songs instead of stretching and bending phrases as he once did. But he resourcefully keeps finding outlets of expression; on Saturday, it was in the interplay of his excellent band, Dylan's and Larry Campbell's guitars twisting through each other like barbed wire one minute, satin strands the next. Bucky Baxter's pedal steel introduced a few ghosts to the arrangements, while drummer Dave Kemper and bassist Tony Garnier kept the tempos swinging like a Mississippi roadhouse on Saturday night.

"Maggie's Farm," "If Not for You" and "Stuck Inside of Mobile with the Memphis Blues Again" were pulled apart and reassembled, with new intros, different tempos, long codas. Only "Rainy Day Women #12 & 35" was tossed off with a perfunctory smirk. "Tangled Up in Blue" was recharged by a bluegrass arrangement, with Dylan taking two acoustic guitar solos. "Highway 61 Revisited" turned into an apocalyptic Texas boogie, and Dylan resolutely refused the singalong possibilities inherent in "It Ain't Me Babe" by playing it as a fast blues shuffle, then cutting the tempo in half.

Even better were the new songs—and when was the last time that could be said about any of Dylan's '60s and '70s contemporaries? "Cold Irons Bound," "Can't Wait," "Love Sick" and especially "'Til I Fell in Love with You" were ravaged by doubt and fired by need. "I've been hit too hard, seen too much / Nothin' can kill me now . . . but your touch," he declared, roaming the space between knowledge and desire, love and disgust, risk and resignation.

Instead of looking to his past for answers, Dylan hunkered down, legs splayed, leaned into the microphone and let a smile crease his face, a searcher still enjoying the uncertainty of the ride.

ROBERT HILBURN

REBORN AGAIN (1997)

Los Angeles Times, December 14, 1997

This interview with Bob Dylan marked the occasion of the release of his acclaimed Time Out of Mind *album; Hilburn is one of the most sympathetic, longtime fans of Dylan and his music and always draws forth a good interview.*—CB

In *Time Out of Mind*, Bob Dylan's most acclaimed album in 20 years, there are moments that sound like the reflections of a man who is nearing the last rites.

"When you think that you've lost everything, you find out that you could always lose a little more," Dylan sings in one song that summarizes the soul of the album, which, in contrast to the youthful optimism of his landmark '60s works, focuses on love and life at a time when options and expectations have been greatly lowered.

So it's surprising to see the classic songwriter in an upbeat, even playful mood as he sits this evening on a couch in a private room just off the lower lobby of a Santa Monica hotel.

Dylan, 56, has disliked interviews for years because he's always asked to reveal something about his personal life or to interpret his lyrics, whether from one of his socially conscious folk anthems like "Blowin' in the Wind" or a snarling, self-affirming rock anthem such as "Like a Rolling Stone."

Even now, he quickly deflects questions about how much his songs, some of which express bitterness over relationships, are from his own experience.

Yet a smile accompanies his rejoinder, rather than the icy defiance that he once might have shown. "They are songs meant to be sung," he says when pressed on the autobiographical aspect. "I don't know if they are meant to be discussed around the coffee table."

It's easy to see why Dylan is in good spirits. *Time Out of Mind*, his first collection of new songs in seven years, was not only hailed by critics, but the album, which entered the pop charts at No. 10 in October, has also already been declared gold (sales of 500,000). It's his first gold studio collection since 1983's *Infidels*. The album (his 40th, including retrospectives) brings his total U.S. sales to nearly 31 million.

Dylan, whose songwriting in the '60s revolutionized rock by bringing commentary and literary ambition to a musical form that had chiefly relied simply on attitude and energy, also received the prestigious Kennedy Center Honor last Sunday in Washington, D.C. About Dylan, President Clinton said, "He probably had more impact on people of my generation than any other artist."

But it becomes clear during the interview that there is a deeper reason for Dylan's sense of satisfaction—one that grows out of what he describes as the rediscovery in recent years of the self-identity as a performer that he lost during the acclaim and hoopla of his '70s and '80s arena and stadium tours.

"I remember playing shows [with Tom Petty and the Heartbreakers in the '80s] and looking out [thinking] I didn't have that many fans coming to see me," he says. "They were coming to see Tom Petty and the Heartbreakers."

About that period, he adds, "I was going on my name for a long time, name and reputation, which was about all I had. I had sort of fallen into an amnesia spell. . . . I didn't feel I knew who I was on stage. . . ."

But Dylan says he regained his sense of identity and purpose in the hundreds of concerts he has done in the '90s, an ambitious series of mostly theater dates that has been dubbed by the media the Never-Ending Tour. That invigorating experience apparently contributed to the creative outburst in the new album.

On the eve of a sold-out, five-night stand at the El Rey Theatre, Dylan—who says he feels fine after being hospitalized in May for treatment of pericarditis—speaks about the new album, the "missing" years and, gingerly, about the success of his son Jakob's band, the Wallflowers.

Question: You seem to be in good spirits. Do you think the word "happy" might even apply?

Answer: I think that it's hard to find happiness as a whole in anything. [laughs] The days of tender youth are gone. I think you can be delirious in your youth, but as you get older, things happen. We take our instruction from the media. The media just gloats over tragedy and sin and shame, so why are people supposed to feel any different?

Q: Some of the words used by critics to describe the songs in the album are . . . brooding, gloomy, misery, wary. Do you see the album that way?

A: I don't know. . . . It's certainly not an album of felicity. . . . I try to live within that line between despondency and hope. I'm suited to walk that line, right between the fire. . . . I see [the album] right straight down the middle of the line, really.

Q: Why were your two albums before this one simply acoustic songs by other writers? Did it take this long to write these songs?

A: I had written these songs, but . . . I forgot about recording for a while. I didn't feel like I wanted to put forth the effort to record anything. The acoustic albums were easy enough. I was pretty content to let it be that.

Q: What was different about this album?

A: Part of the—I don't know what you want to call it—maybe the effectiveness of these songs is the fact that they weren't just written and taken into the studio the way so many of my songs have been, where you are stuck with the arrangement, stuck with who's playing on them, stuck with the lyrics. So many of my records were made that way. So many that people elevate on such a high level were in some sense only first drafts of songs . . . and they have changed over the years. I had lived with these songs long enough to know what I wanted.

Q: The 16-minute "Highlands" is the highlight of the album. How did that song come about?

A: I had the guitar run off an old Charley Patton record [in his head] for years and always wanted to do something with that. I was sitting around, maybe in the dark Delta or maybe in some unthinkable trench somewhere, with that sound in my mind and the dichotomy of the highlands with that seemed to be a path worth pursuing.

Q: What about writing the song? Is it something you do in one sitting or is it something you piece together over time?

A: It starts off as a stream of consciousness thing and you add things to it. I take things from all parts of life and then I see if there is a connection, and if there's a connection I connect them. The riff was just going repeatedly, hypnotically in my head, then the words eventually come along. Probably every song on the album came that way.

Q: There are a dozen lines in that song alone that it'd be interesting to have you talk about, but how about the one with Neil Young? "I'm listening to Neil Young / I gotta turn up the sound / Someone's always yelling, / 'Turn it down.'" Is that a tip of the hat or . . . ?

A: It's anything you want it to be. [smiles] I don't give too much thought to individual lines. If I thought about them in any kind of deep way, maybe I wouldn't use them because I'd always be second-guessing myself. I learned a long time ago to trust my intuition.

Q: How do you feel when one album is praised much more than another one? Do you understand why people respond differently to albums or do you think a lot of it seems arbitrary?

A: I never listen to my albums, once they are completed. I don't want to be reminded. To me, I've done them. I find it like looking into a lifeless mirror. I do, however, listen to this album quite a bit.

Q: If you were so pleased with these songs, why didn't you do them in concert before you recorded them if you had them for so long?

A: That's the funny thing. People don't think they can respond to a song that they haven't heard on a record. It didn't used to be that way, but I think we are living in an age where we are so bombarded—everything from satellite news to biological weapons—and people want to be familiar with something before they are ready to accept it.

Q: Even your fans? Aren't they a pretty adventurous bunch?

A: I don't know. I don't think I have the same fans I had earlier. In fact, I know they aren't the same people. Those fans left me years ago. If I was a fan of me back then, I wouldn't [still] be either.

Q: What do you mean?

A: I wasn't giving anybody anything that they felt comfortable with, and I understood that, but I understood it much later than it was happening.

I don't have any one kind of fan or follower of this kind of music, like say, U2, or Bruce [Springsteen] or any of these young groups today who consistently keep their followers because what they are doing is variations of the same things. My situation is peculiar. I didn't come out of the same environment. My tradition is older than all that. I came out of the environment of folk music.

Q: Is there any way to describe your goals when you were starting out?

A: I knew growing up that I wanted to do something different than anybody else. I wanted to do something that no one else did or could do, and I wanted to do it better than anyone else had. I didn't know where that was going to lead me, but where it did lead me was to folk music at a time when it was totally off the radar screen. Maybe there were 12 people in all of America who even heard of Woody Guthrie, Roscoe Holcomb, the Carter Family, Leadbelly—at least 12 people my age. They were free spirits who took chances, and I never wished to annul any of that spirit.

Q: You've never seemed comfortable with your success and acclaim. Is that true?

A: I'm still not. I still don't consider myself in the same realm as someone like James Taylor or Randy Newman, someone who, in my book, is a "songwriter for the times." I feel my stuff is very hard-edged and not everybody's cup of tea.

Q: You've been touring for more than 30 years now. Do you see a time when you might stop? Or do you think you'll be doing it until your final breath?

A: I could stop any time. . . . I can see an end to everything, really.

Q: You did once stop playing for eight years, during the late '60s. Why were you off the road for so long?

A: I didn't want to go on the road. I didn't feel it was as important to me as personal matters. I had a family. It wouldn't work for me if I was on the road. So I stayed off. Then we came to California . . . and I forgot what I did [on stage] . . . totally. . . . When I got back [on tour in 1974], I was looked upon as a songwriter of a generation or mouthpiece of a generation. That was the slogan put on me at the time. I had to meet that head on.

Good As I Been to You: 1990–Today

Q: Was that uncomfortable?

A: Sure, because when I went back [to touring], nothing was working right for me. . . . I had lost my raison d'être. . . . I didn't know what I was doing out there, people throwing flowers and whatever. I didn't know who they expected me to be. It was a crazy time.

Q: So, what turned it around for you?

A: At a certain point [on the Petty tour], I had a revelation about a bunch of things, which is hard to explain [briefly]. . . . I realized that it was necessary to go out and turn things around.

Q: How did you do that?

A: On some night when lightning strikes, this gift was given back to me and I knew it. . . . The essence was back.

Q: So you learned to enjoy yourself again on stage in recent years?

A: Yes, it took a long time to develop back into what it would have been if I hadn't taken the time off. It's a strange story, I'll admit it.

Q: Speaking of joy, what about Jakob's success with the Wallflowers?

A: It's sensational what has happened to the Wallflowers. It's like one in a million or something.

Q: When you heard he was going to start a band, did you worry about him? Did you advise him at all?

A: It was inconsequential what I thought.

Q: As a father, though, were you worried about all he would have to go through, like the pain of being dropped by his label after the first album?

A: I was concerned after the label dropped him and they still were involved in trying to get another record deal, but he made it on his own. If anything, his name would have held him back. I think that held him back on his first record, to tell you the truth. I think that first record would have been accepted if he wasn't who he was.

Q: What about honors, such as the Kennedy honors? Do you appreciate them?

A: It's always nice to be appreciated, especially while you are still alive.

Chronology

1941

May 24   Born at 9:05 P.M. to Beatty and Abraham Zimmerman, at Saint Mary's Hospital, Duluth, Minnesota

1955

Fall   Starts playing (presumably on piano) with high school band, the Shadow Blasters, through mid-1956

1956

Fall   Forms new band, the Golden Chords, which plays at various events in and around Hibbing, Minnesota, through winter 1958, when band breaks up

1959

Sept. 29   Enrolls at University of Minnesota

Oct.   Walks into Ten O'Clock Scholar, a Minneapolis coffeehouse, and asks if he can play there; gives his name as "Bob Dylan"

1960

Feb.   Regularly plays at the Ten O'Clock Scholar with "Spider" John Koerner, local blues guitarist

Summer   Travels to Denver; reads *Bound for Glory*, instantly becoming a Guthrie fan

Fall   Continues to perform at coffeehouses in Minneapolis

Dec.   Travels to Chicago en route to New York; plays at a sorority house at University of Chicago

1961

Jan. 24   Arrives in New York

Jan. 25   Visits Woody Guthrie at Greystone Hospital in New Jersey

Jan. 29   Performs at Izzy Young's Folklore Center

Feb. 13   Makes first appearance at Gerdes Folk City; continues to perform there at Monday hootenannies

Apr. 11–23	Gets first paying job at Gerdes, as supporting act for John Lee Hooker
mid-May	Returns to Minneapolis
June	Visits Boston
July	Returns to New York
Sept. 26	Begins another two-week residency at Gerdes; opening night reviewed by Robert Shelton of *New York Times*, who hails his performance (review appears on Sept. 29)
Nov. 4	Izzy Young presents Dylan at the Carnegie Recital Hall; only 53 people fill 200 available seats
Nov. 20–22	Records first album, for Columbia, with John Hammond producing

1962

Mar. 19	First album released by Columbia
May	Albert Grossman becomes his manager
Aug. 2	Legally changes his name to Bob Dylan
Dec. 14	Columbia releases first Dylan single, "Mixed Up Confusion"/"Corrina, Corrina," and quickly withdraws it
Dec. 18	Arrives in London to tape BBC radio play

1963

Jan. 14	Records in London with Eric von Schmidt and Dick Farinna for the small label Dobell's 77
Jan. 16	Flies back to New York
Apr. 12	Plays at New York's Town Hall
May 12	Rehearses for appearance on *Ed Sullivan Show*; when told he can't perform the song, "Talkin' John Birch Society Blues," storms out and refuses to appear
May 27	*The Freewheelin' Bob Dylan* released
June 26–28	Appears at Newport Folk Festival in workshop performances and, on the 28th, at an evening concert as guest of Joan Baez
Oct. 26	Plays at Carnegie Hall
Dec. 26	Meets Allen Ginsberg

1964

| Jan. 13 | Columbia releases *The Times They Are A-Changin'*, his third album |
| Feb. 22 | Gives legendary concert at Berkeley Community Theatre; Joan Baez is "surprise" guest |

May 17	Performs at London's Royal Festival Hall to sellout audience
July 26	Headlines closing night of Newport Folk Festival
Oct. 31	Soldout concert at New York's Philharmonic Hall

1965

Mar. 22	*Bringing It All Back Home* released
Apr. 26	Arrives in London to begin British tour documented in film *Don't Look Back*
July 25	"Goes electric" at Newport, backed up by Paul Butterfield's band; audience dismayed, and many folkniks disown their favorite son
Aug. 28	Soldout concert at Forest Hills Stadium, half-acoustic and half-electric; fans perplexed, boo during the electric half of show
Aug. 30	*Highway 61 Revisited* released
Nov. 25	Marries Sara Shirley Lowndes
Dec. 3	Famous San Francisco press conference; transcript published in *Rolling Stone* two years later

1966

Apr. 12	Arrives in Australia for tour
Apr. 23	"Rainy Day Women #12 and 35" reaches no. 2 on *Billboard* charts, becoming his biggest hit single
May 16	*Blonde on Blonde* released
May 27	Famous Royal Albert Hall concert
July 29	Mythic motorcycle accident that leads to over a year of self-imposed exile

1967

Apr.–Oct.	Records *The Basement Tapes*
Dec. 27	*John Wesley Harding* released

1968

Jan. 20	First live appearance in twenty months, at Woody Guthrie Memorial Concert at Carnegie Hall

1969

Apr. 9	*Nashville Skyline* released
June 26	Interviewed by Jann Wenner for *Rolling Stone*; first major interview for the magazine
Aug. 31	Isle of Wight festival

1970

June 8	Ill-fated *Self Portrait* appears
Oct. 21	*New Morning* released

1971

Feb. 8	*Eat the Document* premieres at New York Academy of Music
May	*Tarantula* published; Dylan visits Israel
Aug. 1	The Concert for Bangaladesh

1972

Oct. 1–14	Sessions with Doug Sahm for album *Doug Sahm and Band*
Late Nov.	Begins filming *Pat Garrett and Billy the Kid*

1973

Nov. 5–6	Records *Planet Waves* with the Band

1974

Jan. 3	Opens first tour in eight years at Chicago Stadium, accompanied by the Band
Sept. 16–25	Makes initial recordings for *Blood on the Tracks* in New York
Dec. 27–30	Rerecords *Blood on the Tracks* material in Minneapolis with local musicians

1975

June 25	The highly edited, selected *Basement Tapes* finally "officially" released
Oct. 30	First date in Rolling Thunder Revue tour

1976

Apr. 18	Second leg of Rolling Thunder Revue tour opens at the Civic Center Arena in Lakeland, Florida
Nov. 25	"The Last Waltz" concert with the Band

1977

Mar. 1	Sara Dylan files for divorce

1978

Jan. 25	*Renaldo and Clara* opens
Feb. 20	Gives first-ever performance in Japan, beginning a world tour that goes through the summer
Sept. 15	Begins American leg of world tour in Augusta, Maine

1979

Jan.	Is born again
Aug. 18	*Slow Train Coming* released
Nov.	Two-week residency at Fox Warfield Theater, San Francisco, performing only new, Christian-oriented material; audience reaction is mixed

1980

May 21	*Saved* released
Nov.	Returns for another series of shows at Fox Warfield Theater

1981

June 24	Arrives in London for series of shows at Earls Court Theater

1982

June 6	Surprise guest of Joan Baez at anti-nuclear bomb rally at Rose Bowl

1983

June 6	*New York* magazine reports Dylan has been spending time and studying with the Lubavitcher Hasidim in Brooklyn

1984

May 28	Opens European tour in Verona, Italy

1985

Jan. 28–29	Participates in charity recording "We Are the World"
July 13	Appears at Live Aid accompanied by Keith Richards and Ron Woods; performance a disaster as they cannot hear each other
July 25	Appears at Lenin Stadium in Moscow as part of Russian Poetry Festival
Sept. 22	Performs at Farm Aid backed by the Heartbreakers
Oct. 28	Career-retrospective *Biograph* set appears

1986

Feb. 5	First appearance in tour of New Zealand and Australia
Mar. 5	Begins Japanese tour
June 9	Opens his first American concert tour in five years at Sports Arena in San Diego, accompanied by Tom Petty and the Hearbreakers

1987

July 4	First date in Dylan and the Dead tour
Sept. 7	Performs in Israel
Sept. 10	Opens European tour in Switzerland

1988

Jan. 20	Inducted into Rock and Roll Hall of Fame in its second annual ceremony
Early–mid-May	Records first album with "The Traveling Wilburys" (George Harrison, Roy Orbison, Jeff Lynne, and Tom Petty) over a series of ten days
June 7	Begins American tour with three-piece backup band featuring G. E. Smith on lead guitar

1989

Sept. 22	*Oh Mercy* released
Nov. 21	Shoots video to promote song "Political World"

1990

Jan. 18	First South American show at Morumbi Stadium, São Paulo, Brazil
Jan. 29	Begins new European tour in Paris, France

1991

Mar. 26	*The Bootleg Series, Vols. 1–3* issued

1992

Oct. 18	30th Anniversary concert at Madison Square Garden
Nov. 3	Acoustic-folk album *Good As I Been to You* released

1993

Jan. 17	Performs at Bill Clinton's first inaugural
Aug. 20	First show in two-month tour with Santana
Nov. 16–17	Supper Club appearances in New York, filmed for projected MTV show; some material released on the interactive CD-ROM *Highway 61 Revisited*

1994

Aug. 14	Woodstock II
Nov. 17–18	Films *MTV Unplugged*

1995

Nov. 19	Participates in all-star tribute for Frank Sinatra's eightieth birthday

1996

Feb. 2	Plays private concert for Nomura Securities International in Phoenix, Arizona

June 29	Hyde Park concert with Eric Clapton, Alanis Morrisette, and the Who
Sept. 28	Nominated for Nobel Prize in Literature
Nov. 9	Licenses "The Times They Are A-Changin'" to Bank of Montreal for television commercial

1997

Winter	Hospitalized with a heart infection
Sept. 30	*Time Out of Mind* released
Nov.	Performs before the Pope
Dec. 7	Kennedy Center Honoree

Discography

Bob Dylan
Columbia CL 1779/CS 8579
Released Mar. 19, 1962
You're No Good | Talking New York | In My Time of Dyin' | Man of Constant Sorrow | Fixin' to Die | Pretty Peggy-O | Highway 51 Blues | Gospel Plow | Baby, Let Me Follow You Down | House of the Rising Sun | Freight Train Blues | Song to Woody | See That My Grave Is Kept Clean

The Freewheelin' Bob Dylan
Columbia CL 1986/CS 8786
Released May 27, 1963
Blowin' in the Wind | Girl of the North Country | Masters of War | Down the Highway | Bob Dylan's Blues | A Hard Rain's A-Gonna Fall | Don't Think Twice, It's All Right | Bob Dylan's Dream | Oxford Town | Talkin' World War III Blues | Corrina, Corrina | Honey, Just Allow Me One More Chance | I Shall Be Free

The Times They Are A-Changin'
Columbia CL 2105/CS 8905
Released Jan. 13, 1964
The Times They Are A-Changin' | Ballad of Hollis Brown | With God on Our Side | One Too Many Mornings | North Country Blues | Only a Pawn in Their Game | Boots of Spanish Leather | When the Ship Comes In | The Lonesome Death of Hattie Carroll | Restless Farewell

Another Side of Bob Dylan
Columbia CL 2105/CS 8905
Released Aug. 8, 1964
All I Really Want to Do | Black Crow Blues | Spanish Harlem Incident | Chimes of Freedom | I Shall Be Free No. 10 | To Ramona | Motorpsycho Nightmare | My Back Pages | I Don't Believe You (She Acts Like We Never Have Met) | Ballad in Plain D | It Ain't Me, Babe

Bringing It All Back Home
Columbia CL 2328/CS 9128
Released Mar. 22, 1965
Subterranean Homesick Blues | She Belongs to Me | Maggie's Farm | Love Minus Zero/No Limit | Outlaw Blues | On the Road Again | Bob Dylan's 115th Dream | Mr. Tambourine Man | Gates of Eden | It's Alright, Ma (I'm Only Bleeding) | It's All Over Now, Baby Blue

Highway 61 Revisited
Columbia CL 2389/CS 9189
Released Aug. 30, 1965
Like a Rolling Stone | Tombstone Blues | It Takes a Lot to Laugh, It Takes a Train to Cry | From a Buick 6 | Ballad of a Thin Man | Queen Jane Approximately | Highway 61 Revisited | Just Like Tom Thumb's Blues | Desolation Row

Blonde on Blonde
Columbia C2L 41/CS8 841
Released May 16, 1966
Rainy Day Women #12 & 35 | Pledging My Time | Visions of Johanna | One of Us Must Know (Sooner or Later) | I Want You | Stuck Inside of Mobile with the Memphis Blues Again | Leopard-Skin Pill-Box Hat | Just Like a Woman | Most Likely You Go Your Way and I'll Go Mine | Temporary Like Achilles | Absolutely Sweet Marie | 4th Time Around | Obviously Five Believers | Sad-Eyed Lady of the Lowlands

Bob Dylan's Greatest Hits
Columbia KCL 2263/KCS 9463
Released Mar. 27, 1967
Rainy Day Women #12 & 35 | Blowin' in the Wind | The Times They Are A-Changin' | It Ain't Me, Babe | Like a Rolling Stone | Mr. Tambourine Man | Subterranean Homesick Blues | I Want You | Positively 4th Street | Just Like a Woman

John Wesley Harding
Columbia CL 2804/CS 9604
Released Dec. 27, 1967
John Wesley Harding | As I Went Out One Morning | I Dreamed I Saw St. Augustine | All Along the Watchtower | The Ballad of Frankie Lee and

Judas Priest | Drifter's Escape | Dear Landlord | I Am a Lonesome Hobo | I Pity the Poor Immigrant | The Wicked Messenger | Down Along the Cove | I'll Be Your Baby Tonight

Nashville Skyline
Columbia KCS 9825
Released Apr. 29, 1969
Girl of the North Country | Nashville Skyline Rag | To Be Alone with You | I Threw It All Away | Peggy Day | Lay, Lady, Lay | One More Night | Tell Me That It Isn't True | Country Pie | Tonight I'll Be Staying Here with You

Self Portrait
Columbia C2X 30050
Released June 8, 1970
All the Tired Horses | Alberta #1 | I Forgot More Than You'll Ever Know | Days of 49 | Early Mornin' Rain | In Search of Little Sadie | Let It Be Me | Little Sadie | Woogie Boogie | Belle Isle | Living the Blues | Like a Rolling Stone | Copper Kettle | Gotta Travel On | Blue Moon | The Boxer | Quinn the Eskimo (The Mighty Quinn) | Take Me as I Am | Take a Message to Mary | It Hurts Me Too | Minstrel Boy | She Belongs to Me | Wigwam | Alberta #2

New Morning
Columbia KC 30290
Released Oct. 21, 1970
If Not for You | Day of the Locusts | Time Passes Slowly | Went to See the Gypsy | Winterlude | If Dogs Run Free | New Morning | Sign on the Window | One More Weekend | The Man in Me | Three Angels | Father of Night

Bob Dylan's Greatest Hits, Vol. 2
Columbia KG 31120
Released Nov. 17, 1971
Watching the River Flow | Don't Think Twice, It's All Right | Lay, Lady, Lay | Stuck Inside of Mobile with the Memphis Blues Again | I'll Be Your Baby Tonight | All I Really Want to Do | My Back Pages | Maggie's Farm | Tonight I'll Be Staying Here with You | She Belongs to Me | All Along the Watchtower | Quinn the Eskimo (The Mighty Quinn) | Just Like Tom Thumb's Blues | A Hard Rain's A-Gonna Fall | If Not for You | It's All Over

Now, Baby Blue | Tomorrow Is a Long Time | When I Paint My Masterpiece | I Shall Be Released | You Ain't Goin' Nowhere | Down in the Flood

Pat Garrett and Billy the Kid
Columbia KC 32460
Released July 13, 1973
Billy (Main Title Theme) | Cantina Theme (Workin' for the Law) | Billy 1 | Bunkhouse Theme | River Theme | Turkey Chase | Knockin' on Heaven's Door | Final Theme | Billy 4 | Billy 7

Dylan
Columbia PC 32747
Released Nov. 16, 1973
Lily of the West | Can't Help Falling in Love | Sarah Jane | Mr. Bojangles | The Ballad of Ira Hayes | Mary Ann | Big Yellow Taxi | A Fool Such As I | Spanish Is the Loving Tongue

Planet Waves
Asylum S73 1003 (reissued by Columbia as PC 37637 in April 1982)
Released Jan. 17, 1974
On a Night Like This | Going, Going, Gone | Tough Mama | Hazel | Something There Is about You | Forever Young | Forever Young | Dirge | You Angel You | Never Say Goodbye | Wedding Song

Before the Flood
Aslym S 201 (reissued by Columbia as KC 37661 in April 1982)
Released June 20, 1974
Most Likely You Go Your Way and I'll Go Mine | Lay, Lady, Lay | Rainy Day Women #12 & 35 | Knockin' on Heaven's Door | It Ain't Me, Babe | Ballad of a Thin Man | Up on Cripple Creek | I Shall Be Released | Endless Highway | The Night They Drove Old Dixie Down | Stage Fright | Don't Think Twice, It's All Right | Just Like a Woman | It's Alright, Ma (I'm Only Bleeding) | The Shape I'm In | When You Awake | The Weight | All Along the Watchtower | Highway 61 Revisited | Like a Rolling Stone | Blowin' in the Wind

Blood on the Tracks
Columbia PC 33235
Released Jan. 17, 1975
Tangled Up in Blue | Simple Twist of Fate | You're a Big Girl Now | Idiot Wind | You're Gonna Make Me Lonesome When You Go | Meet Me in the Morning | Lily, Rosemary and the Jack of Hearts | If You See Her, Say Hello | Shelter from the Storm | Buckets of Rain

The Basement Tapes
Columbia C2 33682
Released June 26, 1975
Odds and Ends | Orange Juice Blues (Blues for Breakfast) | Million Dollar Bash | Yazoo Street Scandal | Goin' to Acapulco | Katie's Been Gone | Lo and Behold! | Bessie Smith | Clothes Line | Apple Suckling Tree | Please, Mrs. Henry | Tears of Rage | Too Much of Nothing | Yea! Heavy and a Bottle of Bread | Ain't No More Cane | Down in the Flood | Ruben Remus | Tiny Montgomery | You Ain't Goin' Nowhere | Don't Ya Tell Henry | Nothing Was Delivered | Open the Door, Homer | Long-Distance Operator | This Wheel's on Fire

Desire
Columbia PC 33893
Released Jan. 16, 1976
Hurricane | Isis | Mozambique | One More Cup of Coffee (Valley Below) | Oh, Sister | Joey | Romance in Durango | Black Diamond Bay | Sara

Hard Rain
Columbia PC 34349
Released Sept. 10, 1976
Maggie's Farm | One Too Many Mornings | Stuck Inside of Mobile with the Memphis Blues Again | Oh, Sister | Lay, Lady, Lay | Shelter from the Storm | You're a Big Girl Now | I Threw It All Away | Idiot Wind

Street Legal
Columbia JC 35453
Released June 15, 1978
Changing of the Guards | New Pony | No Time to Think | Baby, Stop Crying | Is Your Love in Vain? | Senor (Tales of Yankee Power) | True Love Tends to Forget | We Better Talk This Over | Where Are You Tonight?

At Budokan
Columbia PC2 36067
Released Nov. 22, 1978 (Japan); U.S. and worldwide release on Apr. 23, 1979
Mr. Tambourine Man | Shelter from the Storm | Love Minus Zero/No Limit | Ballad of a Thin Man | Don't Think Twice, It's All Right | Maggie's Farm | One More Cup of Coffee (Valley Below) | Like a Rolling Stone | I Shall Be Released | Is Your Love in Vain? | Going, Going, Gone | Blowin' in the Wind | Just Like a Woman | Oh, Sister | Simple Twist of Fate | All Along the Watchtower | I Want You | All I Really Want to Do | Knockin' on Heaven's Door | It's Alright, Ma (I'm Only Bleeding) | Forever Young | The Times They Are A-Changin'

Slow Train Coming
Columbia PC 36120
Released Aug. 18, 1979
Gotta Serve Somebody | Precious Angel | I Believe in You | Slow Train | Gonna Change My Way of Thinking | Do Right to Me Baby | When You Gonna Wake Up? | Man Gave Names to All the Animals | When He Returns

Saved
Columbia FC 36553
Released June 20, 1980
A Satisfied Mind | Saved | Covenant Woman | What Can I Do For You? | Solid Rock | Pressing On | In the Garden | Saving Grace | Are You Ready?

Shot of Love
Columbia TC 36496
Released Aug. 12, 1981
Shot of Love | Heart of Mine | Property of Jesus | Lenny Bruce | Watered Down Love | The Groom's Still Waiting at the Altar | Dead Man, Dead Man | In the Summertime | Trouble | Every Grain of Sand

Infidels
Columbia QC 38819
Released Nov. 1, 1983
Jokerman | Sweetheart Like You | Neighborhood Bully | License to Kill | Man of Peace | Union Sundown | I and I | Don't Fall Apart on Me Tonight

Real Live

Columbia FC 39944

Released Dec. 3, 1984

Highway 61 Revisited | Maggie's Farm | I and I | License to Kill | It Ain't Me, Babe | Tangled Up in Blue | Masters of War | Ballad of a Thin Man | Girl of the North Country | Tombstone Blues

Empire Burlesque

Columbia FC 40110

Released June 8, 1985

Tight Connection to My Heart (Has Anybody Seen My Love) | Seeing the Real You at Last | I'll Remember You | Clean-Cut Kid | Never Gonna Be the Same Again | Trust Yourself | Emotionally Yours | When the Night Comes Falling from the Sky | Something's Burning, Baby | Dark Eyes

Biograph

Columbia C5X 38830

Released Oct. 28, 1985

Lay, Lady, Lay | Baby, Let Me Follow You Down | If Not for You | I'll Be Your Baby Tonight | I'll Keep It with Mine | The Times They Are A-Changin' | Blowin' in the Wind | Masters of War | The Lonesome Death of Hattie Carroll | Percy's Song | Mixed Up Confusion | Tombstone Blues | The Groom's Still Waiting at the Altar | Most Likely You Go Your Way and I'll Go Mine | Like a Rolling Stone | Lay Down Your Weary Tune | Subterranean Homesick Blues | I Don't Believe You (She Acts Like We Never Have Met) | Visions of Johanna | Every Grain of Sand | Quinn the Eskimo (The Mighty Quinn) | Mr. Tambourine Man | Dear Landlord | It Ain't Me, Babe | You Angel You | Million Dollar Bash | To Ramona | You're a Big Girl Now | Abandoned Love | Tangled Up in Blue | It's All Over Now, Baby Blue | Can You Please Crawl Out Your Window? | Positively 4th Street | Isis | Jet Pilot | Caribbean Wind | Up to Me | Baby, I'm in the Mood for You | I Wanna Be Your Lover | I Want You | Heart of Mine | On a Night Like This | Just Like a Woman | Romance in Durango | Senor (Tales of Yankee Power) | Gotta Serve Somebody | I Believe in You | Time Passes Slowly | I Shall Be Released | Knockin' on Heaven's Door | All Along the Watchtower | Solid Rock | Forever Young

Knocked Out Loaded
Columbia OC 40439
Released Aug. 8, 1986
You Wanna Ramble | They Killed Him | Driftin' Too Far from Shore | Precious Memories | Maybe Someday | Brownsville Girl | Got My Mind Made Up | Under Your Spell

Down in the Groove
Columbia C 40957
Released May 31, 1988
Let's Stick Together | When Did You Leave Heaven? | Sally Sue Brown | Death Is Not the End | Had a Dream about You, Baby | Ugliest Girl in the World | Silvio | Ninety Miles an Hour (Down a Dead End Street) | Shenandoah | Rank Strangers to Me

Dylan & the Dead
Columbia OC 45056
Released Feb. 6, 1989
Slow Train | I Want You | Gotta Serve Somebody | Queen Jane Approximately | Joey | All Along the Watchtower | Knockin' on Heaven's Door

Oh Mercy
Columbia OC 45281
Released Sept. 22, 1989
Political World | Where Teardrops Fall | Everything Is Broken | Ring Them Bells | Man in the Long Black Coat | Most of the Time | What Good Am I? | Disease of Conceit | What Was It You Wanted? | Shooting Star

Under the Red Sky
Columbia CK 46794
Released Sept. 11, 1990
Wiggle Wiggle | Under the Red Sky | Unbelievable | Born in Time | T.V. Talkin' Song | 10,000 Men | 2 times 2 | God Knows | Handy Dandy | Cat's in the Well

The Bootleg Series Volumes 1–3: Rare and Unreleased 1961–1979
Columbia C3K 47382
Released Mar. 26, 1991

Hard Times in New York Town | He Was a Friend of Mine | Man on the Street | No More Auction Block | House Carpenter | Talking Bear Mountain Picnic Massacre Blues | Let Me Die in My Footsteps | Rambling, Gambling Willie | Talkin' Hava Negeilah Blues | Quit Your Low Down Ways | Worried Blues | Kingsport Town | Walkin' Down the Line | Walls of Red Wing | Paths of Victory | Talkin' John Birch Paranoid Blues | Who Killed Davey Moore? | Only a Hobo | Moonshiner | When the Ship Comes In | The Times They Are A-Changin' | Last Thoughts on Woody Guthrie | Seven Curses | Eternal Circle | Suze (The Cough Song) | Mama, You Been on My Mind | Farewell Angelina | Subterranean Homesick Blues | If You Gotta Go, Go Now | Sitting on a Barbed-Wire Fence | Like a Rolling Stone | It Takes a Lot to Laugh, It Takes a Train to Cry | I'll Keep It with Mine | She's Your Lover Now | I Shall Be Released | Santa Fe | If Not for You | Wallflower | Nobody 'Cept You | Tangled Up in Blue | Call Letter Blues | Idiot Wind | If You See Her, Say Hello | Golden Loom | Catfish | Seven Days | Ye Shall Be Changed | Every Grain of Sand | You Changed My Life | Need a Woman | Angelina | Someone's Got a Hold of My Heart | Tell Me | Lord Protect My Child | Foot of Pride | Blind Willie McTell | When the Night Comes Falling from the Sky | Series of Dreams

Good As I Been to You
Columbia CK 53200
Released Nov. 3, 1992
Frankie & Albert | Jim Jones | Blackjack Davey | Canadee-i-o | Sittin' on Top of the World | Little Maggie | Hard Times | Step It Up and Go | Tomorrow Night | Arthur McBride | You're Gonna Quit Me | Diamond Joe | Froggie Went a Courtin'

The 30th Anniversary Concert Celebration
Released Aug. 24, 1993
Like a Rolling Stone | Leopard-Skin Pill-Box Hat | Introduction by Kris Kristofferson | Blowin' in the Wind | Foot of Pride | Masters of War | The Times They Are A-Changin' | It Ain't Me, Babe | What Was It You Wanted? | I'll Be Your Baby Tonight | Highway 61 Revisited | Seven Days | Just Like a Woman | When the Ship Comes In | You Ain't Goin' Nowhere | Just Like Tom Thumb's Blues | All Along the Watchtower | I Shall Be Released | Don't Think Twice, It's All Right | Emotionally Yours | When I Paint My Masterpiece | Absolutely Sweet Marie | License to Kill | Rainy Day Women #12 & 35 | Mr. Tambourine Man | It's Alright, Ma (I'm Only

Bleeding) | My Back Pages | Knockin' on Heaven's Door | Girl of the North
Country

World Gone Wrong
Columbia CK 57590
Released Oct. 26, 1993
World Gone Wrong | Love Henry | Ragged & Dirty | Blood in My Eyes |
Broke Down Engine | Delia | Stack A Lee | Two Soldiers | Jack-A-Roe |
Lone Pilgrim

Bob Dylan's Greatest Hits, Vol. 3
Columbia CK 66783
Released Nov. 15, 1994
Tangled Up in Blue | Changing of the Guards | The Groom's Still Waiting
at the Altar | Hurricane | Forever Young | Jokerman | Dignity | Silvio | Ring
Them Bells | Gotta Serve Somebody | Series of Dreams | Brownsville Girl |
Under the Red Sky | Knockin' on Heaven's Door

MTV Unplugged
Columbia CK 67000
Released May 2, 1995
Tombstone Blues | Shooting Star | All Along the Watchtower | The Times
They Are A-Changin' | John Brown | Rainy Day Women #12 & 35 |
Desolation Row | Dignity | Knockin' on Heaven's Door | Like a Rolling
Stone | With God on Our Side

Time Out of Mind
Columbia CK 68556
Released Sept. 30, 1997
Love Sick | Dirt Road Blues | Standing in the Doorway | Million Miles |
Tryin' to Get to Heaven | 'Til I Fell in Love with You | Not Dark Yet | Cold
Irons Bound | Make You Feel My Love | Can't Wait | Highlands

Bob Dylan's Official Rarities

COMPILED BY ALAN FRASER

Revised list of officially released Bob tracks not so far available on a currently available Bob CD in the United States. There's more than a boxed set-full!

Definition of "official" is that they must have been released legally by a recognized label, e.g., Columbia, Warner Brothers or Vanguard. I have included promotional items issued by these companies that were not made available to the general public at the time, but which are now in circulation.

Bootleg or "gray import" items are not included. I have also omitted:

Tracks where Bob contributes to other artists' albums only instrumentally or with backup vocals (exceptions are three tracks included on the Japanese promo *Mr. D's Collection* volumes)

Bob's appearances on TV and radio shows that have never been officially released on audio albums or videos

Tracks from official albums that appear on "various artist" compilation albums

Interview discs

This is a chronological (as far as I can make it) list of all the rarities that I know about.

Thanks to Roger Ford, Peter Gilmer, David Grossman, John Howells, Masato Kato, Les Kokay, Robert Ovrebo, Vernon Purnell, Andrew Russ, Ben Taylor, Sam C. Visser, Carsten Wohlfeld, Matthew Zuckerman and anyone else who's written to me about this matter that I've forgotten to credit.

Queries

1. Previously unknown version of "When I Paint My Masterpiece" played on the radio in the United States in 1978–79—this sounds like the

live version from *Renaldo & Clara*, but it has not been otherwise reported as a radio station promo.

2. Reputed Brazilian 1979 single B-side version of "Trouble in Mind" with reinstated verse.

If you know of any officially released item not on this list, please let me know.

Alan Fraser
November 1997
Revised April 3, 1998

A Chronological List of Rare Bob Items

Bob's first official recording appearance was playing harmonica in 1961 on the title track of Harry Belafonte's *Midnight Special* album.

Part 1: 1960s

Carolyn Hester's first self-titled album, 1962:
1. "I'll Fly Away." This track is included because it's on the Japanese promo, *Mr D's Collection, Vol. 1*. Bob plays harmonica on this track and two others on the original album. The album was re-released in 1994 on CD, stickered as featuring Bob Dylan, plus two alternate takes with Bob performing. The track "I'll Fly Away" is also available on a 1992 Rhino CD *Troubadours of the Folk Era Vol. 1* (R2 70262).

Broadside Reunion (as Blind Boy Grunt), released 1972 on Broadside/Folkways Records, recordings 1962–63:
2. "Train A-Travelin'"
3. "(I'd Hate to Be You on That) Dreadful Day"
4. "The Death of Emmett Till"
5. "The Ballad of Donald White"

"Mixed Up Confusion" single, Dec. 1962:
6. A-side—"Mixed Up Confusion," now the original single is on the revised *Biograph*; the rarities are the alternate (mono) take found on *Masterpieces* (#86) and the remix of it found on the original *Biograph* (#110)
7. B-side—"Corrina, Corrina," alternate take to *Freewheelin'* version

Test pressing of *The Freewheelin' Bob Dylan*, Apr. 1963:
8. "Rocks & Gravel"
9. "Talkin' John Birch Paranoid Blues" (not same as *The Bootleg Series* version)

Newport Broadside (Topical Songs), Vanguard, July 1963:
10. "Ye Playboys & Playgirls" (with Pete Seeger)
11. "With God on Our Side" (with Joan Baez), now also on *Joan Baez Live at Newport* CD #175

Fontana 7" EPs (UK), 1963
12. "Ye Playboys & Playgirls" (with Pete Seeger) (same as #10)
13. "With God on Our Side" (with Joan Baez) (same as #11)

Evening Concerts at Newport Vol. 1, Vanguard, July 1963:
14. "Blowin' in the Wind" (with Joan Baez)

We Shall Overcome, Aug. 1963:
15. "Only a Pawn in Their Game"

Broadside Ballads Vol. 1 (as Blind Boy Grunt), released Broadside Records (Folkways), Oct. 1963, recordings Jan.–Feb. 1963:
16. "Talkin' Devil"
17. "John Brown" (original version)
18. "Only a Hobo" (not same version as on *The Bootleg Series*)
(Happy Traum also performs "Let Me Die in My Footsteps" on this album)
19. "With God on Our Side," Parts 1 & 2: A- & B-sides of single, 1964
20. "It Ain't Me, Babe," 1964: different mix on promo

Columbia Miami Convention Message promo, May 1965, recorded in U.K.:
21. "If You Gotta Go, Go Now" (excerpt)

Don't Look Back video, 1965:
22. Live footage from the 1965 England tour, but only fragments of songs
23. "Can You Please Crawl Out Your Window?" July 1965: early version released as "Positively 4th Street" by mistake

24. "Like a Rolling Stone," 1965: radio station promo with the song split over the A- & B-sides (Evidence of this item's existence is disputed.)

Early withdrawn pressing of *Highway 61 Revisited*, Aug. 1965; also Japanese release of album:
25. "From a Buick 6" (alternate take with harmonica intro)

Columbia Disco Teen 66 compilation album, 1966:
26. "Positively 4th Street" (alternate mix, longer)
27. "(Sooner or Later) One of Us Must Know," 1966: unfaded single edit (also included on mono release of *Blonde on Blonde*)
28. "Rainy Day Women #12 & 35," 1966: single edit
29. "Pledging My Time," 1966: single edit
30. French EP (5660): includes #28 & #29 plus the single/mono album version of "(Sooner or Later) One of Us Must Know"
31. "Just Like Tom Thumb's Blues," June 1966: live at Liverpool, May 1966, B-side of "I Want You" (also on *Masterpieces*)
32. "If You Gotta Go, Go Now," July 1967: recorded in 1965, not same as *The Bootleg Series* version: Benelux only

Dutch Greatest Hits album, 1967:
33. "Pledging My Time" (alternate mix)
34. "4th Time Around" (alternate mix)

Tribute to Woody Guthrie with the Band, Jan. 1968:
35. "I Ain't Got No Home"
36. "Dear Mrs. Roosevelt"
37. "Grand Coulee Dam"

Columbia compilation *The Music People*, 1968:
38. "Grand Coulee Dam" (with the Band, Jan. 1968; same as #37)

Johnny Cash: The Man and His Music video:
39. Includes Bob and Johnny duetting on "One Too Many Mornings," 1969 (song incorrectly titled as "A Thousand Miles Behind")

Part 2: 1970s

New Morning, Oct. 1970:
40. Early copies of the album have Bob saying "OK, here we go" at start of title track; later deleted

"Spanish Is the Loving Tongue," June 1971:
41. B-side of "Watching the River Flow," not version #52 on *Dylan* (also on *Masterpieces*)

Earl Scruggs Performing with His Family & Friends, Columbia, mid-1971:
42. "Nashville Skyline Rag" (Earl Scruggs on banjo and Bob on guitar, recorded at Tom Allen's home, Carmel, N.Y.)

Concert for Bangladesh, Aug. 1971:
43. "A Hard Rain's A-Gonna Fall"
44. "It Takes a Lot to Laugh, It Takes a Train to Cry"
45. "Blowin' in the Wind"
46. "Mr. Tambourine Man"
47. "Just Like a Woman"

George Jackson single, Nov. 1971:
48. A-side, "George Jackson"—Big Band version
49. B-side, "George Jackson"—acoustic version
(#48 is on *Masterpieces* and also on the Japanese promo items *Mr. D's Collection*, Vols. 1, 2 & 3, #49 is on Vols. 1 & 3 of *Mr. D's* only)

Doug Sahm & Band, Dec. 1972:
50. "Wallflower" (with Doug Sahm)

Roger McGuinn's first self-named solo album, 1973:
51. "I'm So Restless" by Roger McGuinn—again included because it's on the Japanese promo *Mr. D's Collection, Vol. 1*. Bob plays harmonica and gets a name check in the lyrics. The album is now available on CD (Edsel ED CD 281). "I'm So Restless" is also available on the McGuinn solo Columbia compilation CD *Born to Rock and Roll*.

Dylan, Nov. 1973:
52. "Spanish Is the Loving Tongue"
53. "Lily of the West"
54. "Sara Jane"
55. "A Fool Such As I"
56. "I Can't Help Falling in Love"
57. "Mr. Bojangles"
58. "Big Yellow Taxi"

59. "Mary Ann"
60. "Ballad of Ira Hayes"
This album has never been issued on CD in the United States, although it has been released in Europe as *Dylan (A Fool Such As I)* and is available from import sources

"All Along the Watchtower" (single with the Band), summer 1974:
61. Reputedly not same version as on *Before the Flood*.

Quadraphonic release of *Nashville Skyline*, 1974:
62. Many tracks were mixed differently; "Country Pie" is 16 seconds longer

Quadraphonic release of *Planet Waves*, 1974:
63. Many tracks were mixed differently; the second "Forever Young" has a longer intro

Test pressing of *Blood on the Tracks*, Nov. 1974, (unreleased alternate versions):
64. "Lily, Rosemary & the Jack of Hearts"
65. "You're a Big Girl Now" (original version, remixed on *Biograph*)
66. "Idiot Wind" (not *The Bootleg Series* version)
67. "If You See Her, Say Hello" (not *The Bootleg Series* version)
68. "Tangled Up in Blue" (not *The Bootleg Series* version)

Eric Clapton, *No Reason to Cry*, 1976:
69. "Sign Language" (with Eric Clapton)

Bette Midler, *Songs for the New Depression*, 1976 (recorded late 1975):
70. "Nuggets of Rain (Buckets of Rain)" (with Bette Midler)

Quadraphonic vinyl version of *Desire*, Jan. 1976; has mistakes in:
71. "Joey"
72. "Romance in Durango"

"Hurricane" singles, 1976:
73. Parts 1 & 2: A- & B-sides of single
74. Parts 1 & 2: A- & B-sides of single (radio station version with swear-word beeped)

"Stuck Inside of Mobile with the Memphis Blues Again" single, Nov. 1976:

75. "Stuck Inside of Mobile with the Memphis Blues Again": A-side—edit of live version from the *Hard Rain* album

76. "Rita May": B-side—*Desire* outtake, recorded July 1975 (also on *Masterpieces* #90)

The Last Waltz with the Band, Nov. 1976:

77. "Baby Let Me Follow You Down"

78. "I Don't Believe You"

79. "Forever Young"

80. "Baby Let Me Follow You Down" (reprise)

81. "I Shall Be Released"

Four Songs from *Renaldo & Clara* promo EP, Jan. 1978, with the Rolling Thunder Revue:

82. "People Get Ready"

83. "It Ain't Me, Babe" (released on 2nd European "Dignity" CD single #165)

84. "Never Let Me Go"

85. "Isis" (B-side of "Jokerman" single, 1984, also released on *Biograph*, 1985)

Masterpieces, Australia, 1978:

86. "Mixed Up Confusion," 1962 (alternate mono take of single #6)

87. "Just Like Tom Thumb's Blues," June 1966 (live at Liverpool, May 1966; same as #31)

88. "Spanish Is the Loving Tongue," June 1971: B-side of "Watching the River Flow," #41, not version #52 from *Dylan*

89. "George Jackson"—Big Band version, Nov. 1971, same as #48

90. "Rita May," July 1975 (same as #76)

90a. "Baby Stop Crying," July 1978—Columbia 3–10805 promo 45 has long (album) version on one side, short version (radio edit) on the other

"Gotta Serve Somebody" single, Aug. 1979:

91. Columbia 1–11072 promo 45 has long (album) version on one side, short version (radio edit) on the other

91a. "Trouble in Mind," Aug. 1979: B-side of regular single with one verse omitted (It is reported that the Brazilian issue of this single had the full song.)

Mr. D's Collection Vol. 1—LP (Japanese promo):
92. "I'm So Restless"—Roger McGuinn (same as #51)
93. "I'll Fly Away"—Carolyn Hester (same as #1)
94. "Mixed Up Confusion"—this is reportedly the version that appeared on the original issue of *Biograph*, #110, namely a remixed stereo version of #86 from *Masterpieces*, and not the original single #6
95. "From a Buick 6"—alternate take with harmonica intro (same as #25)
96. "George Jackson"—acoustic version (same as #49)
97. "Can You Please Crawl Out Your Window?"—version mistakenly released as "Positively 4th Street" (same as #23)
98. "Just Like Tom Thumb's Blues"—live version B-side of single (same as #31)
99. "Spanish Is the Loving Tongue"—single version (same as #41)
100. "Nashville Skyline Rag," Feb. 1969—Earl Scruggs version (same as #42)
101. "George Jackson"—Big Band version (same as #48)

Mr. D's Collection Vol. 2—4-song Japanese promo EP (same versions as on the LP):
102. "Mixed Up Confusion" (#94)
103. "Just Like Tom Thumb's Blues" (#98 = #31)
104. "Can You Please Crawl Out Your Window?" (#97 = #23)
105. "George Jackson"—Big Band version (#101 = #48)

Part 3: 1980s

106. "Let It Be Me," July 1981: B-side of "Heart of Mine," recorded May 1981, not *Self Portrait* version (Europe only)

Infidels European singles, Oct. 1983—The U.K. and some countries have "Union Sundown" as A-side, rest of Europe has "I & I" as the A-side:
107. "Angel Flying Too Close to the Ground"
108. "Jokerman," Apr. 1984: single edit
109. "We Are the World," Jan. 1985: Bob contributes vocals to "USA for Africa" single

Original version of *Biograph*, 1985:
110. "Mixed Up Confusion": same version as #94 on *Mr. D's Collection*,

Vol. 1, i.e., a stereo remix of alternate version #86 on *Masterpieces*, not the original single #6

111. "Tight Connection to My Heart," 1985: single edit
112. "When the Night Comes Falling from the Sky," 1985: single edit
113. "Ain't Gonna Play Sun City," Dec. 1985: Bob contributes vocals to "Artists United Against Apartheid" single
114. "Hard to Handle," the HBO special from the 1986 Australian tour with Tom Petty and the Heartbreakers; also released on VHS.

Band of the Hand film soundtrack, 1986:
115. "Band of the Hand" (single version, non-Bob instrumental track as B-side)
116. "Band of the Hand" (album version; different mix and longer)

Hearts of Fire film soundtrack, 1986:
117. "The Usual"
118. "Night after Night"
119. "Had a Dream about You, Baby" (different mix from *Down in the Groove* version)

Kurtis Blow, *Kingdom Blow*, Sept. 1986:
120. "Street Rock" (Bob contributes vocals)

Down in the Groove promo cassette, May 1988:
121. "Important Words"

Argentinean version of *Down in the Groove* album, June 1988:
122. "Got Love if You Want It"
123. "Handle with Care," 1988: Wilbury single, longer on CD and 12"
124. "End of the Line," 1988: Wilbury single, longer on CD and 12"

U2, *Rattle & Hum*, 1988:
125. "Love Rescue Me"
126. "Hawkmoon"

Flashback film soundtrack, Nov. 1989:
127. "People Get Ready" (new recording, not *Renaldo & Clara* version #82)

Woody Guthrie/Leadbelly tribute album *Folkways: A Vision Shared*, 1989:
128. "Pretty Boy Floyd"

"Series of Dreams," 1989:
129. Edit on promo single (second verse missing)
130. Five-track promo CD has alternate take with second verse present, but several lyric differences from the version on *The Bootleg Series* and *Greatest Hits Vol. 3*.
131. "Dead Man, Dead Man," 1989: live version from New Orleans, Nov. 1981, on *Everything Is Broken* CD and 12" European singles, also B-side of U.S. cassette single
132. "Nobody's Child," 1989: Traveling Wilburys, included on *Romanian Angel Appeal* charity album, also single (Dave Stewart track as B-side)

Part 4: 1990s

Blonde on Blonde CD versions:
133. The album was remixed in the 1970s, and the difference is especially noticeable on "Fourth Time Around" (no bass harmonica), for instance. Then when the album was released on CD, the mix used was closer to the original, but "Sad-Eyed Lady of the Lowlands" and "Temporary Like Achilles" were edited to fit both albums on one CD. When the allowable length increased, "Achilles" was restored, and then a later remastering restored "Sad-Eyed Lady of the Lowlands" also. These are both still in shortened form on the U.K. CD; baffling, as this is pressed in Austria, and the same plant also presses a version with a different catalogue number which has the full-length tracks—presumably this is for the rest of Europe, though it occasionally turns up in England (Andrew Russ and Roger Ford).

General agreement is that, in addition to the improved quality, the mix on the gold CD version of *Blonde on Blonde* is closest to the '60s original (AF).

Mr. D's Collection, Vol. 3 (Japanese promo CD):
134. "Just Like Tom Thumb's Blues" (same as #103, #98 & #31!)
135. "I Ain't Got No Home" (from Woody Guthrie Tribute, Jan. 1968; same as #35)
136. "The Grand Coulee Dam" (from Woody Guthrie Tribute, Jan. 1968; same as #37)

137. "George Jackson"—Big Band version (same as #105, #101, #89 & #48!)
138. "George Jackson"—acoustic version (same as #96 & #49)
139. "Rita May" (same as #90 & #76)
140. "People Get Ready" (from *Renaldo & Clara*; same as #82)
141. "It Ain't Me, Babe" (from *Renaldo & Clara*; same as #83)
142. "Never Let Me Go" (from *Renaldo & Clara*; same as #84)
143. "Dead Man, Dead Man" (live; same as #131)
144. "The Usual" (*Hearts of Fire* soundtrack; same as #117)
145. "Pretty Boy Floyd" (same as #102)

"Nice Price" cassette reissue of *Desire*:
146. "Oh Sister" (Unfaded edit with unexpurgated exchange between Emmylou Harris & Bob. Most of this is cut on the CD version.)
147. "Most of the Time," 1990 (promo single recorded Mar. 1990, produced by Don Was)
148. "Runaway," 1990 (B-side of Traveling Wilburys' single "She's My Baby")
149. "New Blue Moon," 1990 (instrumental version—B-side of Traveling Wilburys' single "Wilbury Twist"; also on B-side of 12" single "She's My Baby")

For Our Children charity album, 1991:
150. "This Old Man"

Dylan Originals, four-track promo CD, celebrating *Thirty Years on Columbia*, 1992:
150a. "Big Yellow Taxi" (same as #58)
(The other tracks were "Knockin' on Heaven's Door," "The Man in the Long Black Coat," and "Handy Dandy"—all the regular album versions. Of course, "Big Yellow Taxi" is a Joni Mitchell song; it's not a Dylan original at all!)

Willie Nelson, *Across the Borderline*, 1993:
151. "Heartland" (with Willie Nelson)

The Byrds, boxed set, 1993:
152. "Mr. Tambourine Man," with the Byrds, recorded Feb. 1990

Joan Baez, *Rare, Live & Classic* boxed set, 1994:
153. "Troubled & I Don't Know Why" (with Joan Baez, Aug. 1963)

154. "Mama You've Been on My Mind" (with Joan Baez, Oct. 1964, wrongly attributed to Aug. 1964)
155. "Blowin' in the Wind" (with Rolling Thunder Revue, May 1976, not Newport duet #14—from Fort Collins, Colo., wrongly attributed to Fort Worth, Texas)

Mike Seeger, *3rd Annual Farewell Reunion*, 1994:
156. "Ballad of Hollis Brown" (with Mike Seeger)
Various artists compilation, *Woodstock '94*:
157. "Highway 61 Revisited"

Natural Born Killers film soundtrack, 1994:
158. "You Belong to Me"

Recalled European copies of the *MTV Unplugged* album, Nov. 1994:
159. "Knockin' on Heaven's Door" (mistake edit with loop of cheering overdubbed)

MTV Unplugged, Nov. 1994:
160. "Love Minus Zero/No Limit" (additional track on European copies of album only, also on *Unplugged* video)
161. "I Want You" (additional track on broadcast *Unplugged* program only, not on video)

European *Dignity* CD singles, 1995:
162. "Dignity" (*Unplugged* edit), first single 662076 2
163. "A Hard Rain's A-Gonna Fall" (recorded at Great Music Experience, Japan, 1994), first single 662076 2
164. "Dignity" (studio version), second single 662076 5
165. "It Ain't Me, Babe" (with Rolling Thunder Revue, *Renaldo & Clara* version, same as #83 & #141), second single 662076 5

Bakhalls litterara roster (*The Ambush's Literary Voices*), Swedish album, 1995:
166. "Wade in the Water," 1961 (from the *Minnesota Hotel Tape*)

Highway 61 Interactive CD-ROM, Graphix Zone, 1995:
167. Electric version of "House of the Rising Sun," 1964 overdub
(There are also a number of rare tracks in the digitized files on this CD-ROM, including several takes of "Like a Rolling Stone," an instrumental

with the Band, an alternate take of "I Shall Be Free No. 10" with an extra verse, many clips from other unreleased tracks such as the first version of "My Blue-Eyed Jane," plus three songs on video from the Supper Club shows in 1993.)

Till the Night Is Gone: A Tribute to Doc Pomus, Rhino, 1995:
168. "Boogie Woogie Country Girl"
The Concert for the Rock and Roll Hall of Fame, Sept. 1995:
169. "All Along the Watchtower"

CD-plus version of *Greatest Hits Vol. 3*, 1996:
170. Includes video clip of live version of "Tangled Up in Blue" from *Renaldo & Clara*, 1975

Feeling Minnesota film soundtrack, 1996:
171. "Ring of Fire"

Jerry Maguire film soundtrack, 1997:
172. "Shelter from the Storm," 1975 (alternate version)

European *Best of Bob Dylan* compilation, June 1997:
173. "Shelter from the Storm," 1975 (alternate version from *Jerry Maguire* soundtrack, same as #172)

Joan Baez Live at Newport, 1997:
174. "It Ain't Me, Babe" (with Joan Baez, July 1963; previously unreleased)
175. "With God on Our Side" (with Joan Baez; same as *Newport Broadside*, #11)

Recalled *Biograph*, Aug. 1997:
176. "Mixed Up Confusion" (original single, same as #6) (This change has actually been retained in the "corrected" reissue, Oct. 1997.)
177. "Baby, Let Me Follow You Down" (clipped start)
178. "I'll Be Your Baby Tonight" (unfaded edit)
179. "I Don't Believe You" (live Manchester, May 1966)

The Songs of Jimmie Rodgers tribute album, Sept. 1997:
180. "My Blue-Eyed Jane"

Live '96 Promo Columbia CD (recorded at House of Blues, Atlanta, Aug. 1996), Dec. 1997:

181. "My Back Pages"
182. "Tombstone Blues"
183. "Ballad of a Thin Man"
184. "Boots of Spanish Leather"
185. "Love Sick": promo CD single with edited and album versions of track

Not Dark Yet Scandinavian CD single, Feb. 1998:

186. "Tombstone Blues" (House of Blues, Atlanta, Aug. 1996, version; same as #182)
187. "Ballad of a Thin Man" (same as #183)
188. "Boots of Spanish Leather" (same as #184)

Ronnie Wood's book *Every Picture Tells a Story* with bonus CD, Mar. 1998:

189. "Interfere," with Ronnie Wood, recorded in Ireland, 1996

Exclusive Tracks

Featured on the Columbia Internet Web site www.bobdylan.com

Dec. 1997:

BDC1 "I'm Not There" (1956) (unreleased track from *The Basement Tapes*, 1967)
BDC2 "Blind Willie McTell" (live, Jones Beach, N.Y., Aug. 17, 1997)
BDC3 "Visions of Johanna" (live, Minneapolis, Minn., Sept. 3, 1992)
BDC4 "Mr. Tambourine Man" (live, Wolftrap, Vienna, Va., Aug. 23, 1997)

Jan. 1998:

BDC5 "Lay Down Your Weary Tune" (live, Carnegie Hall, New York City, Oct. 26, 1963)
BDC6 "John Brown" (live, Town Hall, New York City, Apr. 12, 1963)
BDC7 "Cold Irons Bound" (live, El Rey Theatre, Los Angeles, Dec. 16, 1997)
BDC8 "You're a Big Girl Now" (live, El Rey Theatre, Los Angeles, Dec. 17, 1997)
BDC9 "I'm Your Teenage Prayer" (unreleased track from *The Basement Tapes*, 1967)

BDC10 "From a Buick 6" (alternate take with harmonica intro; same as #25)

BDC11 "Percy's Song" (live, Carnegie Hall, New York City, Oct. 26, 1963)

BDC12 "The Lonesome Death of Hattie Carroll," (live, El Rey Theatre, Los Angeles, Dec. 16, 1997)

Feb. 1998:

BDC13 "Seven Curses" (live, Carnegie Hall, New York City, Oct. 26, 1963)

BDC14 "'Til I Fell in Love with You" (live, El Rey Theatre, Los Angeles, Dec. 16, 1997)

BDC15 "Idiot Wind" (live, Orpheum Theatre, Minneapolis, Aug. 30, 1992)

BDC16 "Tight Connection to My Heart" (live, Supper Club, New York City, Nov. 17, 1993, second show)

BDC17 "Weeping Willow" (live, Supper Club, New York City, Nov. 17, 1993, second show)

Mar. 1998:

BDC18 "Love Sick" (live, Grammy Awards, Radio City Music Hall, New York City, Feb. 28, 1998)

BDC19 "Girl of the North Country" (live, Madison Square Garden, New York City, Jan. 20, 1998)

Apr. 1998:

BDC20 "The Man in Me" (live, Landmark Theater, Syracuse, N.Y., Jan. 28, 1998)

Bibliography

Bauldie, John. *Wanted Man: In Search of Bob Dylan*. New York: Citadel Press, 1991

Cable, Paul. *Bob Dylan: His Unreleased Recordings*. New York: Schirmer Books, 1980.

Cott, Jonathan. *Dylan*. New York: Doubleday, 1984.

DeTurk, David A., and A. Poulin, Jr., eds. *The American Folk Scene: Dimensions of the Folksong Revival*. New York: Dell, 1967.

Dylan, Bob. *Tarantula*. New York: Macmillan, 1971.

————. *Writings and Drawings*. New York: Knopf, 1973.

————. *The Songs of Bob Dylan from 1966 through 1975*. New York: Knopf, 1976.

————. *Lyrics, 1962–1985*. New York: Knopf, 1986.

————. *Drawn Blank*. New York: Random House, 1994.

Flanagan, Bill. *Written in My Soul*. New York: Contemporary, 1987.

Heylin, Clinton. *Bob Dylan: Behind the Shades*. New York: Summit, 1991.

————. *Bob Dylan: The Recording Sessions: 1960–1994*. New York: St. Martins, 1995.

————. *Bob Dylan Day by Day: A Life in Stolen Moments*. New York: Schirmer Books, 1996.

Humphries, Patrick, and John Bauldie. *Absolutely Dylan*. New York: Viking Studio, 1992.

Kramer, Daniel. *Bob Dylan*. New York: Citadel, 1967.

Landy, Elliot. *Woodstock Visions*. San Francisco: Continuum, 1994.

Marcus, Greil. *Invisible Republic: Bob Dylan and the Basement Tapes*. New York: Henry Holt, 1996.

McGregor, Craig. *Bob Dylan: A Retrospective*. New York: William Morrow, 1972.

Miles, Barry, ed. *Bob Dylan in His Own Words*. New York: Quick Fox, 1978.

Riley, Tim. *Hard Rain: A Dylan Commentary*. New York: Knopf, 1992.

Scaduto, Anthony. *Bob Dylan: An Intimate Biography*. New York: Grosset and Dunlap, 1971.

Shelton, Robert. *No Direction Home*. New York: Beech Tree, 1987.

Shepard, Sam. *Rolling Thunder Logbook*. New York: Viking, 1977.

Spitz, Bob. *Bob Dylan: A Biography*. New York: McGraw-Hill, 1989.

Thomson, Elizabeth M., and David Gutman, eds. *The Dylan Companion*. London: Macmillan, 1990.

von Schmidt, Eric, and Jim Rooney. *Baby Let Me Follow You Down*. New York: Anchor Press, 1979.

Permissions

Grateful acknowledgment is made for permission to reprint the following:

"The Missing Singer" by Izzy Young. Originally published in *Other Scenes*. Copyright 1968 by Israel G. Young. Reprinted by permission.

"Bob Dylan: A Distinctive Folk-Song Stylist" by Robert Shelton. Copyright 1961 by The New York Times Company. Reprinted by permission.

"Records: Bobby Dylan" by J. R. Goddard. Originally published in *The Village Voice*.

"Tomorrow's Top Twenty?" By R. Gilbert. Originally published in *Scene*.

"Northern Folk Singers Help Out at Negro Festival in Mississippi." Copyright 1961 by The New York Times Company. Reprinted by permission.

"Bob Dylan, 22, A Folknik Hero." Copyright 1963, 1998 by Variety, Inc. Reprinted by permission.

"Flat Tire" by Paul Nelson and Jon Pankake. Originally published in *The Little Sandy Review*. Reprinted by permisison.

"Times They Are A-Changin'" by J. R. Goddard. Originally published in *HiFi-Stereo Review* (May 1964). Copyright Hachette Filipacchi Magazines, Inc. Reprinted by permission. All rights reserved.

"An Open Letter to Bob Dylan" by Irwin Silber. Copyright 1964 by *Sing Out!* Reprinted by permission. All rights reserved.

"Replies to Silber's Open Letter." Copyright 1964 by *Sing Out!* Reprinted by permission. All rights reserved.

"Dylan on Dylan" by Bernard Kleinman. Transcribed from Westwood One (Radio Station Discs).

Index